The Two Majorities

INTERPRETING AMERICAN POLITICS
Michael Nelson, Series Editor

Gerald S. Strom, *The Logic of Lawmaking: A Spatial Theory Approach*

John P. Burke, *The Institutional Presidency*

Marc Allen Eisner, *Regulatory Politics in Transition*

Mark J. Rozell, *Executive Privilege: The Dilemma of Secrecy and Democratic Accountability*

Thomas S. Langston, *With Reverence and Contempt: How Americans Think about Their President*

Byron E. Shafer and William J. M. Claggett, *The Two Majorities: The Issue Context of Modern American Politics*

Patricia Wallace Ingraham, *The Foundation of Merit: Public Service in American Democracy*

John Anthony Maltese, *The Selling of Supreme Court Nominees*

The Two Majorities

THE ISSUE CONTEXT

OF MODERN

AMERICAN POLITICS

Byron E. Shafer

William J. M. Claggett

The Johns Hopkins University Press   Baltimore and London

© 1995 The Johns Hopkins University Press
All rights reserved. Published 1995
Printed in the United States of America on acid-free paper
04 03 02 01 00 99 98 97 96 95   5 4 3 2 1

The Johns Hopkins University Press
2715 North Charles Street
Baltimore, Maryland 21218-4319
The Johns Hopkins Press Ltd., London

Library of Congress Cataloging-in-Publication Data will be found
at the end of this book.
A catalog record for this book is available from the British Library.

ISBN 0-8018-5018-5
ISBN 0-8018-5019-3 (pbk.)

For

Ivy and the late Clayton Claggett

and

Doris and Henry Shafer

The thesis is that we will never understand politics unless we know what the struggle is about.

—E. E. Schattschneider, *The Semi-Sovereign People*

CONTENTS

FIGURES

TABLES

SERIES EDITOR'S FOREWORD

Is American party politics in turmoil? By themselves, the three consecutive national elections of 1990, 1992, and 1994 produced three of the four possible combinations of Republican and Democratic control of the presidency and Congress: a Republican president and a Democratic Congress (1990), a Democratic president and a Democratic Congress (1992), and a Democratic president and a Republican Congress (1994). On the eve of the 1996 elections, many predicted that the voters would choose the only remaining combination, a Republican president and a Republican Congress. To appreciate the anomalous character of the early and mid-1990s, compare them with, say, the period from 1932 to 1952, when a Democratic president governed with a Democratic Congress 90 percent of the time, or the 1920s, when Republican presidents and Republican Congresses were the unbroken rule.

The answer, then, is yes, American party politics is in turmoil. But such an answer only yields two further questions: Why such turmoil? And how deeply into the political system do its roots extend?

In *The Two Majorities*, Byron E. Shafer and William J. M. Claggett provide the basis for addressing these latter questions. Drawing on their sophisticated statistical analysis of a massive survey of more than 8,000 Americans, conducted by the Gallup organization for the Times-Mirror newspaper syndicate, Shafer and Claggett argue that the recent turbulence of American politics is in some ways superficial. Just as the violent waves on the ocean surface mask the great body of deeper and stiller water beneath, so does the political conflict of recent elections mask the deep—that is, stable and salient—political preferences of the American people which help to form the issues context of American politics. Ironically, however, it is the very stability of these deep preferences that has produced 1990s-style waves on the political surface.

Shafer and Claggett find, in particular, that American public opinion is organized around two clusters of issues: social welfare, social insurance, and civil rights, which constitute an *economic/welfare factor*, and cultural values, civil liberties, and foreign relations, a *cultural/ national factor*. The party system forged during the New Deal, which the Democrats dominated well into the 1960s, was constructed mainly on the issues that comprise the economic/welfare factor, especially social insurance issues such as Social Security. Democratic candidates still generally prevail when, as in 1992, economic circumstances combine with an effective candidate like Bill Clinton to make the economic/ welfare factor dominate an election.

Since the 1960s, however, the issues that comprise the cultural/ national factor also have risen to prominence in the minds of Americans. Because Democratic activists, often in conflict with the rank-and-file voters of their party, have taken mostly unpopular positions on these issues, the stable pattern of Democratic control has been undermined. When, as in 1988, the cultural/national factor is brought successfully to the fore by a candidate such as George Bush, the Republicans enjoy their greatest advantage.

Provocatively, Shafer and Claggett conclude from their analysis that each party's best strategy for success is not to try to take popular positions on the whole range of issues that face the voters, but rather to focus the voters' attention on the party's most successful cluster of issues—the economic/welfare factor for the Democrats, the cultural/ national factor for the Republicans. The failure of either party to exploit consistently the relatively stable issues context of American politics in recent years explains why, so far at least, neither the Democrats nor the Republicans have been able to replace the recent period of political turmoil with a new era of political stability.

Michael Nelson

PREFACE

Imagine a nation whose politics can be described in terms of two great underlying concerns in the policy preferences of its citizens. Imagine, however, that this nation features numerous further social divisions, such that many of its most consequential subgroups do not share the national preference pattern. Imagine, moreover, that the political parties charged with converting individual wishes into aggregate politics, and especially their most active operatives, put these preferences together in yet a different fashion, one which is theoretically rather than socially based. Imagine, finally, that all this—these issue dimensions, their social roots, a partisan translation, and some further activist distinctions—effectively constitutes the framework for political conflict in the modern era.

For anyone willing to entertain these possibilities, one way to introduce the book which follows is simply to suggest that such a nation is not imaginary. It is, in fact, the contemporary United States. American political opinion in our time is characterized by two grand, underlying, and essentially independent principles, an economic/welfare principle and a cultural/national principle. These principles, however, are gathered very differently in different social sectors of the nation, in subgroups distinguished by race, by religion, and by social class. Despite these group preferences, partisan activists, the moving force within the two main political parties, insist on their own distinctive combinations of political opinion; such combinations are, after all, what motivate them to be active. As a result, it is not just the contradictions between independent dimensions of opinion, but the tensions between political activists and their own rank and file, which inform and energize American politics.

Probably, all political eras revolve around some analogous set of central policy concerns. Call them "great issues" or just recurring conflicts, these substantive considerations, in effect, *organize* the politics around them. In any case, this book is an attempt to talk about such a substantive framework—an issue context—for our era, too. The problems in doing so, without the benefit of hindsight, are legion, and many will be painfully apparent in the pages that follow. If there are compensating virtues, these will necessarily lie in three broad areas:

1. most importantly, in bringing substance—"what the struggle is about," to quote Schattschneider—to the forefront of political analysis;

2. in revealing the dominant strategic context for political maneuver in our time, a context which operates—indeed, dominates—whether strattegists acknowledge it consciously or not; and

3. in highlighting the coherence of such a context across an extended political era, so that its outcomes can be seen as a connected historical whole, rather than as just "noise."

A small set of persons, organizations, and institutions have abetted this enterprise, though none in a way that they should be blamed for its product. The data, with their peculiarly stiff requirements, were provided by the Times Mirror newspaper syndicate, from an early part of what became a running—and stimulating—portrait of the American public. Andrew Kohut, Director of Surveys for the Gallup Organization, was extremely gracious in facilitating access to the key survey, and Margaret Petrella, Assistant to the Director, not only managed the practical details of such access but answered questions and provided further advice with unfailing patience.

Analysis of the data was then powerfully facilitated by the Andrew Mellon Funds at the university and college levels at Oxford University, and by the Politics Group, Warden, Bursar, and Fellows generally at Nuffield College. The fact that the two of us could spend a number of summers working together in Oxford—discussing this work with others as we went—is due largely to an ongoing commitment by these organizations, funds, and individuals to just such an outcome. While it would be invidious to name some and not others in the associated intellectual network, David Cox, Geoffrey Evans, and Anthony Heath among the permanent fellows, along with Robert Lane, a "permanent visitor," did comment upon specific aspects of the enterprise along the way. Among more intermittent visitors, Gary King provided a detailed commentary on the entire manuscript. Paul Sniderman and Edward (Ted) Carmines then offered a penultimate reading of the result.

As the analysis evolved, a number of other organizations provided crucial forums for reports on this work-in-progress. The American Political Science Association, through a plenary session at its meetings in 1989, provided an early opportunity to focus some of our historical and theoretical hypotheses. The British Association for American Studies, in a plenary lecture in 1991, offered a forum for the first public exposition of findings from these data. And the American Politics Group of the Political Studies Association has offered so many chances for subsequent exposition—its collective patience has been tried so many times—as to fall in a class by itself in the case of this manuscript. Indeed, it was an extended conversation at lunch after one of these presentations, in 1993, that generated the title.

Finally, "blame" for the whole enterprise, if that is the ultimate verdict, can come closest to being shifted to the two individuals who have seen it through to published form. Michael Nelson, series editor for Interpreting American Politics at the Johns Hopkins University Press, came looking for a book on elites in American politics. It is testament to his larger intellectual principles that, when what he got was this instead, he not only welcomed it but supported it actively. Henry Tom, Executive Editor at the Press, also came out in support of this project early, on the basis of a prospectus which was necessarily long on promise but short on everything else. He has seen it through every step of the process since then. Carolyn Moser provided a copyedit noteworthy for its gentle deftness, and Kimberly Johnson then brought the copyedited version to production.

While they might reasonably recoil at the thought, we think the influence of our teachers, especially Nelson Polsby and William Flanigan, is present at every point. We dedicate the result, of course, to those who must take a kind of ultimate responsibility for it.

The Two Majorities

1 THE NOTION OF AN ISSUE CONTEXT

Public Wishes and the Two Majorities

An issue context, as we conceive it, is the grand substantive framework for political conflict. As such, it consists of the more stable, underlying concerns that organize the politics of its era, along with the more changeable, surface concerns that give these underlying influences expression. On their way to *being* the "great issues" of an era, however, these underlying concerns almost inevitably acquire roots in key social groups; are then gathered by political parties, in additionally distinctive ways; and achieve further contours from the continuing preferences of the most active participants. In contemporary terms, across society, such a context creates a comprehensive political framework by linking elite strategies, mass public responses, and random interventions by events of the day. In historical terms, across time, such a context creates a comprehensive (and extended) political *era* by linking a succession of policy conflicts—and outcomes.

That is an introduction at its most definitional. The process of putting empirical detail (and hence political reality) back into such a definition is, accordingly, the main task of succeeding chapters. Seen from one side, this is an attempt to set out the structure of American political opinion in the late twentieth century: the central and continuing concerns of this opinion, their roots and the distribution of preferences on them, the partisan gathering (and dividing) of these preferences, along with their preliminary fate among the more specialized actors who ordinarily play an outsized role in issue transmission. Such an enterprise has a rich and distinguished tradition.[1] If this book has something further to contribute, it must lie in a more comprehensive embodiment than was previously possible, thanks largely to direct advantages in size of sample and in substantive reach of the questionnaire, but also, we hope, to some added conceptual power.

Seen from the other side, however, such an enterprise is also an attempt to sketch the issue context for practical politicking in our time, and thus to write political history as it unfolds. Viewed this way, the structure of American political opinion becomes not so much a focus in its own right as the putative framework, often ill-perceived yet insistently present despite that, within which political operatives craft (and test) their strategies. In turn, the character and durability of this framework go a long way toward determining the character and durability of extended political eras. This is surely the most difficult and potentially fraught side of the undertaking, albeit the one with the more provocative implications.[2] As elaborated here, it will produce suggested answers to, among other contemporary queries,

- how the social backgrounds of ordinary citizens can produce *patterns* of policy preference so different from what theoretical analysts—and often, practical strategists—otherwise expect;

- why active Republicans are led to talk about *race*—why, in the strategic sense, they "must" do so—contrary to the views of some internal advisors and many external critics;

- why active Democrats are led just as consistently *away from* the one realm—social insurance—where the general public is most in agreement with them;

- how a "minority party" can win nationwide contests consistently, while the "majority party" nevertheless remains on the apparent verge of reducing the minority party to irrelevance; and

- why the partisan outcomes of the last quarter-century—sometimes split partisan control of national government in the stereotypical sense, always the possibility of "divided governance," rightly understood— follow logically and ineluctably from an underlying issue context.

Promises and Presuppositions

The scholarly mission, then, in the vocabulary of the social sciences, is to tease out the structure of American political opinion. Yet the further intellectual mission of such a book, on grounds where social scientists, practicing journalists, and political operatives meet, is to consider the implications of an opinion structure for the practical behavior of current political actors. In truth, key political actors are occasionally able, collectively and convulsively, to alter the very implications of this structure—its incentives and its constraints—so as to accomplish precisely what they themselves desire. More often, they are strongly channeled in what they actually undertake by the character of an existing issue structure. Sometimes (and surely more than a self-respecting activist would admit) what they hope to accomplish is itself effectively determined by this issue context.[3]

Sophisticated readers, on the other hand, those concerned with substance and not just those concerned with approach, should be alerted to two fundamental presuppositions behind any effort to uncover this context. Both may seem nearly intuitive and thus self-evident; all of what follows is, in any case, further evidence for their defense. Yet at the beginning, the aspiringly sophisticated reader must in effect be willing to treat these two postulates at least as assumptions, to see where they lead.

The first is that the general public does indeed possess major and continuing policy predispositions. These are not constant responses to the details of policy promotion, which may vary widely from time to time or even, when assessed, from question to question. Nor are they immediate recognitions of the interrelatedness, and hence the appropriate priorities, of various continuing policy concerns. But they are the "deep preferences" to political opinion; they are comparatively confirmed and stable; and they can be tapped by the successful policy entrepreneur—and presumably the successful survey analyst as well—on the average and over time.

Among scholars, a propensity to treat opinions in isolation, measured by themselves and outside any operational realm, often serves to mask the power and continuity of such predispositions. Among practitioners, the need to depend for a livelihood on manipulating these predispositions—on the part especially of modern campaign consultants, though aided and abetted by some scholars of modern campaigning—has produced evident incentives to minimize the regularity and constraints of underlying public preferences. Moreover, the fact that operating politicians are always only more or less successful in activating these predispositions means that their partial successes (and failures) further muddy the picture.

Nevertheless, a deep and continuing structure to public preferences is probably present for most societies, and while it certainly evolves, it also evolves slowly. The reasons for this, in turn, lie more in the realm of social structure than of opinion and its measurement per se. To wit: The social situation of individual members of the general public, and hence both the preferences they inherit and the experiences through which they evaluate (and presumably revise) these preferences, change far more slowly than do, for example, question formats. As long as social structures show continuity, then, opinion structures should show a counterpart consistency.[4]

The second presupposition fundamental to what follows is that the politics of our time does possess an overarching issue context as well. Again, this is not to assert that some small set of influential preferences are constantly and directly decisive during our (or any) political era. Nor is it to assert that a diagnostic issue context should (or can) ultimately determine most of the outcomes of individual consequence. Obviously, much of practical politicking, in our time as presumably in most others, is a matter of finding ways to pursue lesser, circumscribed goals within whatever the overarching issue structure may be, adapting strategy but not substance to an existing issue context.

Yet, again, the initial presumption is that larger organizing concerns—not necessarily attractive, despite their power—ought to characterize our era, as they have previous eras. This too is frequently masked by the normal, ongoing character of politics, and especially of its reportage. Politicians, for their part, describe (and often visualize) their activities in terms of immediate opportunities and constraints, immediate allies and opponents. Journalists, for their part, augment this sense of constant flux (and infinite possibility) by treating the news of the day as simultaneously unprecedented and portentous, unexpected and important.

Individual policy outcomes from a specific contemporary conflict will surely reflect the idiosyncrasies of key actors as well as chance interactions among events of the day. But in any extended period, including ours, the issues which come repeatedly to the fore, the coalitions which can be built around them, the arguments mobilized in their pursuit, and even, ultimately, the outcomes which they permit— all should actually vary within certain crucial and recurring limits, deriving in turn from a larger issue context. And how could they not? If social institutions in the grand sense (economic units, residential geographies, family structures, and so on) change only gradually, or else in response to dramatic but rare outside stimuli, then the organizing concerns of their politics should—they almost must—share that character.[5]

On the one hand, then, actors, strategies, institutions, and resources still matter. On the other, they also still put themselves in the service of the larger political concerns of their age. Nevertheless—and here is the last consumer warning—if all this seems balanced and unexceptional on its face, it is worth recalling the extent of work on contemporary American politics that implicitly begins from other premises. Or at least, it is worth recalling the amount of work in which politics is, in effect, a partial epiphenomenon of something else—the simple extrusion of its own mechanics—whether that means fund-raising, media attention, or naked ambition, whether it be incumbency, advertising, or reapportionment.

This book intends to tilt the balance the other way. It thus aspires to be an explicitly "political" look at modern American politics, in the sense in which most respondents to public opinion surveys would probably use that term: looking at the preferences which individuals bring to practical politics and at the conflicts which follow from those (differing) preferences. Intrinsically apolitical influences do not disappear as potential subsequent elements of such an analysis, nor should they. But the analysis begins with (and then returns to defend) the premise that such influences at most reinforce and channel a larger issue context, and that in the absence of change in fundamental public preferences, alterations in these other, admittedly more tangible phenomena are not themselves likely to shift the contours of an enveloping political framework.

The larger result of such a focus, by extension, is nothing less than a description (and explanation) of temporal *eras* to American politics, extended periods which are organized by, and reciprocally shape, an overarching issue context. This is a result which would raise few eyebrows when derived historically, at least after passage of enough time, but which sits oddly athwart many efforts to explain contemporary politics by way of its own machinations. On the one hand, then, we do believe that substance disciplines mechanics, and that *institutionalized* substance disciplines history. On the other hand, eras last, but not forever; underlying issue concerns last, but not forever; social coalitions, built upon policy preferences, last, but not forever either.

Perspectives and Applications

The most prosaic way to introduce the contents of such a book is just to provide short chapter summaries, and such summaries will in fact close this introductory chapter. But a slightly less pedestrian approach is to set out five of the major available perspectives on what follows, five major associated themes which run at least implicitly throughout, and to which each of these chapters could be explicitly applied. They constitute, in effect, five perspectives on the specific contents of the individual chapters, and thus five aspiring answers to the unavoidable introductory question, "What is this about?"

Two of these are little more than self-conscious restatements of the larger goals of the book, intended here to help readers assess their realization (or not) as the argument progresses. Two others are separable subaspects of these larger efforts, aspects which will not, in truth, be disentangled in the text, but which might be of central importance to some other readers. And a fifth is in some sense a prospective theme, the beginnings of a further argument which could reasonably proceed when this book ends. All are continuing elements in the search for a structure to American political opinion and for its contribution to the character of contemporary American politics. Ideally, signposting them provides additional uses for the chapters which follow.

The first and most scholarly of the explicit perspectives among these involves the pursuit of a *structure* to political opinion in the contemporary United States.[6] At a minimum, such a structure has one or (probably) more underlying dimensions upon which individuals can be arrayed. Fully developed, such a structure has social roots, that is, a distribution of opinions on its dimensions that is associated with differences in social background and current position. Fully developed, such a structure also features some patterned transmission—usually a differential transmission—between those who hold these opinions in a general public and those who hold them in a more active substratum of this public, one normally more central to politics.

That, then, is the first way to describe the contents of this book: careful data analysis organized through accepted summary concepts to produce a coherent larger picture. Implicit in such a focus, however, is a second, intimately related way to think about what follows. This would emphasize instead the geographic and cultural *location* of this structure—that is, the characteristics which make it distinctively American.[7] These characteristics need not (though of course they might) mark the product as "exceptional." Indeed, addressing the question of any putative exceptionalism would require a different, explicitly comparative focus. All that this particular work can do in this realm is to raise possibilities and stimulate curiosity.

Nevertheless, such a perspective is always implicitly present. From the start, our hypotheses about the underlying dimensions of American political opinion are derived—as they must be derived—from recent *American* history. The exceptionalist possibility continues with a potential distinctiveness in the social roots of these opinions, as, for example, with the comparatively large role (relative to other developed democracies) of religious belief or racial status. And this possibility remains inherent in the potentially distinctive contribution of a weak two-party system to the structuring of political opinion, especially a system in which partisan elites are so generally voluntaristic and self-motivated.

A third, clearly different route into what follows, and the other intendedly explicit perspective, is to focus on the *implications* of this structure of public opinion for the practical politics which plays out within it. Such a structure can hardly escape having powerful implications in the realm, for example, of partisan strategy or even partisan success.[8] As a result, the chapters which follow can hardly escape suggesting what Democrats or Republicans should (and should not) emphasize, along with how each set of partisans should counter normal emphases by the other, as long as this particular context obtains. In passing, the specifics of this continuing strategic advice become a further incentive toward split partisan governance, one emanating from the preferences of the American public.

Yet what this also implies, by extension and perhaps less obviously, is that there is indeed a *political*—an ideational and programmatic— underpinning to politics in our time. Legislators could be districted differently; funds could be raised differently; public officials could be tenured differently; and yet the basic partisan and substantive contours of politics would be remarkably little changed. As long as the structure of public wishes does not shift, and as long as party strategies remain roughly stable within it (as they are very likely to do), there is no reason to expect potential reforms to become more than ancillary influences. "Politics," again in the form of a struggle over the translation of public wishes, should remain central.

This leads on, quite naturally, to a fourth connecting thread, involving arguments which are larger but more deeply buried. Indeed, these are both sufficiently intrinsic and sufficiently submerged that they could not, even in principle, be made central themes of the book without reorienting it in a major way. Yet they are inherent to it; they do acquire some evidence for their own validity along the way; and they surely deserve, in consequence, an early signpost. Most of what follows, accordingly, revolves around an apparently central dynamic to politics, around the apparent essence of successful *politicking*. And this dynamic suggests, indirectly but persistently, that success in such politicking may lie more in achieving priority for favorable issues than in deducing the optimal position on an issue raised by (and presumably intended to favor) the opposition.

Much writing about political conflict, both journalistic and professional, proceeds on the (unstated) opposite assumption, that the essence of the underlying combat lies in picking the best available response to the issues of the day. Superficially, the logic of this is undeniable. Outside forces often do set the agenda; a given candidate had better know how to respond intelligently. Our analysis, however, provides ammunition for a different approach, with both positive and powerfully negative reinforcements. Positively, a candidate may still be better advised to try to shift the *grounds* of the debate; negatively, a candidate who cannot, will probably lose. In short, if an opinion structure is stable, or at least if there are stable majorities in given issue-areas, there appears to be more—much more—advantage in seizing the high ground and avoiding the low, rather than in skillfully battling uphill.[9]

Finally, the whole analysis affirms, again and again, the centrality of two great underlying dimensions to American politics in our time. From there, it is but a short step to two further, prospective, comparative analyses. Neither of these is pursued in the material which follows; this material, nevertheless, contributes a necessary first step toward their pursuit. The first such comparative possibility is that the same dimensions might underpin the politics of some, but not all, other modern nations. These dimensions do appear fundamental enough to suggest (and acquire) functional counterparts elsewhere. Their incarnation also remains sufficiently—distinctively—American as to limit the prospect of any automatic transfer.[10]

A related, equally inescapable possibility is that these dimensions might be isolated in other periods in American history; this is the internal comparative possibility. Its pursuit, too, would not involve some automatic extrapolation, since the specific conflicts which embody (and carry) these underlying dimensions would surely change from period to period. Indeed, the relationship between these two dimensions and even their respective emphases could plausibly differ in different political eras. In our time, these underlying dimensions are essentially unrelated—geometrically at right angles—creating a diagnostic array of political tensions, strategic opportunities, and partisan outcomes. In other times, a different relationship would presumably produce a different array of outcomes as well.

An Outline

All these perspectives, in any case, weave in and out of six further chapters plus a conclusion.

Chapter 2 canvasses postwar political history for hypotheses about an issue context for American political opinion and applies a newly available data set to the result. The product of that application is six immediate and very familiar issue dimensions, along with two key underlying concerns.

Chapter 3 examines the relationship between a position on these issue products and the personal characteristic most closely linked to politics, namely, partisan self-identification. The extent to which partisan attachments structure all these dimensions proves surprising, though the serious links center on one underlying concern.

Chapter 4 turns to the main alternative source of societal roots for political opinion, namely, membership in social groups. What emerges here is the extreme diversity, and the potential both for political conflict and alternative strategy, inherent in the American society behind and around its political parties.

Chapter 5 asks how group membership and party identification interact. On the one hand, such interactions prove to be highly dependent on particular issues of the day. On the other, they nevertheless give rise to continuing strategies for dealing with the resulting environment, while they isolate a few strategically critical subgroups that are especially susceptible to issue-based cross-pressures.

Chapter 6 goes on to investigate the issue preferences of party operatives, comparing them both with activists from the other party and with the rank and file of their own. The existing—and striking—disjunctions go a long way toward completing the substantive framework for American politics in our time.

Chapter 7 focuses on factional struggles within the active parties over policy options to be presented to the general public. The two parties actually feature quite different internal struggles, producing very different strategic problems.

The final chapter, Chapter 8, then reassembles all of this to consider issue contexts, not for their composition, but as influences on the outcome. Specific electoral contests and extended political eras across the entire postwar period prove to be strongly and directly rooted in an overarching issue context.

2 DIMENSIONS OF POLITICAL OPINION

"Great Issues" for the Modern Era

Propositions about the issue context of modern American politics actually abound, though they are often not acknowledged as such. Social scientists who work on public opinion are, of course, enjoined to be explicit about such propositions. But commercial analysts of public opinion—professional pollsters of all sorts—work with what are, in effect, operating hypotheses too, about substantive realms of consequence, about the character of public preferences within them, and about the best ways to assess these elements. Lastly, journalists, more implicitly but just as insistently, work with—and indeed need—assertions about public opinion in order to explain the daily events of politics: so-and-so was elected because he "touched a public nerve"; such-and-such failed because "the public would not go for it."

Many of these assertions remain untested. Events of the day succeed each other rapidly; attempts to explain them must move with equal speed. Most of the rest are tested mainly within their own confines. Thus, the ordinary operational goal is to write accurately and intelligently about economic dislocation, defense technology, race relations, family values, and so forth, or about opinions thereon. The goal is not to see whether these are related to each other, much less whether they represent a continuing (or changing) structure of opinions and preferences, least of all whether they are temporary embodiments of some underlying framework, within which they are predominantly "indicators" rather than consequential influences in their own right.

Nevertheless, much of this effort contributes not just propositions about the issue context of modern American politics, but evidence—data—toward a test. Seen one way, then, the burgeoning efforts of social scientists, professional pollsters, and practical journalists to explain the events of contemporary politics contribute—they really constitute—both preliminary hypotheses about the structure of political opinion and preliminary evidence toward a test. What they lack is some further effort to integrate these hypotheses into a more comprehensive framework, capable of acquiring defensible surrogate measures *and capable of shaping the politics of our time.* A working version of such an issue framework is thus the purpose of this chapter.

Surface Hypotheses about the Contemporary Issue Context

Recent American history contains numerous major themes for such a putative issue context. There is, of course, no guarantee that these themes, abstracted from major political conflicts, will find a central resonance in mass political opinion, much less that they will continue to be central. On the other hand, these themes do constitute an obvious starting point. Moreover, they are associated, in every case, with a succession of events which could potentially both register and reinforce them. Finally, all have in fact migrated into scholarly work as well, so that there are at least incipient formal tests of their centrality and staying power.

Even the crudest reading of recent American history, one oriented solely toward isolating a dominant concern or theme for each recent decade, provides an array of assertions—a largely consensual array— about the contemporary issue context. In such a reading, the 1930s would surely appear as the decade of the Great Depression and the New Deal, of the arrival of the welfare state in American life and of the centrality of issues of *social welfare.*[1] In the same way, the 1940s would appear as the era of World War II and then of the Cold War, of the emergence of the United States as a world power and hence of the centrality of *foreign relations* to American public life.[2] Moreover, nothing about the intervening years suggests that such concerns have gone away, at least as matters for public political struggle.

The same sort of potted recent history would make the late 1950s and early 1960s into the period when issues of *civil rights and racial policy* became central to modern American politics.[3] Again, a student of political history could hardly miss the arrival of these concerns, and that same student would be unlikely to assert that they had been resolved and relegated. By extension, the late 1960s and early 1970s would be the period of *cultural* (and countercultural) *issues,* of conflict over private morality and public order, personal deportment and community prerogatives, individual responsibility and group entitlement.[4] Once more, a sudden intensification of these concerns in public politics would be hard to ignore; once more, most have hardly disappeared.

Accordingly, all four of these issue-areas—social welfare, foreign affairs, civil rights, and cultural values—meet certain minimal preconditions as dimensions shaping politics and potentially commanding an opinion. All are, at a minimum, arguably (and often dramatically) central to recent political life in the aggregate. Beyond that, all are constituted from a further large variety of theoretical subconcerns. Foreign relations, for example, comprises alliance behavior, military emphasis, international trust, defense expenditure, and so on. Similarly, civil rights involves procedural guarantees, discrimination remedies, demographic targeting, racially based trade-offs, and potentially much more.

By the same token, all four issue-areas, especially as elaborated through their subconcerns, permit embodiment in a nearly infinite array of specific events, which can both elicit public preferences on them and reinforce those preferences. In social welfare, battles over unemployment insurance and retirement benefits can be succeeded by battles over occupational training and medical benefits, which can be succeeded by conflicts over guaranteed employment and child-care provisions—and back around again.[5] Cultural values offers an even more dizzying prospect, with abortion, euthanasia, public prayer, public protest, criminal procedure, drug enforcement—to take only some of the subjects now common to any given term of the U.S. federal courts—as elements in an apparently unending supply of concrete vehicles to embody the general issue-area.[6]

Fortunately, lest this impressionistic way of isolating the major putative dimensions of modern political opinion seem just too crude, scholarly attention—self-conscious social science—has followed roughly the same trajectory. In one sense, it is hardly surprising that social scientists of the time integrated what they took to be the central developments in society at large into their work. Yet what resulted was, again fortunately, a "double record." The explicit part of this record consisted of the specific findings which emerged from this research, concrete evidence on the reality of public opinion in these various realms. The implicit part lay in the very questions themselves, which tie an impressionistic historical survey to self-conscious social science by marking the points at which given political concerns—our ostensible decadal themes—crossed into serious scholarly work.

The great cornerstone of research on the political attitudes and behavior of the American public, *The American Voter,* can actually be used to begin demonstrating this link.[7] Published in 1960 but drawing on data from the two presidential elections of the 1950s, *The American Voter* limned a world in which partisan identifications, largely built upon class coalitions which were originally formed around social-welfare issues, were the dominant organizing factors of politics. The specific issues most likely to affect these established coalitions, in turn, were naturally related to domestic policy, especially to social welfare and economic benefit. Issues of foreign policy and defense, while present in a secondary sort of way, remained just that—secondary.

> It is noteworthy that the total volume of comment about war and peace and other issues of foreign affairs was small relative to the level of other sorts of responses in these years. The Second World War as well as the Korean War had intervened between the experience of the Depression and the years 1952 and 1956. Yet the number of responses reflecting the Great Depression and its political aftermath was much greater than the number referring to issues raised by these wars or by any other aspect of foreign affairs.[8]

Intellectually, *The American Voter* contributed the dominant model for thinking about mass attitudes and mass behavior in the social science research that followed. Historically, it contributed a specific portrait of mass public politics during the period of its data collection, the 1950s. Practically, it made yet a third great contribution: It led directly to the institutionalization of regular surveys of the American electorate, through a biennial series now recognized as the National Election Study. The substantive content of these further surveys thus provides a further scholarly link with (and recapitulation of) a general historical summary of the succeeding decades.[9] In other words, larger historical interpretations of the essence of a decade are again paralleled by and made immanent in self-consciously scientific measures.

What those measures reveal is that into the 1960s substantive questions about politics managed to remain tightly focused around economics and social welfare, with international affairs a distant second. Civil rights then entered these surveys in preparation for the 1964 election and has remained there ever since. Foreign relations increased in importance in preparation for the 1968 election, first through a focus on the Vietnam War but later through a sequence of other concerns which moved in and out of the series. By the 1972 election, cultural issues had arrived with a large and explicit array—crime and public safety, gender roles and the place of women in society, the appropriate ease or difficulty of abortion—and these, too, were never to be absent thereafter.

Again, seen not for what these questions reveal about actual social divisions, where they tapped intense divisions at various points, but for what their very appearance suggests about perceptions at the time, the implication is clear enough. By the late 1960s, scholars concerned with surveying public attitudes, especially those attitudes having a potential impact on politics, could no longer content themselves with a focus on social welfare, however broadly drawn or precisely elaborated. Rather, they felt that they owed—they felt that real politics pressed them toward—increased attention to international relations and sharply increased attention to civil rights and cultural values.

Deeper Hypotheses, a Data Set, and a Method

There is, accordingly, a collection of nearly inescapable, roughly consensual, implicit hypotheses about the central surface stimuli for contemporary political opinion. Seen from the other side, these are also the putative implicit dimensions of contemporary public preference, which then require some practical measure if they are to be useful in investigating a larger opinion context. To call them "surface" hypotheses is merely to note that they do sit, broadly and dramatically, on the surface of recent American history. It is not otherwise to diminish them, for they bid, in fact, to be nothing less than the "great issues" of American politics in our time.

Yet if the historical net had been cast differently, to permit a longer time perspective, there might well have been deeper hypotheses too, propositions about fundamental issue-areas which underlie even these grand and extended issue-clusters of the day, and which impart a further structure to them. A longer time perspective might, of course, have encouraged a variety of such (deeper) propositions. But one, involving two great and potentially independent summary dimensions, seemed both easy to observe across much of American history and persistently in the background of modern surface concerns. While there are any number of ways to summarize this deep hypothesis about the fundamental structure of political opinion, the simplest way might be to stereotype it as the distinction between opinions on the "quantity" and opinions on the "quality" of social life.

In essence, the (putative) distinction is between a concern with the material conditions of daily life versus a concern with the intrinsic character of that life, its specific components rather than its aggregate level. There is no direct and obvious body of continuing opinion surveys, a counterpart to the National Election Study, that can immediately confirm the existence of these two deeper factors, much less show their evolution across the postwar years. Yet here too, there is a welter of analogous theorizing and research—if we will only acknowledge it as such—embracing recurrent attitudinal divisions, basic societal cleavages, and even fundamental distinctions in the organization of social life itself.

Moreover, much of this work is (or can be) unified across these diverse domains by the discovery that two underlying dimensions are necessary to understand the impact of these domains on politics, within most nations and over time.[10] A good deal of such work is additionally and incorrectly unified, in our reading (though the items cited in note 10 do escape this failing), by a tendency to conceive the more directly economic dimension—distributional attitudes, class cleavages, or marketplace conflicts—as either naturally or historically dominant. At a minimum, it is easy enough to argue that the second of these dimensions, the one involving the character of national life, has been at least a constant and continuing theme (and thus a recurrent political worry) in the United States.

Said differently, what makes such concerns seem less cataclysmic but more continual in American politics is an arguably different way of constituting the nation itself. Even the modern United States is ultimately the product of external immigration and internal migration, so that a concern with guaranteeing a reliable *character* of life, alongside a concern with guaranteeing the physical essentials, is arguably inherent. Such concerns (and such a distinction) were all the more pressingly evident during the late nineteenth and early twentieth centuries, the period which served as evidence for the argument that what distinguished the United States as a nation was that America was itself an ideology, rather than a birthright. In this construction, newcomers could be "Americanized" and natives could be "un-American," a fact which struck a remarkably diverse range of analysts as characteristic, and distinctive.[11]

These analysts went on to differ powerfully over the specific values which went into this American ideology. Nevertheless, the point here is simply that an enveloping concern with national integration, with ensuring the essence and continuity of daily life, has been a recurring theme across American history, in both its finest and its grimmest moments. While this concern can sometimes be linked to a focus on dividing up the concrete benefits of society, the two foci are not inherently the same. The latter is essentially a distributional concern, involving economics and social welfare. The former is much more a cultural concern, involving the values which govern ordinary social exchange, in the nation and, perhaps, the wider world.[12]

In any case, the great problem in looking for a comprehensive structure involving such putative deep dimensions of political opinion has long been a data problem. The search is, by definition, not just for some usable measure of the surface dimensions, though this aspect of the problem is difficult enough, given that these dimensions are numerous and aspire to constitute the great issues of an era. Yet that search is also for some working measure of their putative deeper counterparts, wellsprings not just for a particular incarnation in the modern era, but potentially in other eras, too. Moreover, such a search ideally proceeds in a manner permitting both surface dimensions and deeper influences to be tied back to their social roots and then taken forward toward key political intermediaries.

It requires a large number of survey items even to allow for the possible appearance (and hence initial validation) of four or more hypothesized dimensions simultaneously, quite apart from then being able to subject that product to a second-order analysis. Or at least, a structure of this character cannot even potentially be isolated without opinions on a number of policy items which are superficially associated with each of the hypothesized dimensions, all within the same (simultaneous) survey. The presence of such a survey (or, again ideally, surveys) hardly guarantees the appearance of these dimensions; their original hypotheses may simply prove false. But the absence of such a survey obviously forecloses the hunt.

Compounding the problem is the political and societal, rather than the more strictly attitudinal, side of the same task. For in fact, searching for the political and social attachments of opinions on these or other key dimensions requires the further ability to subdivide any sample into a number of serious subgroups and to conduct at least some minimal analysis within each. That translates into a demand for a sample which is large in terms of the number of respondents, rather than just in the number of questions asked. To date, this combination has proved elusive. The few previous samples with a sufficient breadth of questions offered too few respondents for subsequent analysis, just as the few previous samples with enough respondents to permit detailed internal breakdowns tended to concentrate on one or two issue-areas.

This is true even of the National Election Study, that otherwise much-revered progenitor, whose prior influences certainly made work like this possible. Nevertheless, both sample size and substantive content were always insufficient for even a preliminary test. A possible alternative appeared in the late 1980s with a series of national surveys, funded by the Times Mirror Company and executed by the Gallup Organization, examining American attitudes on a succession of contemporary issues *and* examining the social groups associated with various preferences. Indeed, the first round of this series asked an additionally large national sample about numerous opinion items in numerous surface domains, including (but hardly limited to) the issue dimensions hypothesized here. That is the survey upon which our analysis is based.[13]

The intended logic of our analysis then determined the specific technical method to be used. In formal terms, our obvious intention was to use a broad array of individual policy preferences as indicators of a smaller set of underlying dimensions, ideally so that the resulting dimensions could be subjected to a second-order analysis, to permit the appearance of even deeper factors. The relevant method needed to be formally analogous to this empirical structure, permitting it to appear without providing it by definition, and thereby permitting a comparison between initial hypotheses and observed dimensions, without insisting that the latter be related to each other in any given way. The most common method of choice for such an exercise, a method both mimicking this logical structure and in fact created for just such purposes, is factor analysis with oblique rotation. Gary King captures the desired logic:

> In the factor analysis model, there are many observed variables from which the goal is to derive underlying (unobserved) factors. A common mistake is to view the observed variables as causing the factor. This is incorrect. The correct model has observable *dependent* variables as functions of the underlying and unobservable factors. For example, if a set of opinion questions asked of the political elite is factor analyzed, underlying ideological dimensions are likely to result. It is the fundamental ideologies that cause the observed opinions, and it is precisely because these ideologies are unobservable that we measure only the consequences of those ideologies.[14]

Proceeding in this way should also guarantee that the result is not just the substance preferred by one or another deracinated intellect. Which is to say: Recent political history generates the initial hypotheses, and the general public gets to confirm or disconfirm them. Moreover, elements of that public get to structure the answers in their own way, theoretical logic potentially to the contrary. Indeed, when issues of the day do tap into ongoing concerns which affect portions of the general public in distinctive ways, that is probably because they resonate with key elements of social experience. Those who share this experience thereby form an implicit coalition; outside analysts are, by that time, irrelevant. More to the practical point, such concerns *and* their social alignments do not need to be consciously abstracted (or even explicitly understood) in order to shape political strategy in powerful ways.

Issue Dimensions for the Modern Era

Accordingly, items in the initial Times Mirror/Gallup survey that possessed both an arguable policy content and some evident substantive connection to the hypothesized surface dimensions of political opinion were submitted to a first-order factor analysis. The notion of "policy content" was interpreted broadly, so that personal orientations with prospective policy implications would qualify. The apparent face connection to the four hypothesized dimensions was interpreted broadly as well, to permit the maximum scope for public definition of these issue areas, without surrendering the evident substance of recent politics (and thus, we felt, the practical applications of the analysis) to purely mechanical criteria.

While this manner of proceeding was largely dictated by an insistence on deriving hypotheses from major themes in recent political history, it had the incidental advantage of constraining a major potential problem in factor analysis as the technical method of choice. In this, the outcome of any given factor analysis can be heavily dependent on the particular items available for analysis; filtering those items through the lens of postwar politics provided at least a constraint on that problem. At the same time, broad definitions of policy content and of face connection militated against otherwise premature limitations, against an outcome constrained too tightly by initial hypotheses—though the actual outcome, imposed by survey respondents, was also to prove reassuring in this regard.

In this way, we hoped to go looking for measures of preference on the major themes of postwar politics, while permitting the general public to mix or merge these according to actual public perceptions of their content. The full text of all relevant items is presented in the Appendix. Otherwise, it should probably just be noted, as a way of providing concrete referents for these decision rules, that they encouraged the inclusion of agreement or disagreement with propositions like "Books that contain dangerous items should be banned from public school libraries" or "We have gone too far in pushing equal rights in this country," while excluding, in a survey intended to tap many explicitly nonpolitical attitudes, agreement or disagreement with propositions like "Hard work offers little guarantee of success" or "Even today, miracles are performed by the power of God."

Initially, what emerges from the first-order factor analysis is what would conventionally be recognized as a six-factor solution, providing six further measures for the pursuit of major dimensions to American political opinion, *if* these measures can be given coherent substantive interpretations. Table 2.1 provides the structure matrix for this pursuit, deleting all factor-loadings of less than .3 so as to simplify visual examination, and reordering the items to give them a preliminary visual clustering. The six dimensions presented in Table 2.1 all have initial eigenvalues above 1.0, the minimum conventionally demanded for interpretable factors. All, as will become clear, are subject to very straightforward substantive interpretation.[15]

Table 2.1
Surface Dimensions to American Political Opinion: The First-Order
Factor Analysis

Item No.[a]	Item Identifier[b]	Factor 1: Cultural Values	Factor 2: Social Welfare	Factor 3: Foreign Relations	Factor 4: Social Insurance	Factor 5: Civil Rights	Factor 6: Civil Liberties
1	V 40206	+.67		+.36			−.42
2	V 20101	+.57			+.34		
3	V 20103	+.54		+.38			
4	V 40211	+.52					−.35
5	V 20108	+.47					
6	V 40025		+.74			+.38	
7	V 40026		+.73			+.35	
8	V 40024		+.71			+.32	
9	V 20006		+.45		+.31	+.42	
10	V 40022		+.37		+.32		
11	V 20104			+.66			
12	V 40035			+.60			
13	V 20105			−.57			
14	V 210			−.53			
15	V 212			+.48			
16	V 209			+.47			
17	V 204			+.43			
18	V 20111			+.33			
19	V 20009				+.54		
20	V 20003		+.31		+.53		
21	V 20014				+.49		
22	V 20110				+.43		
23	V 20008		+.38		+.31	+.76	
24	V 40032		+.38			+.61	
25	V 40023	+.38		+.31		−.52	
26	V 40207	+.64					−.68
27	V 40209						−.67
28	V 40210	+.33					−.62
29	V 40213	+.43		+.35			−.47
30	V 20106	+.43					−.44
	Eigenvalue	5.20	3.80	1.64	1.38	1.15	1.07

Note: All entries are structure matrix coefficients; n = 4,820; cum. var. = 47.5%.

[a]As listed in the Appendix, which provides full text for the questions.[b]

To that end, Table 2.2 displays three of the highest-loading items from each of these apparent issue dimensions. For naming purposes only, each item is assigned in Table 2.2 to the dimension on which it has its highest loading. The top three items for each dimension are then presented by content.[16] (Again, full item texts are in the Appendix.) As it turns out, the resulting substance is indeed easily summarized (and

Table 2.2
A Substantive Content for the Surface Dimensions: Three Leading Items
from Each Issue-Area

Factor 1: Cultural Values
    Firing homosexual teachers
    Making abortion more difficult
    Permitting prayer in the schools
Factor 2: Social Welfare
    Helping the needy
    Guaranteeing a place to eat and sleep
    Accepting responsibility for those who cannot
Factor 3: Foreign Relations
    Building Star Wars
    Ensuring peace through strength
    Cutting defense and military spending
Factor 4: Social Insurance
    Improving national health care
    Devoting more to retirement programs
    Providing aid to farmers
Factor 5: Civil Rights
    Programs to assist blacks and other minorities
    Preferential treatment for blacks and other minorities
    Going too far in pushing equal rights
Factor 6: Civil Liberties
    Banning dangerous books from libraries
    Restricting freedom of speech for extremists
    Allowing easy police searches

---

hence interpreted), requiring one unanticipated but familiar addition, and introducing one—but only one—genuine surprise.

Thus, the three leading items on the first of these dimensions are firing homosexual teachers, making abortion more difficult, and permitting prayer in the schools. These are three of the "hot button" concerns in what is often referred to as "the social issue." Along with an array of other items, they are obvious elements for a dimension of *cultural values*, in its orthodox designation from recent political history. Reassurance for this designation comes from the item with the next-highest loading on this dimension as well: returning women to a traditional role.

In the same manner, the three items with the highest loadings on the second of these putative dimensions are helping the needy, guaranteeing a place to eat and sleep, and accepting responsibility for those who cannot care for themselves. These are, of course, classic, effectively stereotypical elements from the concept of *social welfare* as it is normally understood, involving governmental intervention to provide protection and support for the least fortunate in society.

Three main items from the third apparent dimension are building "Star Wars," ensuring peace through strength, and cutting defense and military spending (the last inversely related). Along with a much larger array of items on this same dimension, these are straightforward elements of *foreign relations*, involving appropriate attitudes and behavior for the United States in the outside world. As with the particular incarnation of social welfare, this incarnation of foreign relations is an obvious successor to measures which have been used with public opinion data since it began to be studied systematically.

And a fourth dimension was the main substantive surprise. In one sense, it too was a version of social welfare, since its lead items were improving national health care, devoting more to retirement programs, and providing aid to farmers. These are all, in fact, classic elements of the New Deal, and thus of the American welfare state. On the other hand, philosophically, they are not so much welfare, involving simple redistribution to the truly disadvantaged, as they are insurance, involving protection against the vagaries of life in an economic marketplace. That is, all these items are not so much about providing a guaranteed minimum standard of living as they are about providing the metaphorical "safety net."[17]

To underline this distinction—apparently present in the public mind as measured here and reaffirmed in the social-group analysis of Chapter 4—we have called this dimension *social insurance*. Such a label indicates a substantive and philosophical difference from the second dimension (social welfare), just as it anticipates the possibility that different social groups will combine preferences on these two dimensions in different ways. Additional substantive reinforcement comes from the fourth highest-loading item on the social-insurance dimension: protecting American jobs.

The fifth dimension, by contrast, looks like *civil rights* and racial policy at its most stereotypical. Leading items include programs to assist blacks and other minorities, preferential treatment for blacks and other minorities, and going too far in pushing equal rights (related inversely). In principle, these items could have been parceled out among the second, fourth, and (as we shall see) sixth dimensions. Recent history, however, would argue that such a parceling is unlikely, and in practice, the sampled population apparently agreed.[18]

The sixth and last dimension is instantly recognizable, even if it does not possess one particular decade to anticipate it. This final dimension looks to be an orthodox embodiment of *civil liberties*, with main items including banning dangerous books, restricting freedom of speech, and allowing easy police searches. If such concerns cannot claim to be the "story" of any single decade, that is in part because they have surfaced, dramatically and insistently, in all. Moreover, scholarly work using survey research has been bound up with civil liberties concerns for so long that the realm can hardly be argued, in any conceivable sense, to be lacking in scholarly attention.[19] So, while this dimension did just struggle above the conventional minimum required for statistical reliability, it remains easily interpretable and very familiar in substantive terms.

Surface Dimensions and Deeper Factors

These six dimensions provide six major measures for pursuit of the implications of an issue context for recent American politics. Procedurally, these measures are the principal product of a first-order factor analysis of numerous and diverse policy items. Conceptually, these items were selected to conform, on their face, to a set of hypotheses drawn from both recent political history and contemporary social science. Practically, because the resulting dimensions did bear some evident relationship to these original guiding hypotheses, as judged simultaneously by their clustering and their substantive content, it seemed reasonable to name them accordingly.

By this designation, then, self-evident issue dimensions (and accompanying measures) did appear for the issue-areas of cultural values, social welfare, foreign relations, and civil rights. Civil liberties, while an unhypothesized issue-area, was instantly recognizable on all the same grounds. The exception, the unhypothesized appearance which might not have been anticipated on these grounds, came in the form of a division *within* the broad realm of social provision, where a further issue-area of social insurance also seemed appropriate. Such a distinction is apparently justified both in statistical and substantive terms, though whether it would hold up in subsequent analysis—whether it would prove to have distinguishable social roots along with distinguishable political attachments—was of course dependent on the analysis itself.

In the meantime, however, these six dimensions did contribute six surrogate measures for the pursuit of that analysis. On the other hand, what will serve as "findings" in one sense, and as "instruments" in another, can serve as "data" in yet a third. Which is to say that if there is indeed a deeper (and presumably simpler) structure to these putative issue dimensions, serving to gather and abstract them in the same way they gather and abstract individual opinion items, then those six surface dimensions must serve as the data for an analysis which will reveal this deeper structure. Once more, the technique of factor analysis provides the mechanism in principle for revealing such a struc-

Table 2.3
Deep Factors to American Political Opinion: The Second-Order Factor Analysis

Factor	Cultural/National Factor	Economic/Welfare Factor
1. Cultural values	+.90	+.08
6. Civil liberties	+.75	−.17
3. Foreign affairs	+.57	+.42
2. Social welfare	−.02	+.78
5. Civil rights	+.30	+.77
4. Social insurance	−.33	+.53
Eigenvalue	2.39	1.97

Note: Varimax rotation; N = 4,820; cum. var. = 59.7%.

ture, by permitting a second-order analysis, in effect a factor analysis of these first six factors.[20]

Table 2.3 sets out the product of such a second-order analysis. Here, what emerges is overwhelmingly a two-factor solution, with two of these putative deep factors possessing eigenvalues far above 1.0, and no others anywhere near that figure. Moreover, it is not difficult to impute substantive interpretations to both of these two aspiring deep factors. Each is in fact principally associated with three of the six original issue dimensions, and each cluster of three has commonalities sufficient to posit a general identity. This identity, finally, is sufficiently close to the original deep hypothesis, in face content, that this hypothesis can again be used to name the resulting measure.

The first of these alleged deep factors to American political opinion is built principally upon cultural values, civil liberties, and foreign relations. If these are read as being about domestic policy, procedural norms, and external affairs, respectively, then they have *no* evident substantive commonality and can be dismissed as an intricate statistical artifact. But if the focus is drawn instead from the initial operating hypothesis, about *the implementation of American values*—the values which define appropriate social behavior, in the small and in the large—then they can easily be viewed as having a simple and inherent congruence.

Cultural values is the domestic entree to this, as well as being the most straightforward embodiment, thematically and statistically. Foreign relations then becomes the means both of projecting these values into the non-American world *and* of proceeding so that the outside world does not hobble them at home. Civil liberties, finally, represents the central domestic means by which one or another conception of these values will either be implemented or thwarted. Given the initial deep hypothesis, the resulting composite dimension is perhaps most

accurately summarized as the *cultural/national factor,* gathering conflicts over the operational character of social life.

The second of these putative deeper factors to American political
opinion is built principally upon social welfare, civil rights, and social
insurance—and shares all the opening perceptual difficulties and all
the ultimate analytic advantages of the first. Once again, it is not
difficult to describe its three component elements so that they appear
not to have a common core. Social welfare and social insurance had to
be created as separate issue dimensions, after all, because a previously
hypothesized commonality did not emerge; and civil rights is, in the
philosophical sense, more a matter of procedures and liberties than of
entitlements and disbursements.

On the other hand, if it is possible to read these clustered dimensions as a mere statistical artifact, it is not difficult to work the other way
around: to search for a reading which would make this an appropriate,
deeper, organizing principle drawn from the other side of the initial
operating hypotheses—and to find it. In this light, social welfare and
social insurance remain, at bottom, different aspects of the same overarching concept, tapping arguments over the appropriate (re)distribu-
tion of economic benefits to the less fortunate, whether they are argued
to be in that category as a result of marketplace inequities (social insurance) or personal disabilities (social welfare). By this light, the first-order
factor analysis emphasized an important internal distinction; the second-
order analysis then restores the overarching commonality.

It is only another step to the perception that civil rights, however
the *analyst* might hypothesize its essence, is conceived by the general
public—and even more so, it develops, by black Americans (see Chapter 5)—as principally a distributional and not a libertarian matter.
Again, there is a disadvantaged population, delineated this time by
race; again, it deserves (or not) compensating benefits. In such a reading, civil rights clearly belongs with this second deep cluster even on
substance, where, in any case, it actually resides. Given the initial deep
hypothesis, the resulting deeper dimension is perhaps most accurately
summarized as the *economic/welfare factor,* gathering conflicts over the
distribution of material goods in society.

Strategic Implications: The Generic Options

If these deeper factors and surface dimensions actually constitute the
issue context for modern American politics, then the overarching strategic question is obvious: How could a political operative—a partisan
activist, a professional advisor, an electoral aspirant, or a public official—
respond strategically within such an issue context? In answering, it

will be necessary to set out their larger strategic options in the abstract, so as to establish the available repertoire of responses, before converting those responses into specific actions. In doing so, it will be easier to speak in terms of "candidates" and "campaigns" than of "office-holders" and "policy-making," though it should be noted at the outset that the underlying logic is essentially the same.

It must also be noted that many of the strategic implications of this issue structure, the putative issue context of modern American politics, need to wait upon the introduction of social groups and political parties. Or at least, preferences on such issue dimensions have often been tied quite powerfully to social groups, so that the need to operate through (or countervail) this tie is a potentially powerful constraint upon strategic options. Even more to the practical point, political parties have ordinarily served to structure the options on such issue dimensions, so that party positions—and party behavior—are likely to be an even stronger constraint. Chapters 3 and 4 will show that both considerations remain powerfully relevant and thus remain central aspects of the strategic landscape.

On the other hand, a basic framework, this putative issue context, already encapsulates the *generic* strategies available to the politically active. This framework goes on to provide structured incentives toward the deployment of these strategies. It also goes a long way toward specifying their precise application. So it should be possible, first, to set out the strategic options inherent in any issue structure, once that structure has been identified. And it should be possible, second, to put specific instructions alongside these abstract possibilities, thereby elaborating the available concrete strategies with some precision. The remainder of this chapter will do this abstractly; the chapters that follow will do it much more concretely, giving intended strategic "bite" to these abstract possibilities.

Yet it is possible to talk about generic strategies, as an introduction to all that follows, because there are, at bottom, only two general responses to any specific issue, once it has broken through to public attention. Having chosen one mode of response or the other, the candidate then has a range of additional choices. But at the start, there is only the basic option. In essence, a candidate can either reposition on the issue(s) which the larger environment has presented, considering and/or adjusting a personal stance, or can attempt to shift the terms of the debate, devoting strategic energies to propelling some *other* issue(s) to public attention.

Much writing about political issues and political conflict assumes the first of these overarching choices, and not without good reason.[21]

That is, it assumes that adjusting a position in response to the rise of a specific issue is either the simplest tactic or is otherwise unavoidable. A candidate can, in principle, be directly responsible for a personal position; in any case, the *statement* of that position is clearly under his or her control. Moreover, the perceived need to respond reflects the fact that the matter in question has already become a public issue, either because some other candidate has successfully propelled it to public attention or because external events have effectively accomplished the same thing.

On the other hand, there are good and inherent reasons why any candidate would prefer not to be stuck with the option of positioning (or repositioning) on some existing matter of conflict. At a minimum, the preferred public position may be genuinely unclear, perhaps even to the general public. Hence, even the most self-conscious attempt to cater to that public may prove ultimately harmful to the caterer. Beyond that, when there is a clear public preference on the conflict in question, some other candidate may already have staked it out. Having previously taken that position in a high-profile manner, this other candidate is already, in effect, a more likely beneficiary of this association than are any successors. Finally, even when a clear public preference exists but a prior candidate claim does not, a given candidate may be *unable* to take the preferred public position, being constrained either by a personal political history or by a current personal base of support.

Under any or all of those conditions, the wise hypothetical candidate takes the other grand option and attempts to shift the focus of debate. Politics being a relentless business with more losers than winners over the long run, it is worth emphasizing that neither branch of this fundamental choice is automatically superior: both can entail major costs. Moreover, actually changing the substance of political debate is always more easily said than done. Existing issues of the day already have the presumption of some public attention, along with some public resonance. As a result, failing to address them can have its own costs, especially where there is no guarantee of success in shifting the debate. Nevertheless, repositioning on an established issue may be even more reliably harmful, when it merely serves to emphasize an item on which another candidate already controls the optimal position.

So, some candidates will always try, in principle, to shift the substance of debate. And when they do, they will essentially have three— and apparently, only three—further options. Once again, the first may be the simplest, in the narrow sense of being easiest to execute. Faced with a specific issue of the day which is associated with a given surface dimension of political opinion, and knowing that some other candidate is favored by its specifics, the remaining candidate (or candidates) can look for a different issue *within the same surface dimension.* Faced with, for example, an issue from the dimension of cultural values, one upon which there is a conservative majority, a more liberal candidate searches for another issue from the same dimension, one where there is a liberal majority instead. Or, faced with an issue from the dimension of social welfare, one where there is a liberal majority, a more conservative candidate searches for another issue, still from the dimension of social welfare, where there is a conservative majority instead. And so on.

That is, then, the first obvious and logical option. Presumably, it has certain inherent advantages. If public attention is actively engaged by something within the dimension of cultural values (or social welfare, etc.), it may well be easier to shift attention within that dimension than to get the public to abandon it entirely. Nevertheless, such a response also shares some of the dilemmas inherent in the prior choice, between repositioning on one issue or shifting the debate to another. Indeed, in the case of this first suboption, the shared dilemma may be particularly acute.

From one side, a candidate attempting to shift the issue focus *within* a particular surface dimension may simply not succeed, failing to garner public attention for his or her preferred alternative, while simultaneously failing to present a useful position on the issue which the candidate was trying to avoid. From the other side, by concentrating energies and resources on one or more other issues within the *same* surface dimension, this candidate may actually emphasize the dimension itself, thereby (re)emphasizing the original issue which gave rise to the need for a strategic response.

That situation leads, quite naturally, to the second subcategory of response within the general option of shifting the debate. Faced with an unattractive issue of the day from a specific surface dimension of political opinion, an opponent (or opponents) can of course attempt to shift not just the specific issue but the entire dimension—in the first instance, to one of the other surface dimensions within the same, organizing, deep factor. Again, to convert the abstract point into a concrete case, if the issue of disadvantage is within the dimension of cultural values, an opponent can attempt to shift the focus of debate to an issue within the dimension of foreign relations or civil liberties instead. Alternatively, if the issue of disadvantage is within the dimension of social welfare, an opponent can attempt to shift the focus of public conflict to an issue within the dimensions either of social insurance or civil rights. Both changes are still within the underlying factor, yet away from the specific dimension of disadvantage.

Once more, while this is likewise a major abstract possibility for strategic response, it offers no inherent (abstract) guarantee of success. At a minimum, an obvious and potentially countervailing issue, one which can plausibly be elevated to a similar level of public attention, may not be available within the same deeper opinion factor. Moreover, if it is, it still needs to be available in a fashion which does not simultaneously contribute further emphasis to the *original* issue, which created the need for a specific evasion.

The truth of this situation—the actual existence of such a specific alternative—always depends on the particular aspects of the contest in question, be it an electoral or an institutional contest. There is, however, reason to believe that such issues are not, in principle, reliably present. Or at least, the very fact that various surface dimensions are partial expressions of some underlying factor suggests that an assault on one issue that has acquired public attention, by way of another issue with lesser attention *within the same general factor*, always risks emphasizing the initial problem, rather than ducking it.

This leads, naturally and finally, to the third great suboption within the overarching strategic decision to (try to) shift the center of debate. That is, of course, the strategy of trying to counter a disadvantageous issue of the day which falls within one of the two deep factors of political opinion with an advantageous (aspiring) issue of the day which falls within the other. In concrete terms, this either means displacing a specific issue within the cultural/national factor with one from the economic/welfare factor, or it means the opposite.

Further Implications: Contexts as Constraints

That is the strategic side of the equation. In the abstract, it constitutes a response to the question, Within the contemporary issue context, what are the available alternative strategies? More concretely, the same strategic overview constitutes an answer to the question, What can *political actors* do with the world as they find it? We shall return to these opening queries in the concluding chapter, with pointed applications from recent presidential elections. Yet it would be just as easy, now, to summarize this situation more abstractly, asking instead, What does such an issue structure permit—and demand? Or again, somewhat more concretely, what does the contemporary *issue context* elicit from—and allow to—those same political actors?

The raw materials for an answer to both sets of questions are, of course, identical: two deep factors to political opinion, a cultural/national and an economic/welfare factor, which gather and organize six surface dimensions to that opinion—namely, cultural values, social welfare, foreign relations, social insurance, civil rights, and civil liberties—which in turn gather and organize a welter of individual policy issues. Looking at these materials from the candidate side produces an array of potential strategies. Looking at them as a structure encourages seeing them instead as *constraints upon* such strategies—that is, as incentives for some responses and disincentives for others, or even as predictors that some gambits will prosper and others will fail.

Said differently, viewing these policy items as an issue context underlines the extent to which candidates are not free, for example, to talk about social welfare as a means of emphasizing their cultural/national credentials, or to talk about civil liberties as a means to damage an opponent on economic/welfare matters, or, indeed, to escape the influence of economic/welfare alignments by talking about civil rights or the influence of cultural/national alignments by addressing foreign affairs. Such abstracted strictures are still hardly the whole of constraints on practical politics. Partly, this is just because practical politics occurs, by definition, in a particular place and time. But also, it is because applied politicking grows out of a particular social context and because it ordinarily occurs by means of—within and through—political parties.

Yet if both this opinion structure and its associated strategies remain a trifle abstract and hence ethereal, that is in large part because they still need to be immersed in the major political institutions charged with drawing them into aggregate politics, namely, political parties, and because they still need to be associated with the major social institutions normally expected to give individual preferences on these matters a collective shape, namely, social groups. Nevertheless, this general issue structure will never hereafter be absent in the analysis of parties, groups, or specialized actors within them—just as the general options for responding *within* this issue context will only be refined, not changed, by adding these critical further elements.

3 A STRUCTURE FOR POLITICAL OPINION

Political Parties and Partisan Preferences

How does this opinion structure find its way into practical politics? Indeed, where do individual positions within this structure originate, before they ever find their collective way in? The conventional answer to the first question is "by way of political parties." And the conventional answer to the second is "from social experience," an experience differing, inevitably, for different social groups. Chapter 3 thus attempts to tie this opinion structure to political parties. Said differently, it attempts to place individual Americans within this structure by means of their partisan attachments. Chapter 4 then attempts to tie this opinion structure to social groups, placing individuals within it by means of their group memberships instead.

Opinion data alone—or, for that matter, any slice of the actual opinions being measured—can hardly resolve the question of how political parties contribute to translating public wishes into governmental policy. That is, in large part, an institutional question. Nor can such data (or the actual opinions) confirm the evolution of individual preferences, along the way to manifesting a group connection. That is, in turn, a matter for longitudinal analysis. What such data can potentially do is to comment systematically on the question of how political parties and social groups "structure" political opinion. Which is to say: What such data can do is to comment upon the *association between* preferences on the deep factors or surface dimensions of political opinion and the bedrock institutions for shaping or transmitting those preferences.

In the case of social groups, this is initially a question of *which* group memberships actually possess distinctive preference patterns on the deep factors and surface dimensions of American political opinion. Thereafter, it is a question of the content of these (group) profiles. In the case of political parties, the matter of key institutions is effectively settled: it is the Democratic and Republican parties which will offer the critical opinion profiles, if such profiles exist at all. If they do, the question then becomes which policy preferences actually have a clear association with partisan attachments and, by subtraction, which do not.

Political Parties as a Structural Focus

It is no surprise, by hindsight, that the first great round of attempts to study public opinion and its structural attachments self-consciously, by means of sample survey data at the immediate beginnings of the postwar period, reflected these apparently inherent alternatives—reflected, in fact, a tension between them. As opinion data from scientific samples of the American public became increasingly available, immediately after World War II, social scientists perhaps inevitably looked to these same two theoretical principles (and these same two institutionalizing devices) for organizing their own first empirical investigations.[1]

These foci were never, of course, practically inconsistent. Indeed, it was a rare scholarly work that did not bring social groups into an analysis beginning with political parties, or political parties into an analysis beginning with social groups. Yet the simple process of writing about political opinion required some editorial—and in truth, intellectual—priority. Not surprisingly, then, with the arrival of survey research, there were two clear conceptual starting points, with two clear procedural approaches following from them, though these are surely much easier to distinguish (and stereotype) forty years later than they would have been at the time.

The first of these grew out of a basically sociological tradition, in which first social background and then social groups shaped individual opinions, including political opinions. This was not, even initially, a purely—a mechanistically—sociological approach, in that the degree of individual identification with the relevant social backgrounds and social groups was also consequential. But society, not polity, was still the focus of what would sometimes be described, after the fact, as the "Columbia school" of research on public opinion and voting.

Two landmark works came to symbolize this school. The first, *The People's Choice: How the Voter Makes Up His Mind in a Presidential Campaign*, appeared in 1944; the second, *Voting: A Study of Opinion Formation in a Presidential Campaign*, followed in 1954.[2] Their conclusions are diagnostic of a view of the structuring of political opinion which concentrates on social background and on the social groups most intrinsic to individual identity. Thus, *The People's Choice* concluded that

> there is a familiar adage in American folklore to the effect that a person is only what he thinks he is, an adage which reflects the typically American

notion of unlimited opportunity, the tendency toward self-betterment, etc. Now we find that the reverse of this adage is true: a person thinks, politically, as he is, socially. Social characteristics determine political preference.[3]

A decade later, *Voting* (still) came to the same general conclusion:

> In Elmira, then, it is the socioeconomic classes, on the one hand, and the religious and ethnic groups, on the other, that serve as the social carriers of political traditions. In the country at large, to these two kinds of differentiation in the population is added the ecological division of region or size of community (e.g., the metropolitan area as against the small town). In contrast, there are only minor differences in voting between men and women or between young and old or, indeed, on any other characteristic.[4]

By the time *Voting* was published, however, work had already begun on another major "characteristic," in what would be the centerpiece of the alternative approach. This grew principally from social psychology (rather than sociology), where the attitudes, perceptions, and preferences of the individual were the starting point. Again, this was not a purely social-psychological approach, even at the outset, since it was being utilized by self-conscious political scientists who were focusing, naturally and inherently, not just on political opinions but on political *parties.* When their data appeared to affirm the importance of parties and partisanship—of "party identification"—this second group was confirmed in their alternative approach.

Once more, these particular founding figures were often referred to, after the fact, as the "Michigan school" of research on political attitudes and voting behavior, though this again overstates the intellectual distance between two schools of thought and, indeed, the social isolation between two groups of scholars. In any case, by the time *Voting* was published in 1954, extending the basically sociological approach, it was joined by the precursor of the major works of the Michigan school, which consciously differed. The key preliminary work here, *The Voter Decides,* asserted instead:

> The experience of the last two presidential elections has shown us, however, that the simple classification of voters into sociological categories does not have the explanatory power that at first appeared . . . Many a political prognosticator has been led into difficulties by the confident assumption that the major population classes will vote in the next election as they have voted in the recent past, and seldom has this been more true than it was in 1952 . . .
>
> Additional information regarding the dynamics of voting behavior can be obtained by an approach at the level of attitudes, expectations, and group loyalties, the psychological variables, which intervene between the

external events of the voter's world and his ultimate behavior. Successful identification and analysis of these "intervening variables" should provide insights into the problem of voter motivation beyond anything we can hope to achieve through attempting to relate specific campaign events to the vote, or by classifying the votes of the major demographic classes.[5]

The very first "intervening" device tested in *The Voter Decides*—indeed, the title for the very next chapter—was "party identification." It proved promising there, and two landmark works subsequently realized its promise, thereby putting the basic framework into place and ultimately symbolizing the entire approach. These were, of course, *The American Voter*, appearing in 1960 (with a widely used, abridged edition four years later), followed by *Elections and the Political Order* in 1966.[6] Practically, these books were instrumental in institutionalizing the study of American electoral behavior. Conceptually, they also contributed what was to become the dominant framework for such study. Effective institutionalization, in turn, probably reinforced intellectual dominance. All followed on from a fundamental conclusion: "Apparently party has a profound influence across the full range of political objects to which the individual voter responds. The strength of relationship between party identification and the dimensions of partisan attitude suggest that responses to each element of national politics are deeply affected by the individual's enduring party attachments."[7]

The ascendancy of political parties (and party identification) in the study of American political opinion thus had multiple roots. It began, at bottom, with the fact that an explicit partisan approach appeared simply to fit the data better. The presidential election of 1952 brought a powerful change in partisan outcomes from 1948 but far more limited change in the social background of its electorate, while the presidential election of 1956 actually brought differing swings in congressional versus presidential voting from the *same* electorate. While both research frameworks made use of social groups and political organizations in addressing these elections, electoral outcomes were simply better handled, for most purposes, by the "Michigan" rather than the "Columbia" framework. As *The American Voter* noted,

> Most Americans have an enduring partisan orientation, a sense of party identification, which has wide effects on their attitudes toward things that are visible in the political world. Were party identification the sole determinant of the psychological forces on behavior, the attitudinal components of the vote would agree in their partisan direction with the party loyalties of a majority in the electorate. But we know that party identification is not the sole influence on how the voter appraises the things he is acting toward. In some elections the public's evaluations of the current

elements of politics may not agree with its predominant partisan allegiances, and when they do not, in a system where the standing balance of party identification is not too uneven, the difference between evaluations of current political objects and long-term partisan loyalties may be wide enough to elect the candidate of the minority party.[8]

Yet there was more to it than that, for disciples of *The American Voter* went on to establish a further conceptual framework, by way of partisan self-identification, which was to prove capable of integrating a broad array of political phenomena. These ranged all the way from the impact of "cross-pressures," in the form of defection rates or of the actual timing of candidate choices, to the very occasional but always decisive, grand shifts in the distribution of party preferences themselves. The concept of a "normal vote," built essentially on elaboration of (and differentiations within) party identification, rather than on social background and group membership, was central to all of this and exemplified the simplicity and power of the approach. Yet even it was only the keystone of a much larger conceptual edifice.[9]

By hindsight, two generations later (and two generations of research later as well), this seems a natural outcome. On the one hand, social background may well be more individually formative than partisan attachment, and one or more key social groups are often more central to current personal opinions than even that great political intermediary, the political party. Yet on the other hand, and more to the practical point, political parties are just much more proximate to the actual operation of governmental institutions. From one side, they are indeed a major organizing *mechanism* for those institutions. From the other, they are inevitably more proximate to explicitly political opinions, or at least to those opinions which parties are likely to nurture in practical politics.

Party Identification and the Deep Factors

The orthodox means of measuring mass partisanship—of distinguishing the aggregate of self-described Republican and Democratic identifiers—was contributed by *The Voter Decides*.[10] This involves a two-step, branching question, which permits a variety of (re)combinations afterward, depending on the purpose of the analysis; the Times Mirror survey, too, adopted this procedure for assessing partisan attachment. In it, the orthodox opening query is, "Generally speaking, do you think of yourself as a Republican, a Democrat, an independent, or what?" For those accepting a partisan designation, its strength is probed with "Would you call yourself a strong [Republican/Democrat] or a not very strong [Republican/Democrat]?" For those initially claiming partisan independence, there is an alternative probe, "Do you think of yourself as closer to the Republican or Democratic party?"

Our purpose was to isolate the two great parties-in-the-electorate and then pursue the role of identification with one of these two parties. Accordingly, we have classified all those who accepted a Republican or Democratic self-designation under the first question, along with all those who confessed to being closer to the Republican or Democratic party under the third, as Republicans or Democrats, respectively. Which is to say: all those with at least Republican *leanings* have been classified as Republicans, and all those with at least Democratic leanings as Democrats. Again in the standard manner, this leaves as pure independents only those who claimed independence under the first question, and then denied any partisan closeness under the third.[11]

The results, beginning at Figure 3.1 for the opinion relationships with party identification, are actually presented in terms of weighted scale scores, which are derived from the original factor analysis (at Table 2.1 ff.). Use of factor scores as a main measure has a major drawback in the demands they make on the overall sample: every item used in the analysis must be answered by every respondent. Said differently, only respondents who answer all the items used in the analysis can make their way into the effective sample, thereby often sharply reducing its total size. This was true in our case as well, since a respondent would have had to answer all thirty items in order to appear in tables based on factor scores.

A simple correction is to use factor loadings (from the original factor analysis) to create weighted scale scores, and that is what we have done here. For these, participating individuals need only answer (all) the questions in each individual scale, so that sample size is likely to be greatly restored. In our case, we constructed five-item scales for each of the two deep factors and six surface dimensions, taking the five items which loaded most heavily on these factors or dimensions, and then weighting them according to their individual loadings.[12] As expected, this radically reflated the sample, thereby promising much greater reliability to positions and preferences for particular subsections within it.[13]

Accordingly, in the figures that follow, we have gone on to use weighted scale scores, standardized (to a mean of 0 and a standard deviation of 1.0) for ease of comparison. For immediate comprehension, we have also converted these so that the positive side is "liberal" and the negative side "conservative" throughout.[14] Within this initial division of the general public by party identification, three simple points characterize the relationship between the political parties in the

Figure 3.1.A
Mass Party Position on the
Deep Factors of Political Opinion

Cultural/National

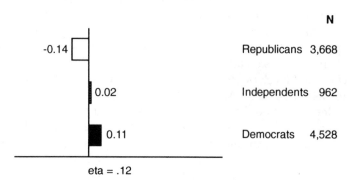

eta = .12

Figure 3.1.B
Mass Party Position on the
Deep Factors of Political Opinion

Economic/Welfare

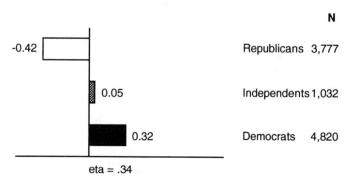

eta = .34

electorate and the deep factors of political opinion (Fig. 3.1). Each merits a summary and some elaboration, not just for its own sake, but because each will also characterize relationships between the mass parties and the six surface dimensions of political opinion:

1. Both deep factors to American political opinion show a clear relationship to aggregate partisanship.

2. This relationship is ideologically parallel across the factors, with Republi-

cans more conservative and Democrats more liberal on both cultural/national and economic/welfare matters.

3. There is nevertheless an important distinction in the strength of association, with the economic/welfare factor distinguishing mass identifiers much more clearly than the cultural/national factor.

Even the first of these findings—the mere fact that the parties as aggregates differ on both deep factors or, said differently, that each deep factor can distinguish the two parties—probably deserves comment. By comparison both to political parties in other nations and to their own history, modern American parties are usually argued to be "weak." Unlike parties in other developed democracies, they cannot formally impose a nominee chosen by the party hierarchy. Unlike their own situation in the immediate postwar years, they no longer possess the informal resources necessary to command an army of party workers in the wards, precincts, townships, and towns across the nation. Indeed, the two major American political parties appear to have declining power even as a focus of psychological attachment for the general public, at least if their share of self-described strong partisans is any indication.[15]

Nevertheless, despite all that, they are obviously focused enough to feature distinguishable partisan profiles on the deep factors of political opinion. Said differently, they are hardly so inconsequential that these deep factors cannot distinguish the parties in the electorate, even just as mass aggregates. Moreover, not only do the parties manage to present different issue positions on both underlying factors of American political opinion; they also offer these positions in an ideologically parallel fashion. That is, Republican identifiers are collectively more conservative on both, and Democratic identifiers are more liberal. Such labels—"liberal" and "conservative"—are in truth not ideal for either factor. "Progressive" versus "traditionalist" might be better for the cultural/national factor, "redistributive" versus "market-oriented" for the economic/welfare factor.

In conventional intellectual usage, however, an ideological parallelism does obtain across both deep factors within the two mass political parties, despite the fact that these factors are clearly independent of each other in the nation as a whole. This is not the same as asserting that social experience will or should move any given group or individual to this same combination of preferences, jointly liberal or jointly conservative. Indeed, some major American social groups do put them together quite differently. (See Chapter 4.) But it *is* to say that students of political ideology have conventionally used the terms "liberal" and "conservative" as shorthand in just this fashion, and that the two parties link them in this (theoretical) fashion as well.[16]

On the other hand, and finally, none of this should be allowed to mask a crucial difference *between* partisan links to the two deep factors. Party identification—thinking of oneself as a Republican or a Democrat—is just much more closely tied to the second deep factor, to economic/welfare concerns, than it is to the first, to cultural/national matters. The distance between the overall partisan means tells the story one way: a major gap (.74) between mass party positions on economic/welfare matters (−.42 to +.32), a much more minor gap (.25) between mean party positions on cultural/national concerns (−.14 to +.11). The difference between measures of association (of issue position and partisan attachment) then affirms that this is not artifactual: an eta of .34 with economic/welfare matters, but of only .12 with cultural/national concerns.[17]

In perspective, this comparative partisan standing may seem natural and appropriate. Or at least, economic/welfare matters were central to the reshaping of partisan self-identification at the time of the Great Depression and the New Deal. There has been no similarly cataclysmic set of events since, and there has certainly been no similarly dramatic shift in public attachments to the parties, rivaling the one which apparently converted a Republican majority into a Democratic majority within a few years in the 1930s. Accordingly, the continued centrality of economic/welfare matters (rather than cultural/national concerns) to partisan attachments seems straightforward.[18]

Party Identification and the Surface Dimensions

The six surface dimensions of American political opinion add a variety of elaborations—twists and turns—to these original relationships, between mass partisanship and the deeper factors of opinion (Fig. 3.2). The same three basic points can nevertheless still be made, succinctly and accurately: Every dimension still shows some partisan connection, though this can now be quite attenuated. Every connection is still in the (same) ideologically parallel direction, Republicans to the right and Democrats to the left. Finally, these surface dimensions, too, can still be distinguished as between the strongly partisan and the far less partisan, between the more and the less party-related. Yet with this last point, the number of conditions and permutations also grows.

Thus, among the surface dimensions principally associated with the economic/welfare factor, there is a further hierarchy of partisan attachment—one suggesting a new, and not the old, partisanship. In

Figure 3.2.A
Mass Party Positions on the
Surface Dimensions of Political Opinion

Cultural Values

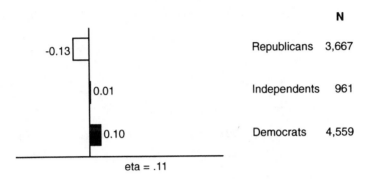

	N
Republicans	3,667
Independents	961
Democrats	4,559

-0.13

0.01

0.10

eta = .11

Figure 3.2.B
Mass Party Positions on the
Surface Dimensions of Political Opinion

Social Welfare

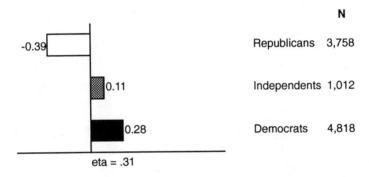

	N
Republicans	3,758
Independents	1,012
Democrats	4,818

-0.39

0.11

0.28

eta = .31

this, *civil rights* is now marginally the leading partisan concern (Fig. 3.2.E and Table 3.1). It would be surprising, given recent (and apparently continuing) political history, if the civil rights dimension had not acquired a mass partisan attachment.[19] Clearly it has, and with a vengeance. Yet it is only just ahead of social welfare, which shows the same sharp partisan distinctions, with the party mean well to the right of the national average for Republicans, well to the left of that average for Democrats (Fig. 3.2.B and Table 3.1). In the same "new partisan-

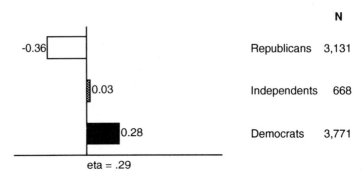

Figure 3.2.C
Mass Party Positions on the
Surface Dimensions of Political Opinion

Foreign Relations

eta = .29

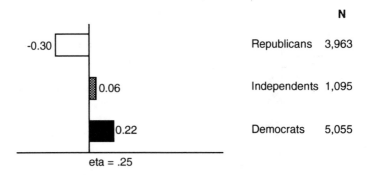

Figure 3.2.D
Mass Party Positions on the
Surface Dimensions of Political Opinion

Social Insurance

eta = .25

ship," then, social welfare has apparently become the main embodiment of partisan difference on *explicitly* distributional concerns.

That leaves social insurance as a modest anomaly (Fig. 3.2.D and Table 3.1). On the one hand, it does retain a partisan attachment, of the orthodox sort. On the other, it was really social insurance, not social welfare, which etched the great partisan differences of the New Deal era—yet social insurance no longer matches the partisan bite of a number of other dimensions. Chapter 5 will suggest that this dimen-

Figure 3.2.E
Mass Party Positions on the
Surface Dimensions of Political Opinion

Civil Rights

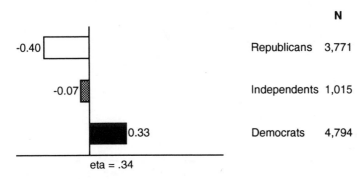

eta = .34

Figure 3.2.F
Mass Party Positions on the
Surface Dimensions of Political Opinion

Civil Liberties

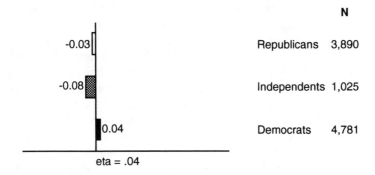

eta = .04

sion has become invested, in our time, with strongly group-related (rather than just party-related) considerations. Chapters 6 and 7 will go on to suggest that its peculiar status among economic/welfare dimensions is also rooted in elite-mass tensions internal to the political parties.

The component dimensions of the cultural/national factor present almost a mirror image of this partisan situation, albeit one which is actually exaggerated by the mirror. Civil liberties is archetypal, offer-

Table 3.1
Comparative Partisanship of Contemporary Issues

	Distance between Partisan Means (range)[a]	Strength of Association (eta)
Deep Factor		
Economic/Welfare	.74	.34
Cultural/National	.25	.12
Surface Dimension		
Civil Rights	.73	.34
Social Welfare	.67	.31
Social Insurance	.52	.25
Civil Liberties	.07	.04
Cultural Values	.23	.11
Foreign Relations	.62	.29

[a]Ranges may differ slightly from a calculation based on Figs. 3.1 and 3.2 due to rounding.

ing only the barest of partisan connections (Fig. 3.2.F and Table 3.1). But cultural values is not that far behind (Fig. 3.2.A and Table 3.1). On the one hand, both do show some minimal partisan distinction, which deserves mention precisely because cultural/national concerns were *not* central to the formation of the New Deal party system—were, indeed, arguably slanted in the other direction, with more traditionalistic Americans being disproportionately attracted by the newly invigorated Democratic program. On the other hand, these partisan links remain impressively weak, the one with civil liberties being nearly nonexistent. Once more, Chapter 5 will suggest that these are classically group-dominated (rather than party-dominated) dimensions, with some individual distinctions involving particular social groups.

Yet the cultural/national factor also contains its own striking internal exception. For among the surface dimensions associated with cultural/national concerns, foreign relations actually demonstrates a strong partisan attachment (Fig. 3.2.C and Table 3.1). Earlier scholarship on public opinion would have judged this, too, to be anomalous. Foreign policy was normally bipartisan in practice; mass partisan differences on it were normally quite secondary to counterpart differences on social insurance. Yet events in the recent history of foreign relations, from the Vietnam conflict through the Gulf War, suggest that the two parties *have* polarized on this dimension; and recent research on political opinion suggests a concomitant rise of mass partisan attachment in the foreign-policy arena.[20] Respondents to the Times Mirror survey obviously belong in that more recent world.

None of these distinctions (among the surface dimensions) even threatens to alter the underlying relationship between the economic/welfare factor or the cultural/national factor and ultimate partisan *impacts*. Indeed, this relationship will remain one of the strongest, and thus most strategically relevant, through all sorts of further elaborations and refinements—by membership in social groups, for example, and by level of political activity as well. What the surface dimensions will do, within that larger relationship, is to provide different ways of *implementing* concrete policy appeals, and thus different strategic elaborations and implications as a result. These latter must await the introduction of social groups and of elite-mass distinctions before they can be accurately interpreted. Further implications from the fundamental and underlying difference between the partisan impacts of economic/welfare versus cultural/national concerns, on the other hand, do not need to wait.

Strategic Implications: A Partisan Structure

Obviously, political parties, even of the much-maligned American variety, do provide an organizing principle for public preferences on policy concerns. Partisanship—personal identification with one or the other of the two major political parties—is clearly and straightforwardly associated with both the deep factors and the surface dimensions of political opinion. As a result, preferences on both these underlying factors and their surface translations can be used to differentiate the mass base of the two political parties. The strength of these relationships still varies from realm to realm, and this variation itself has potential consequences. Yet there is some partisan association everywhere; it reaches impressive levels in a number of domains; and it runs in a parellel fashion across them all.

There are grounds for considering all this to be a genuine surprise. Or at least, the conventional view of what makes American political parties nationally distinctive could be read to conduce toward different expectations. That view focuses programmatically on social overlap and ideological convergence. It focuses operationally on weak party organizations and formally democratized procedures.[21] Whatever the truth of these individual perceptions—and each seems fully defensible on its own—they are obviously not so strong in the aggregate as to void a clear and consistent programmatic connection between partisan self-identification and personal preference on the great issues of our time by the general public.

Indeed, in a different sense, elements of American distinctiveness in the *institutional* realm of partisan politics only increase the potential consequence of these issue relationships. For it has long appeared necessary, in dealing with American political parties, to talk about them in a tripartite fashion: party in the electorate, party as organization, and party in government. These issue relationships are a crucial element of the party in the electorate. Moreover, there is an institutional distinctiveness to American parties—genuinely exceptional by world standards—which helps to explain the need for this tripartite conception, while it goes on to magnify the consequences of any mass partisan structure to political opinion.[22]

This is, of course, the process of nomination to public office by means of public primary election, rather than by way of internal (semi-private) party procedure. Many elements of the American party system can best be understood as ramifications of this central and unique institutional way of proceeding. For our purposes, however, the point is merely that both in theory and in formal process (though to varying degrees, as ever, in actual practice), nomination by primary election places the selection of public officials in the hands of the general partisan public, into precisely the two great embodiments of the party in the electorate that have been at the center of Chapter 3. So, the issue context for American politics acquires further, potentially major, structuring principles from the mass base of the two political parties. And these are in fact institutionally augmented through the device of the primary election.

The generic fundamentals of partisan strategy remain unchanged in the face of the contemporary issue (and now institutional) context. Which is to say, the basic choice is still among (a) repositioning on a given issue of the day, (b) shifting away from that issue toward a related concern within the same surface dimension, (c) shifting out of one surface dimension and into another within the same deep factor, or (d) attempting to shift out of one deep factor entirely. (See the concluding sections of Chapter 2.) As ever, the *ease* of any one of these maneuvers—its possibilities even for execution, much less for success— is powerfully dependent on particular forces of the day. Yet now, with political parties entered onto the issue landscape, it is possible to see some further channeling principles to strategic choice, and some further constraints upon it as well.

The first of these is elementary. At a minimum, it is now clear that the mass base of the two major parties—the two political parties in the electorate—makes it very likely that partisan operatives will begin any strategic maneuvering from opposite sides of the ideological spectrum. It will surprise few to learn that Republicans will ordinarily start from the conservative and Democrats from the liberal sides, though the link between that fact and an issue context structured additionally by mass partisans is perhaps less widely appreciated. In any case, party strategists, were they not themselves inclined to approach politics from opposite ideological sides, would find that this is, in fact, where their median party supporters reside.

Seen one way, this is the territory most likely to *generate* party candidacies; seen the other way, it presumably sets limits on candidate deviations. In other words, aspiring elected officials who differ strongly from these mass partisan preferences need other, presumably substantial, countervailing assets in order to put themselves forward in what is, substantively, the "wrong" party. When they nevertheless do, they should expect an uphill fight. Mass partisanship alone, then, would give a further ideological cast to the political landscape, and this is before the proclivities of partisan activists contribute their powerfully reinforcing effects (see Chapter 6).

On the other hand, two reliable sources of variation do modify this picture. In the first, a geographically large and socially diverse nation should still permit substantial variation within the parties across the nation as a whole. With, for example, 435 congressional districts, some minority of these will *not* have mean policy preferences close to those of their national (Republican or Democratic) parties. And in a second source of variation, it should be emphasized that partisan ideological attachment is much stronger in the case of economic/welfare than of cultural/national concerns. Median party positions differ far more on the former than on the latter: that is, party identification and economic/welfare preferences are much more strongly associated than are party identification and cultural/national position. Accordingly, the mass party in the electorate presumably constrains variation in candidate strategies far more on economic/welfare issues than it does on cultural/national matters.

Nevertheless, despite the power of the basic relationships between party identification and positions on the deep factors of political opinion, and despite the further channeling effects inherent in the *difference* between this relationship for economic/welfare as opposed to cultural/national concerns, it is worth returning to two other facts. One is that politics retains substantial room for simple strategic error. If things other than issue positions can determine the outcome of political contests, it is also true that politicians (or electorates) can simply read a situation wrongly and offer (or endorse) issue positions which then merely lose. The other key fact, however, is that these initial partisan implications contain within them a set of further, implicit, second-level strategic admonitions, which offer even more pointed—and this time, differing—advice to the two political parties.

Further Implications: Interparty Conflict

The first of these further, second-level implications involves the manner in which political competition should occur. Put simply, it ought to be easier to enforce partisanship by emphasizing economic/welfare issues, just as it ought to be easier to violate partisanship—and hence to shift partisans between parties—by emphasizing cultural/national issues instead. Not only are economic/welfare preferences more strongly associated with party identification than are cultural/national preferences, but the two parties in their mass incarnations also stand much farther apart on the former than on the latter. Their candidates ought accordingly to have a much easier time reinforcing partisanship on—and by way of—economic/welfare than cultural/national concerns. Indeed, emphasized successfully, the former provide an automatic approximation to partisan attachments.

It is always possible to get the application wrong, choosing inappropriate issue embodiments or inappropriate positions on otherwise appropriate issues. Yet if the task is to activate partisan identifications, economic/welfare concerns are clearly the issues of choice. Conversely, if the task is to violate partisanship and encourage deviations from normal partisan attachments, then cultural/national concerns come into their own. Their association with party identification is much weaker; the distance between the median positions of the two parties in the electorate is much closer as well. Such a profile, again barring inappropriate or inefficient application, is thus conducive—and probably essential—to facilitating issue-based partisan defections.

Yet that is hardly the end of this particular chain of (partisan) impacts. For in fact, the basic strategic choice, between activating partisanship or encouraging deviation, is not (in our time) a generic option, whose application depends only on the issue or candidate situation of the moment. This would be true if both parties in a two-party system were of roughly equal size. But as soon as one is reliably larger than the other, the larger one acquires an inherent incentive to activate partisanship, while the smaller one acquires an equally inherent (and in many ways more pressing) incentive to obfuscate partisan attachments instead. And in the United States, during all the postwar years, despite constant and ongoing partisan fluctuations, the Democratic party has been larger than the Republican party in the electorate.[23]

Accordingly, when these abstract imperatives are crossed with the modern political landscape—when these two alternative strategies are applied to the current issue context *as it is attached to the Republican and Democratic parties*—specific imperatives for each of these parties appear. For the Democrats, the statistically dominant party, the evident principal strategy is to see that political conflict is focused on economic/welfare matters. Concentrating time, organization, advertising, and finance on economic/welfare matters is presumably one way of securing effective emphasis. Offering a sufficiently clear-cut position, so that no one should confuse the outcome from voting Democratic (or Republican), is presumably the—coordinate—other.

In this sense, the Democratic party has an incentive not to move too close to the competition. The party can still, of course, move too far away, creating an incipient Republican majority even on this most favorable factor. But it needs to remain sufficiently distinctive to provide the prerequisites of emphasis for economic/welfare matters.[24] The evident secondary element to this strategy, then, is to see that cultural/national matters stay simultaneously and solidly in the background. By extension, this requires either sufficient detachment from cultural/national concerns to provide no implicit emphasis on them, or sufficient moderation on cultural/national concerns to offer no incentive to defect when they *are* receiving emphasis.

Obviously, these strategic incentives also have a converse, a combination strategy that would, if adopted, be minimal rather than optimal. For this, the Democratic party would deemphasize economic/welfare matters, either by "assuming" them and not bothering to focus on them or by moving sharply toward the Republicans on these concerns. Simultaneously, it would put more emphasis on cultural/national matters *and* move off to the left on these. Such a strategy—the ultimate Democratic minimum—would provide no overriding issues by which the dominant partisans would be encouraged to assert their partisanship, while providing obvious incentives for those closer to the Republicans on cultural/national matters to defect.

Needless to say, the Republicans have their own, sharply different version of the same overarching strategic advice. Its evident principal demand, for the statistically smaller of the two political parties, is that cultural/national matters move to (and then stay at) the center of politics. These are the matters which would cause Democratic identifiers to defect, and if a focus on these issues runs some risk that Republican identifiers will defect in the opposite direction—as some surely would—the cold fact remains that in the absence of serious defections, the Republicans should normally lose, at least nationwide.

The evident secondary element to this strategy is thus equally

Figure 3.3.A
Attitude Combinations within the Political Parties

The Republican Party

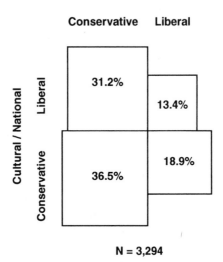

Economic / Welfare

Conservative   Liberal

N = 3,294

clear, and involves seeing that economic/welfare matters disappear, if possible, from public attention. One way to foster such a disappearance is to be sure that Republicans themselves do not attend powerfully and publicly to such matters. Presumably, an even better (though by no means mutually exclusive) way is to moderate party positions. Which is to say, a mainstream Democrat can hope to create a partisan majority from his or her "natural" party positions here, while a mainstream Republican cannot.

This dual strategy also has its destructive converse, an incarnation which promises to minimize Republican prospects. This would begin by emphasizing economic/welfare matters, while staking out a clear-cut Republican position well to the right of the national average. It would then be extended by ducking cultural/national concerns where possible and by moving to determinedly moderate positions when they did arise. There must be individual constituencies within the nation where this would actually be the right Republican strategy. But

Figure 3.3.B
Attitude Combinations within the Political Parties

The Democratic Party

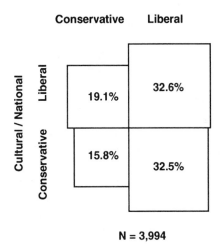

Economic / Welfare

Conservative   Liberal

N = 3,994

in most constituencies and surely for the nation as a whole, it is the best available way to guarantee that the smaller party is also the loser.

The structural incentives for these distinctive approaches show up even more strikingly when the two deep factors of American political opinion are displayed in conjunction (Fig. 3.3) The relationship of these factors to the two political parties, factor by factor, appeared sufficient to condition strategy. Their relationship to these parties, when displayed jointly, confirms that the resulting advice is not the mere product of treating individual factors in isolation. Indeed, even more vividly than with individual portraits, a two-dimensional portrayal of the mass base of the political parties shows the powerful "organizing" role of economic/welfare concerns, and the potentially powerful "confusing" role of cultural/national matters.

Both parties are, not surprisingly, defined (in issue terms) principally by way of the economic/welfare factor, though the extent of this effect may seem surprising even then. Over two-thirds of Republicans are more conservative than the national average on these matters;

nearly two-thirds of Democrats are more liberal than that average. By contrast, when cultural/national concerns are the focus, there is only the slightest recapitulation of the pattern, featuring only a modest majority of Republican identifiers as conservative and the barest majority of Democratic identifiers as liberal.

This gives rise, of course, to the same strategic environment, now seen collectively rather than factor by factor: If economic/welfare concerns are at the center of politics, and if cultural/national concerns are muted (either through moderation or through inattention), voters are maximally encouraged to assert their traditional party preferences—and Democrats ought to be at their zenith. By contrast, if economic/welfare concerns should be muted, again either through moderation or inattention, then near-majorities of each party ought to be potentially susceptible to blandishments from the other on cultural/national themes—and a huge share of the electorate ought to be potentially up for grabs.

This combination—of the basic issue context of American politics plus the structuring of that context by political parties—goes a long way toward establishing the contours within which the strategic conflict of politics can be (and must be) constructed. The basic issue context itself puts definition into a set of generic options for electoral or institutional strategy. The political parties, and party identification, begin to fill in the details of the resulting strategies. Whether these strategies can be executed successfully, however, or whether they can actually be executed at all, is also dependent on developments among the subgroups which make up the political parties. Chapter 4 turns to the first and largest aspect of this question.

4 A STRUCTURE FOR POLITICAL OPINION

Social Groups and Group Preferences

Political parties did displace social groups as the main organizing device, conceptual and practical, for empirical research about politics in the era of the sample survey. Moreover, party identification, even in its modern (and debilitated) form, retains an evident and consistent association with policy preferences. Yet none of this suggests—or ever suggested—the irrelevance of social groups. These groups, of course, hardly disappeared as elements on the social landscape or as research foci in their own right. In turn, even at the point when political parties were achieving priority over them as the organizing focus of research on politics, sensible scholars moved immediately on to social groups in their partisan analysis.

As well they might. Membership in social groups can, after all, impart a conscious social identity. It can also be a deliberate means of acquiring information about (and positions on) political events and public policy. Yet even when such developments are not intentional, membership in social groups serves as a kind of shorthand for shared experiences, and these provide both a means for judging the impact of policy options and an institutionalized *interest*, a common stake, in their outcomes.[1] Moreover, as the organizational integrity of American political parties and as the strength of public identification with them have declined, the potential for social groups to organize political opinion has only grown.

Social groups, then, still serve as the obvious next conceptual and practical stop in the search for social devices that reveal a structure to political opinion. Indeed, any attempt to ignore them would fly in the face of major and continuing strands in the interpretation of American history and of the contemporary American experience. Racial, religious, economic, and geographic diversity, in particular, along with the struggle to produce something consensually "American" from it, have been central themes in the interpretation of American life from the founding to the present.[2] The distinctions which comprise them can hardly be avoided in the search for a group structure to political opinion.

On the other hand, social groups present a difficulty in this regard which political parties did not. A focus on political parties as a generic category effectively determines the identity of the parties in question: we mean the Republican and Democratic parties. A focus on social groups, however, permits a huge array of further individual possibilities, even when limited to the categories creating racial, religious, economic, and geographic divisions. So, once these grand divisions have themselves been introduced, some further and specific means of narrowing—really, of constructing—the group universe for subsequent analysis will be required.

Social Groups as a Structural Focus

The continuity of (sub)group themes in American life has not implied that work based upon these themes lacks specificity about the *sorts* of groups which have, at each stage, provided major internal contours to society. Indeed, certain major means of categorizing—of "grouping"— American society have long served as tools for interpreting its development. Accordingly, it seems worth introducing each as a general category, and then introducing the subcategory most often argued to be central to politics in our time, before going on to the actual relationships between group membership and policy preferences, between social groups and political opinion.

Thus, *ethnicity and race* have long been a central means of placing individual Americans into social groups, not just for social analysts but, evidently, for those individuals themselves.[3] A nation built substantially through immigration, and immigration from a variety of other nations at that, provided great inherent scope for the organizing power of ethnic identifications. The persistence of ethnicity in subsequent generations was effectively indexed by the arrival of "hyphenated Americans"—Irish-Americans, German-Americans, Italian-Americans, and so on. More all-encompassing in its aggregation of ethnic groups, but also potentially in its ability to organize opinions, is race. European-Americans of various ethnic backgrounds, along with Asian-Americans of various ethnicities, contributed major racial strands to the United States. But the focal point of writings about race in American history was most often African-Americans, especially because they arrived not as classic immigrants, but as slaves.

Religion and (sub)culture have long been a second great means of placing individual Americans in a group context, and if this categorization has been blurred by ethnicity in some respects, it has remained crucially distinctive in others.[4] Many immigrant groups were themselves further divided by religious background, a fact which was equally true of the "native" population, however that is defined. Regardless, religion as a worldview *and* religion as an institution have shaped politics in the United States throughout its history. From the very beginning, religious and/or cultural dissidence served as motives for coming to the United States. Throughout the nation's subsequent development, a church or churches were reliable early institutions in any new community. And at various specific points, the great denominational distinctions—Catholic versus Protestant, of course, but also Christian versus non-Christian and even "high church" (liturgical) versus "low church" (pietistic) within the dominant Protestantism—were central dimensions of political conflict.

Social class occupied a more ambivalent position in the pantheon of American social divisions.[5] One of the principal moving causes for the founding of the American colonies, and then of an independent nation as well, was a rejection of the social stratifications of an older Europe. Nevertheless, conflict along just such lines surfaced early in the new nation, providing some of the differences in orientation toward the Revolution itself and providing a crucial distinction between, for example, the pro- and anti-Jackson forces at the point when political parties began seriously to organize mass politics. The subsequent arrival of a vast, successful, but comprehensive industrial economy meant that social class in the modern sense came inevitably to characterize the larger society: American life might soften the edges associated with the phenomenon elsewhere, but class was nevertheless integral to a mature industrial order. The New Deal is normally taken to be the high point of class association with partisan politics, yet that fact, too, serves only to emphasize the way in which class links to politics can both rise and fall, as well as operate both more and less directly.

Finally, simple geographic growth—that is, the regional diversity inherent in continental dispersion—served to introduce divisions of real consequence to the larger society, divisions involving distinctive geographic identities and underpinned by composite differences in *region.*[6] The great historical incarnation was "North" versus "South," precipitating the Civil War as this division deepened and then troubling national politics for generations thereafter. But differing patterns of immigration, differing economic possibilities in different geographic areas, differing social structures developing from different settlement patterns, along with simple differences in the sense of being allied to (or distinct from) other geographic areas—all these contributed further potential principles for structuring mass political opinion.

These great American social divides—race and ethnicity, religion and culture, class, and region—were broad, deep, and historically extended. It would be strange if they did not extend into our time as well. Yet if each is a continuing thread across American history, each has also come to the fore in specific eras, where a certain intrinsic virulence or a critical interaction with other influences has served to make it a peculiarly diagnostic division. Accordingly, if each of these has some intrinsic claim on analytic attention, each can also be assumed to possess more organizing power in some times than in others—including, presumably, our own.

For example, the great waves of European immigration have receded historically, and as the possibilities of a further European stream have been deliberately circumscribed, ethnicity has receded as a touchstone for political analysis. In part, this is an artifact rather than a true change, however, reflecting a situation in which many of the newer immigrant groups can be distinguished by race and not just by national origin. By extension, then, race itself should be receiving more attention as an analytic focus, courtesy of this same development. Yet what has really kept race as a category alive in our time has been the civil rights revolution and then the continuing centrality of race *policy* to American politics. Accordingly, black Americans would appear to have a particularly strong claim on any group focus within the general category of race and ethnicity.[7]

The place of religion and its associated subcultures probably generates less consensus among social analysts. From one side, those who believe in the long-run secularization of developed societies also believe that religious background must—and therefore will—decline as an explanation of the character of American life. From the other side, events of the last generation certainly argue that this process is not automatic, or at least not linear. Phenomena as close to the grass roots as the mobilization of religious evangelicals for electoral politics, or as distant from those roots as constitutional battles at the Supreme Court over the public observance of religion, attest to a continued vitality. In particular, the pietistic Protestants at the center of both of these examples—"born-again" Christians, the social bedrock of an ostensible "new Christian right"—appear to have an especial claim on any contemporary group focus within the general category.[8]

Social class offers an analogous version of the same ambiguity. From one side, at the grand level, there is the argument—perhaps akin to the secularization hypothesis for religion—that the shift from an industrial to a "postindustrial" economy should logically fracture the old class arrangements. Beyond this, there is the inescapable fact that the class-based electoral alignments of the New Deal have frayed substantially over time. Yet from the other side, there is the obvious (counter)argument that the class structure appearing in a postindustrial society (if indeed that is our world) should simply be different, not absent. Moreover, certain aspects of class in the old-fashioned sense, especially those involving *education*, appear actually to be on the increase as an influence on attitudes and behaviors.[9]

Finally, region presents the same possibilities for argument, though the balance, as with ethnicity, appears more clearly to favor the side asserting a decline. In this, if there is an ongoing "nationalization" to the focus not just of American politics but of American life more generally, then there is simply less room for some growing, simultaneous attitudinal regionalization. Presumably, greater economic growth in the previously less developed areas of the United States, along with greater migration in and out, only accelerate this trend. The distinctive casualty in all this, in turn, is the regional separation of the American South, as subculture rather than just geographic entity. Yet there are not only defenders of a residual Southern distinctiveness. There are also new, putative regional substitutes, as with the notion of a "bicoastal" America, a United States where the East and West Coasts are in effect allied against the broad geographic middle.[10]

Locating Critical Social Groups

Four great principles of social differentiation have thus been argued to divide American society into its most relevant social groups. Needless to say, proof of the value of such distinctions, for us, lies ultimately in their contribution to the analysis of political opinion, and especially of an issue context. Yet analysis first requires some usable measures, presumably distributed across these four social realms, and these require further distinguishing categories within them, along with associated measurement "cuts."

With ethnic and racial distinctions, despite an aspiration for a variety of further divisions, we ended by cutting the sample, simply, into "black" and "nonblack." The Times Mirror survey did collect background information on ethnicity in general. Yet the resulting European-American groups within this were each comparatively small. Moreover, in summary examination (as supported by the algorithm in Fig. 4.1), most showed little noteworthy difference from the national average, except where this was a surrogate for non-Christian religion, which is registered more effectively elsewhere. Hispanic-Americans and Asian-Americans also produced very small collectivities, and that was before further national distinctions could be introduced. Again, summary examination also suggested, at least, less stark differences from the national average than for blacks. Given recent events and recent research, then, which argued for a priority on black Americans as a potential group for analysis, we settled for the black/nonblack division.

In the case of religious distinctions, we chose a fourfold cut, given the historical background and the benefit of sufficient numbers. The great cut would traditionally have been between Protestants and Catholics, or perhaps between Protestants and everyone else. More recent history, however, suggested the importance of permitting "low" (pietistic) Protestants to emerge separately, if indeed they possessed separable combinations of preferences. Accordingly, the religious dimension was divided into Catholics, high (liturgical) Protestants, low Protestants, and non-Christians.[11] The last category blended subgroups additionally distinctive in their theology, being comprised principally of nonbelievers and secondarily of Jews. Yet within this particular conceptual approach to cutting the category, they did "belong together," and in fact, their positions on the various opinion measures were to show an impressive coherence, such that while the category retained a high internal variability—and thus a high standard deviation to its opinion scores—this still represented a consistent difference (and distance) from the other three groups.

Social class (and its relevant internal distinctions) presented a different kind of measurement problem. Ideally, this would have been solved through some mix of occupation, income, and education; failing that, it would have turned on some complex measure of occupation alone. The Times Mirror survey, however, allowed respondents to place *themselves* in broad and general occupational categories, which appeared to overlap ambiguously even then, so that the product suggested extreme problems of reliability. As a result, we felt compelled to use education alone as a surrogate. This was at least familiar and regular, and we chose to cut it into four equally familiar pieces: did not complete high school ("high-school dropouts"), completed high school ("high-school graduates"), undertook some education or training beyond high school (the "some-colleges"), and completed college ("college graduates").

Finally, for regional distinctions, while the Times Mirror survey was easily large enough to permit further subclassification, we chose to remain with the traditional cut, as used in the U.S. Census: "Northeast" (New England plus Middle Atlantic states), "Midwest" (East North Central plus West North Central), "South" (South Atlantic, East South Central, plus West South Central), and "West" (Mountain plus

Pacific).[12] We were reinforced in this, somewhat perversely, by the growing literature on the "nationalization" of American politics. In that literature, regional categories as genuine autonomous influences are in serious decline—and this includes that perennial candidate for an exemption, the American South.[13]

In any case, even these further and pointed internal cuts left a huge array of abstract possibilities for social groups that might carry the subsequent analysis—the multiplicative product, in effect, of two cuts on race, by four cuts on religion, by four cuts on class, by four cuts on region. Had we been forced to proceed by choosing among these possibilities—"weighing" recent work to see what group bases appeared to be closest to actual political *conflicts*—such an exercise might well have yielded a group universe comprising some mix of blacks, white low Protestants, high-school dropouts, high-school graduates, some-colleges, and college graduates, probably with the additional isolation of (white) non-Christians and possibly with the additional isolation of the South. Yet in the case of these social groups, this putative grand hypothesis would still be far less consensual than the hypothesis, say, that social-insurance issues characterized the 1930s and then continued on, or that civil rights issues characterized the 1960s and did likewise.

As a result, we felt the need for some additional, neutral means of testing the claims of various hypotheses about the relevant group universe, before making any single version the ultimate vehicle for a confrontation with political parties, political activists, and especially, an issue context. We needed, in short, some simple procedural algorithm. In order to create it, two further operational steps were required:

First, criteria for selecting among potential groups needed to be defined more precisely. The goal, as ever, remained the isolation of specific groups with distinctive opinion profiles. In an analysis of the impact of an issue context, after all, the social groups most clearly associated with *differentiating* that context were the appropriate focus. The final justification for any specific product would still lie in the substantive contribution the resulting universe of groups could make. Yet some clear and straightforward definition of "distinctiveness" was necessary to guide subsequent operations.

That said, testing these social groups also required some essentially *mechanical* translation, an effectively automatic procedure to apply this prior definition. Such a procedure needed to produce its groups for further analysis in line with a preceding substantive definition, of course. Yet it had to produce them more or less automatically as well, that is, so that they could be argued to be selected by the data, rather than by the historical accounts or recent events that had given rise to this particular set of group hypotheses in the first place. Once again, hypotheses derived from postwar political history had to permit their own refutation.

Conceptually, given our purposes, we sought the social groups that were most clearly distinguishable in their political opinions *in the sense of holding composite preferences most distant from the overall national average.* In proceeding in this fashion, it was not our intention to limit recognizable groups to those with extreme opinions, and in fact, the actual positions of the resulting groups on both the surface dimensions and deep factors varied substantially in this regard. (See Figs. 4.2 and 4.3.) On the other hand, it clearly was our intention that no ostensibly diagnostic pattern of consistent *moderation* result solely from the averaging of more extreme scores for two otherwise highly distinguishable subcategories within a group, as isolated by these same divisions on race, religion, class, and region. Again, if an issue context was to be revealed as shaping political possibilities (not to mention behavior), then issue differences needed to be elucidated, not suppressed.[14]

Operationally, in turn, we fell back on a simple arithmetic algorithm to infuse this definition into the universe of abstract possibilities (Fig. 4.1). This algorithm was applied, specifically, to group scores on the two deep factors of political opinion, which were calculated and summed—and then constantly recalculated and resumed—for all remaining cuts within the four grand principles of social differentiation (black, nonblack; low Protestant, high Protestant, Catholic, etc.). At each step, the category with the greatest composite difference from the national average was isolated and removed, while scores for the remaining categories were recalculated, summed, and compared, in preparation for the next, repetitive step in the same sequence. Where there were overlapping social segments, these were assigned, in similar fashion, to the social group from whom they had the *least* composite differences on opinion scores.

Formally, the algorithm also required some minimum standard, below which a given (sub)population could no longer represent the category from which it had been originally derived. On simple statistical grounds, there was inevitably a point—normally about 40% of the original membership, in our sample—where such a population became too small for the required range of subsequent internal analyses. On more directly substantive grounds, there was also a point where any given subpopulation could neither reasonably elaborate the preferences of a (putatively much larger) social group nor, especially, link those preferences to an associated historical and theoretical literature.

The precise figure for such a standard is effectively arbitrary. But because we wanted to retain maximum scope for essentially mechanical operationalization, we preferred to keep this figure low, and chose a practical cut-off—a floor—of 40%. Under these instructions, when the remnant of a category (as continually recalculated) fell below 40% of its original size (as registered at step 1 [Fig. 4.1]), it was excluded from subsequent recalculations. In practice, none of the categories distinctive enough to survive into our ultimate analysis fell anywhere near this minimum standard, so that its main practical role was to terminate the analysis (at step 20) when only one remaining category could meet its demands.

Figure 4.1 provides the precise details both of the algorithm itself and of the resulting universe of groups. It is probably the best introduction to this way of proceeding. Before analyzing the product of this algorithm, however, we would emphasize that the algorithm does proceed *sequentially*, thereby throwing the strategic landscape of American politics into particularly stark relief. Along the way, every individual is assigned to a group, but no individual contributes to the scores of more than one group. At the end, the groups themselves are mutually exclusive and jointly exhaustive.

Group Membership and Political Opinion

Figure 4.1 not only shows this process at work; it also reveals the seven social groups which emerged and which provide the group basis for the remainder of the analysis. One advantage in creating such groups purely by means of the deep factors is that it is possible to turn immediately to group profiles on the associated surface dimensions. Said differently, a further profile of each resulting group on the surface dimensions of political opinion can serve not only to describe the social structuring of political opinion. It can also become the first, tentative, substantive contribution from—and thus practical validation of—this approach. Figure 4.2 provides that first product.

Perhaps unsurprisingly, the first subcategory to emerge as a distinctive social group, in terms of its political preferences, was "black Americans." Figure 4.2.A shows their aggregate opinion profile on the surface dimensions. By far the most liberal group on civil rights, black Americans were also wildly liberal on social welfare and solidly liberal on social insurance, the three surface dimensions reflecting the economic/welfare factor. Beyond that, they proved to be modestly liberal on foreign relations, modestly conservative on cultural values, and somewhat more conservative on civil liberties. Such a profile made them massively the most liberal of the seven major groups in American

Figure 4.1

Deriving the Social Groups: An Algorithm

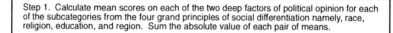

Step 1. Calculate mean scores on each of the two deep factors of political opinion for each of the subcategories from the four grand principles of social differentiation namely, race, religion, education, and region. Sum the absolute value of each pair of means.

Step 2. Q: Which is the largest composite score? A: 1.25 for black Americans. Make "**Blacks**" the first social group for subsequent analysis.

Step 3. Remove all black Americans from the sample. Recalculate mean scores on each of the two deep factors for each of the remaining subcategories from the four grand principles of social differentiation. Sum the absolute value of each pair of means.

Step 4. Q: Which is the largest remaining composite score? A: 0.99 for non-Christians. Make "**Non-Christians**" the second social group for subsequent analysis.

Step 5. Isolate the overlapping segment -non-Christian blacks- and compare its scores on the two deep factors with the scores of (a) all blacks minus their non-Christians and (b) all non-Christians minus their blacks. Sum the absolute values of these differences.

Step 6. Q: Are non-Christians blacks closer to non-Christians generally than to blacks generally? A: No, they are not (2.17 versus 0.42, respectively). Keep black non-Christians with the black social group.

Step 7. Remove non-Christians from the remaining sample. Recalculate mean scores on each of the two deep factors for each of the remaining subcategories from the four grand principles of social differentiation. Sum the absolute value of each pair of means.

Step 8. Q: Which is the largest remaining composite score? A: 0.95 for low Protestants. Make "**Low Protestants**" the third social group for subsequent analysis.

Step 9. There is no overlapping segment, by definition, for the low Protestants versus the non-Christians. Proceed with the search for the largest remaining composite score.

Step 10. Remove low Protestant from the remaining sample. Delete the subcategory "South" (down to 38% of original membership) from subsequent recalculations. Recalculate mean scores on each of the two deep factors for each of the remaining subcategories from the four grand principles of social differentiation. Sum the absolute value of each pair of means.

Step 11. Q: Which is the largest remaining composite score? A: 0.98 for college graduates. Make "**College Graduates**" the fourth social group for subsequent analysis.

Step 12. Isolate the overlapping segment -college graduate low Protestants- and compare its scores on the two deep factors with the scores of (a) all college graduates minus their low Protestants and (b) all low Protestants minus their college graduates. Sum the absolute value of these differences.

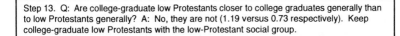

Figure 4.1 (cont.)

Step 13. Q: Are college-graduate low Protestants closer to college graduates generally than to low Protestants generally? A: No, they are not (1.19 versus 0.73 respectively). Keep college-graduate low Protestants with the low-Protestant social group.

Step 14. Remove college graduates from the remaining sample. Recalculate mean scores on each of the two deep factors for each of the remaining subcategories from the four grand principles of social differentiation. Sum the absolute value of each pair of means.

Step 15. Q: Which is the largest remaining composite score? A: 0.53 for the some-colleges. Make "**Some-Colleges**" the fifth social group for subsequent analysis.

Step 16. There is no overlapping segment, by definition, for the some-college versus the college graduates. Proceed with the search for the largest remaining composite score.

Step 17. Remove some-colleges from the remaining sample. Delete the subcategories "Non-black" (down to 33%), "Northwest" (35%), "Midwest" (32%), and "West" (28%) from subsequent recalculations. Recalculate mean scores on each of the two deep factors for each of the remaining subcategories from the four grand principles of social differentiations. Sum the absolute value of each pair of means.

Step 18. Q: Which is the largest remaining composite score? A: 0.49 for the high-school dropouts. Make "**High-school Dropouts**" the sixth social group for subsequent analysis.

Step 19. There is no overlapping segment, by definition, for the high-school dropouts versus the some-colleges. Proceed with the search for the largest remaining composite score.

Step 20. Remove high-school dropouts from the remaining sample. Delete the subcategories "High Protestant" (29%) and "Catholic" (32%) from the subsequent recalculation. At this point, only high-school graduates remain as a subcategory satisfying minimum requirements. Accordingly, make "**High-School Graduates**," with a composite score of 0.17, the seventh and final social group for subsequent analysis.

society on economic/welfare matters. It also distinguished them in the degree of *disconnection* between preferences on civil rights and, on the other hand, civil liberties.

The next group to come out of the analysis was the "Non-Christians"—white non-Christians, since black Americans had already been isolated (Fig. 4.2.B). Within the universe of social groups, these non-Christians would prove to be *comparatively* liberal across the board;

indeed, their Democratic identifiers were destined to provide the sole party faction which was liberal on every dimension (Fig. 5.4). Nevertheless, they too retained substantial variability from one issue dimension to another. Thus, white non-Christians were wildly liberal on all the cultural/national dimensions—on cultural values especially, but really on civil liberties and foreign relations as well. They were at the national average on civil rights and social welfare, dipping to a clearly conservative stance only on social insurance, on those classic social-insurance programs which, ironically, had so often been used to *define* liberalism.

Next out of the analysis was the other great religious category to emerge from this algorithm, the "Low Protestants"—white members of the pietistic Protestant denominations (Fig. 4.2.C). Even they did not fail to offer some internal variation, of potential strategic import. But here, the dominant theme was surely a blanketing conservatism. Thus, the low Protestants were militantly conservative on cultural values, still strongly conservative on foreign relations, and clearly conservative on civil liberties. Likewise, they were strongly conservative on civil rights, still clearly conservative on social welfare, and modestly conservative only on social insurance. That was greater internal variety, in truth, than that to be exhibited by two of the other major social groups (below). But it was also the most consistently conservative profile in the sample.

The remaining four subgroups were all isolated by virtue of their educational backgrounds, though both the order of their appearance and the ultimate composition of their preferences offered substantial further twists and turns. The first of these were the college graduates, followed by the some-colleges, the next group down the educational hierarchy. Yet they were to be followed by the high-school dropouts, at the opposite end of the educational continuum. And the analysis was completed when high-school graduates became the last group to possess both sufficient numbers and an interpretable social reality.

In a sequential process, the first of these groups, the college graduates, inevitably introduced an apparent (and potentially important) overlap. There had already been a tiny overlap between blacks and non-Christians, but it was both statistically unimportant and manifestly closer to blacks as a social group (steps 5 and 6 in Fig. 4.1). On the other hand, the college-graduate *low Protestants* could in principle have belonged in either the college-graduate or the low-Protestant categories, and they were substantially more numerous. Yet these individuals, at least when judged by their policy preferences, were in fact more like low Protestants who had not graduated from college than

Figure 4.2.A
Issue Profiles of Social Groups

Blacks

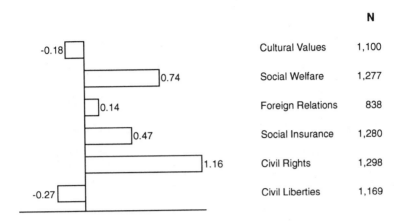

		N
Cultural Values		1,100
Social Welfare		1,277
Foreign Relations		838
Social Insurance		1,280
Civil Rights		1,298
Civil Liberties		1,169

Figure 4.2.B
Issue Profiles of Social Groups

Non-Christians

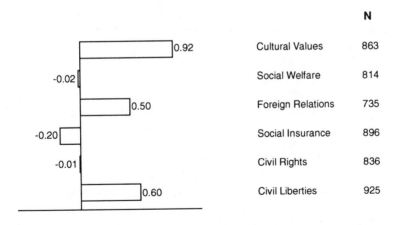

		N
Cultural Values		863
Social Welfare		814
Foreign Relations		735
Social Insurance		896
Civil Rights		836
Civil Liberties		925

Figure 4.2.C
Issue Profiles of Social Groups

Low Protestants

		N
-0.59	Cultural Values	1,950
-0.25	Social Welfare	1,950
-0.36	Foreign Relations	1,595
-0.05	Social Insurance	1,996
-0.44	Civil Rights	1,948
-0.27	Civil Liberties	1,993

they were like college graduates who were not low Protestants (steps 12 and 13 in Fig. 4.1), so that they remained appropriately with their coreligionists.

In any case, the first of the social groups defined by their educational background, the remaining "college graduates," were not just a distinguishable opinion group. They were additionally noteworthy for the internal diversity of their views across the various opinion measures (Fig. 4.2.D). As a group, they were at their most liberal on cultural/national issues, wildly so on cultural values and civil liberties but clearly so on foreign relations as well. Yet they were also the most conservative group in the nation on social insurance, clearly conservative on social welfare, and modestly so even on civil rights.

Those who had gone on to some sort of education or training after high school, but who did not go so far as to complete a college degree, also produced a distinctive opinion profile. Yet if its issue variability was not as great as that of the college graduates, this profile had other distinguishing characteristics (Fig. 4.2.E). On the cultural/national dimensions, these "some-colleges" were merely a more moderate version of their college counterparts: moderately (rather than wildly) liberal on cultural values and civil liberties, and just above the national average on foreign relations. But on the economic/welfare dimensions, they were actually more conservative than the college graduates on civil

Figure 4.2.D
Issue Profiles of Social Groups

College Graduates

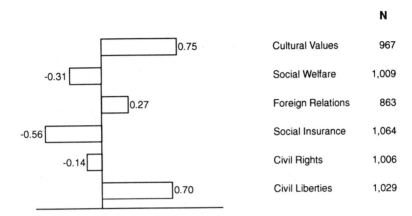

	N
Cultural Values	967
Social Welfare	1,009
Foreign Relations	863
Social Insurance	1,064
Civil Rights	1,006
Civil Liberties	1,029

College Graduates chart values: Cultural Values 0.75, Social Welfare -0.31, Foreign Relations 0.27, Social Insurance -0.56, Civil Rights -0.14, Civil Liberties 0.70

Figure 4.2.E
Issue Profiles of Social Groups

Some-Colleges

	N
Cultural Values	1,307
Social Welfare	1,347
Foreign Relations	1,100
Social Insurance	1,412
Civil Rights	1,352
Civil Liberties	1,363

Some-Colleges chart values: Cultural Values 0.22, Social Welfare -0.31, Foreign Relations 0.04, Social Insurance -0.22, Civil Rights -0.24, Civil Liberties 0.23

rights and equally so on social welfare, being more moderate (and hence more liberal) only on social insurance.

Their counterparts at the opposite end of the educational continuum, the "high-school dropouts," were next out of the analysis (Fig. 4.2.F). These individuals—those who did not complete even a high-school education in a society where over half of all high-school graduates now reliably enter college—were evidently liberal on the economic/ welfare dimensions. In this, they were at their most liberal on social insurance, clearly liberal on social welfare as well, and modestly liberal on civil rights. They were, however, even more evidently conservative on the cultural/national dimensions, especially on civil liberties and cultural values, but also on foreign relations. They thus offered an almost perfect polarity, not just educational and social but also ideological, to the college graduates.

That left the "high-school graduates," those classic Americans-in-the-middle by almost any standard, who were remarkably centrist and moderate on all these measures, too (Fig. 4.2.G). In the mechanical sense, high-school graduates were a "residual" category, because they emerged at a point in the analysis (the final step) when numerical limits and the simple absence of theoretically plausible, alternative social interpretations came into play. Yet there is no principled reason why consistent moderation should not constitute an opinion profile, and that was certainly what these middle Americans offered. They were at their most liberal on social insurance and their most conservative on civil rights, but even these were very moderate scores, and most others hugged the national average.

Strategic Implications: The Group Structure

Seven social groups, then, possessed both a long-standing historical claim on being central to American politics and a contemporary data-based claim on being central to political opinion. These included blacks, non-Christians, low Protestants, college graduates, some-colleges, high-school dropouts, and high-school graduates. Mechanically, they were distinguished by the combined absolute values of their positions on the two deep factors of American political opinion. Substantively, their scores—their preferences—on the six surface dimensions of opinion suggest that further attitudinal distinctions do accompany these initial differences.

Together, these seven constitute the group universe, providing an initial social structure to political opinion and providing a conceptual tool for further analysis as well. Yet because the isolation of these groups proceeded sequentially, with each confirmed group removed in

Figure 4.2.F
Issue Profiles of Social Groups

High-School Dropouts

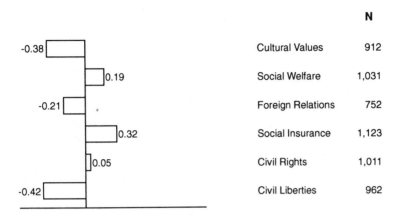

	N
Cultural Values	912
Social Welfare	1,031
Foreign Relations	752
Social Insurance	1,123
Civil Rights	1,011
Civil Liberties	962

-0.38, 0.19, -0.21, 0.32, 0.05, -0.42

Figure 4.2.G
Issue Profiles of Social Groups

High-School Graduates

	N
Cultural Values	1,668
Social Welfare	1,665
Foreign Relations	1,353
Social Insurance	1,821
Civil Rights	1,699
Civil Liberties	1,771

-0.07, 0.02, -0.02, 0.13, -0.19, -0.16

turn from the total sample, and because some (single) dominant characteristic was critical to each removal, it may be worth reassembling the collective product in yet another fashion, to be absolutely clear about the social composition of these analytically critical groups. Figure 4.3 summarizes this group universe, the product of the algorithm underlying Figure 4.1, in this other fashion.

Perhaps the most surprising aspect of the *collective* appearance of these seven groups was the role of religious background. Given recent political history, the presence of fundamentalist Protestants might not really be surprising, though the pull of low Protestantism did prove stronger even than that of a college education, in the sense that college-educated low Protestants were closer to their coreligionists than to their co-educationalists. Yet the low Protestants were actually preceded, in attitudinal distinctiveness, by the non-Christians, an amalgam of unbelievers, Jews, and a handful of others, and a population not as reliably the focus of journalistic attention.

Whether the resulting universe will prove to have additional interpretive contributions and additional strategic consequences when political parties are reintroduced or when parties are further subdivided into their more and less active identifiers must await Chapters 5 to 7. In the meantime, however, such groups *as a collectivity* do offer some immediate and additional descriptive commentary on the American political landscape. This group landscape, in turn, possesses some immediate and further strategic incentives, or at the very least, strategic implications and possibilities.

In the first of these further interpretive contributions, one which marks this collective group universe as evidently American, it should be noted that three different *forms* of social categorization—race, religion, and education—were needed to constitute the American group landscape. Indeed, race, in the form of African-Americanism, along with religion, in the form of both non-Christianity and low-Protestantism, took precedence as organizing devices over most slices of education/class when issue distinctiveness was defined as mean distance from the national average. Which is to say: an African-American racial identity, or a pietistic Protestant or non-Christian religious identity, trumped educational background among those who were members of the former groups. Moreover, these three groups together contributed fully 45% of American society.

As a result, only after blacks, non-Christians, and low Protestants had left the sample did education/class come into its own. On the other hand, this fact must not be overinterpreted. If social class was largely displaced at the beginning by race and religion in the American

Figure 4.3
The Seven Major Social Groups

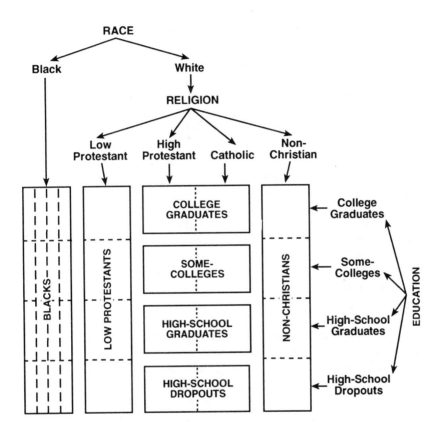

context, it nevertheless managed to claim substantial territory in the end—a clear majority of social groups and group members. Moreover, there is no way to know how different this group universe actually is from those of other nations without comparative data from those nations as well, except to say that it is clearly different from those without substantial racial minorities or without multiple religious traditions. Said another way, it is surely different from those where social class really does have an initial claim on the social structuring of political opinion or a preponderant residual claim because of the absence of these other principles of social differentiation.[15]

Yet there is implicit within the resulting group universe a further "comparative" implication about American society, in this case about change by comparison to itself at an earlier time. For what is also noteworthy about this group universe is the social category which never emerged. That category, of course, is region. At no point did any of the regional subclassifications (Northeast, Midwest, West, or even South) so much as threaten seriously to precede any of those racial, religious, or educational classifications which did ultimately produce recognizable social groups. Instead, regional categorizations overwhelmingly tracked the national average.

Yet this regional nonemergence, too, must be interpreted with care. And here, the American South, as the region most frequently and impressionistically offered as different, provides a particularly instructive warning. From one side, the South did not, in our time, demonstrate substantial differences of political opinion between the dominant elements of its population and individuals *of similar social characteristics* who lived elsewhere. Which is to say: approached through their political preferences, black Southerners or low-Protestant Southerners (to take members of the two most disproportionately Southern social groups) are little different from black or low-Protestant *non*-Southerners.

From the other side, however, a national political leader who went on to assume the lack of any need for a specifically regional approach could still be committing a strategic fallacy of the highest order.[16] For the social composition of the South as a region remains noticeably different, precisely because there *are* both more blacks and more white low-Protestants—far more—than in any other region. In turn, because both these groups have distinctive opinion profiles nationwide, any politician who ignored the strategic requirements of an issue context structured by a concentration of blacks or a concentration of low Protestants—or especially, in this case, by major concentrations of both groups in close proximity—would be running a high (and potentially unnecessary) risk. Southerners, accordingly, need not be distinctive as individuals in order for the South as an aggregate to remain a distinctive environment, suggesting distinctive strategic treatment.

A less noteworthy but more unambiguous nonemergence was the old Catholic/Protestant division. Major distinctions remain, of course, between Catholics and *pietistic* Protestants, but this was not, historically, the main embodiment of this particular religious tension; and in any case, the associated gap within Protestantism (between "high" and "low" Protestants) is every bit as large. There can still be individual policy items that widen the Catholic/high-Protestant gap. But on the larger surface dimensions of political opinion, not to mention the deep factors, that gap is no longer apparently consequential.[17]

Further Implications: Intergroup Conflict

The precise nature of these or any other strategic implications (and fallacies) must await the integration of social groups with political parties, the focus of the next chapter. We note once more, however, the vastly expanded *potential* for strategic initiatives (and conflict) introduced by this social structuring of political opinion, with its various, diverse, and crosscutting group preferences. Whether this potential can be realized in any given situation depends, as ever, on numerous other contextual factors—the issues, coalitions, and even personalities of the day—as well as on a more institutionalized interaction with political parties.

Yet where parties served to restrain and channel opinion differences, along with the strategic options following from them, social groups are obviously working, down below, to open these options out. Or at least, parties reflected ideologically parallel positions on the issues—consistently liberal or consistently conservative—albeit not without differential success and some strain (see Chapter 3). Social groups, on the other hand, reflect no such parallelism. They can join the deep factors of political opinion in far more varied fashion, and they do. They can permit an even wider combination of group preferences on the surface dimensions of political opinion, and this they do as well.

The fact that these groups were isolated through the *strength* of their composite opinion scores does itself conduce toward apparent group differences; it would be hard for such a way of proceeding to produce a universe of indistinguishable groups. On the other hand, the degree of difference is still dependent on the level of inherent differences in society, and seeking groups with distinctive preferences was, after all, precisely the point. Moreover, proceeding in this fashion clearly does not predetermine the actual groups which emerged, nor the actual group *positions* which emerged, much less the composite portrait which emerged as well.

In this composite portrait, these seven groups do provide examples—rough and varied, as they are—of most of the logically possible combinations. At first blush, especially when viewed through specific group scores (the right-hand column of Table 4.1.A), only extreme but idiosyncratic variability may seem to characterize this particular aggregate. Yet if these social groups are instead *ranked* from most liberal to most conservative (as in the first two columns of Table 4.1.A), each of the main abstract combinations comes effectively into view.

Table 4.1
Strategic Possibilities by Social Group

	Deep Factor		
Social Group	Cultural/ National	Economic/ Welfare	Scores[a]
A. Rank Order by Ideology (most liberal to most conservative)			
Blacks	5	1	(−.23, +1.02)
Non-Christians	1	3	(−.95, −.04)
Low Protestants	7	7	(−.58, −.37)
College Graduates	2	5	(+.74, −.23)
Some-Colleges	3	6	(+.22, −.31)
High-School Dropouts	6	2	(−.35, +.12)
High-School Graduates	4	4	(−.08, −.09)
B. Resulting Positional Combinations[b]			
Low Protestants	C	C	
High-School Graduates	M	M	
Non-Christians	L	L	
Blacks	C	L	
High-School Dropouts	C	L	
College Graduates	L	C	
Some-Colleges	L	C	

[a]The first number represents the cultural/national dimension, and the second, the economic/welfare dimension.
[b]C = conservative, M = moderate, L = liberal.

Seen this way, in fact, three of these groups—low Protestants, high-school graduates, and non-Christians—offer ideologically parallel combinations (see Table 4.1.B), analogous to those offered by the political parties, though even these break immediately into further internal distinctions. The other four, the larger share of the group universe, do *not* combine the two deep factors of opinion in an ideologically parallel fashion, being instead conservative on one and liberal on the other (Table 4.1.B). Moreover, each of the resulting pairs itself manifests a different internal weighting.

Of the three groups with ideologically parallel combinations, the low Protestants are consistently and dramatically conservative, as they would be by absolute and not just relative standards. The non-Christians are then consistently liberal, though it should be noted that they are far more liberal on cultural/national than on economic/welfare matters. Finally, the high-school graduates are consistently—almost militantly—moderate, falling near the national average on both deep factors. On the other hand, if the focus is on strategic options and the possibility of alternative strategic appeals, then even this consistent moderation presumably makes the high-school graduates more (not less) amenable to appeals from both parties, and thus more likely to encourage conflict and flux.

The larger share of the group universe, however, both in terms of the number of social groups and in terms of their aggregate membership, does *not* offer this sort of ideological parallelism, so that prospects for issue conflict can only increase in their presence. The Democratic party may be consistently liberal and the Republican party consistently conservative. Yet two of the four remaining groups are ideologically opposite (and potentially cross-pressured) in one direction, while the other two are ideologically opposite (and again incipiently cross-pressured) in the other.

It only ices the cake to note that within each of these pairs, the two resident groups differ additionally as to the factor on which they present their highest group scores.[18] Thus, blacks and high-school dropouts are cross-pressured in the same fashion, being conservative on cultural/national matters and liberal on economic/welfare concerns (Table 4.1.B). Yet blacks have their higher score by far on economic/welfare, while high-school dropouts have their higher score on cultural/national (Table 4.1.A) In turn, college graduates and the some-colleges are cross-pressured in the other main direction, being liberal on cultural/national matters and conservative on economic/welfare concerns (Table 4.1.B). Yet again, the college graduates actually have their (far) higher score on cultural/national, the some-colleges on economic/welfare (Table 4.1.A).

The same situation, leading to the same conclusions, can be seen with a very different kind of graphic representation. If the two deep factors of political opinion are used not in isolation but in conjunction, it is possible to go beyond categorizing each group by its basic tendencies (as above) and to examine the distribution of opinion combinations *within* the group, as well as to compare those combinations across groups. This was done for political parties in Figure 3.3, and it reinforced the sense that economic/welfare concerns provide the main issue reinforcement to partisanship, while cultural/national concerns provide the main means of disruption. Done for social groups, such a display instead reinforces a sense of the (extensive) variety in group profiles, along with their potential for broadening strategic options and hence presumably augmenting conflict (Fig. 4.4).

Because the point of Figure 4.4 is basically repetitive, there is little need to elaborate upon its contents. Once again, measured this way, high-school graduates prove to be profoundly moderate—almost a

Figure 4.4.A
Strategic Possibilities by Social Group:
Combined Positions on the Deep Factors

The Nation

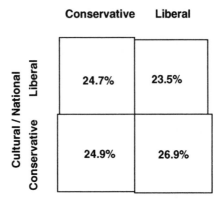

Economic / Welfare

N = 8,072

Figure 4.4.B
Strategic Possibilities by Social Group:
Combined Positions on the Deep Factors

Blacks

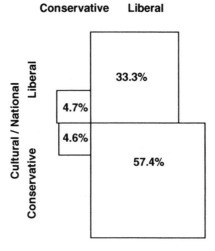

Economic / Welfare

N = 1,018

Figure 4.4.C
Strategic Possibilities by Social Group:
Combined Positions on the Deep Factors

Non-Christians

Economic / Welfare

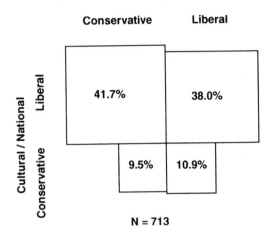

N = 713

Figure 4.4.D
Strategic Possibilities by Social Group:
Combined Positions on the Deep Factors

Low Protestants

Economic / Welfare

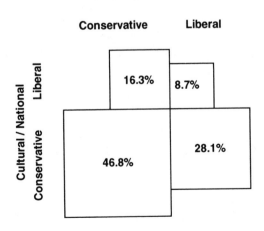

N = 1,701

Figure 4.4.E
Strategic Possibilities by Social Group:
Combined Positions on the Deep Factors

College Graduates

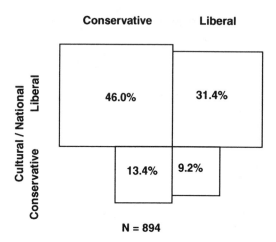

Economic / Welfare

N = 894

Figure 4.4.F
Strategic Possibilities by Social Group:
Combined Positions on the Deep Factors

Some-Colleges

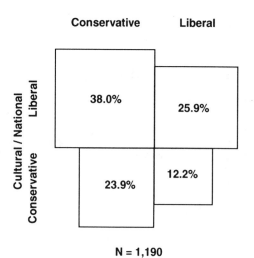

Economic / Welfare

N = 1,190

Figure 4.4.G
Strategic Possibilities by Social Group:
Combined Positions on the Deep Factors

High-School Dropouts

Economic / Welfare

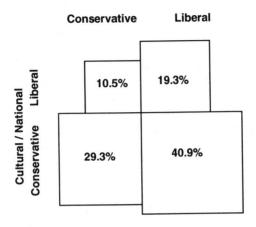

Conservative   Liberal

Liberal
10.5%   19.3%

Cultural / National

Conservative
29.3%   40.9%

N = 781

Figure 4.4.H
Strategic Possibilities by Social Group:
Combined Positions on the Deep Factors

High-School Graduates

Economic / Welfare

Conservative   Liberal

Liberal
24.2%   22.3%

Cultural / National

Conservative
27.9%   25.6%

N = 1,440

national average (Fig. 4.4.H)—when compared to the true national mean (Fig. 4.4.A). And again, the other groups remain wildly varied among themselves. The first three social groups, those categorized by race or religion, give an immediate sense of the scale of this variety (Figs. 4.4.B, C, and D). But in truth, none of these groups looks, in this kind of profile, much like *any* of the education-based groups, which in turn do not look all that much like each other (Figs. 4.4.E, F, and G). It might be noted additionally that, by comparison with the same distribution for political parties (at Fig. 3.3), only one social group puts its collective internal preferences together in the same fashion as the parties do—black Americans (Fig. 4.4.B), in parallel with the Democrats—and it actually presents a much more extreme version of the pattern.

Viewed either way, then, this is the raw material, piece by piece, for a broad array of strategic initiatives. It is also the raw material, collectively, for a politics of perpetual assault on stable coalitions, a rolling and tumbling politics built around the process of raising one or more *other* issues, other than those currently under attention, as a means of constructing some other (ideally winning) coalition. Of course, whether any or all of these patterns and their associated initiatives actually function as strains within the enveloping political parties, and thus whether they serve as strategic opportunities for dislodging and shifting the identifiers within those parties, depends crucially on how group membership interacts with partisan identification.

That is, the effectiveness of any or all of these strategic responses to the social structuring of political opinion depends, first, on the distribution of these social groups within the two political parties. It depends, next, on actual preference patterns among group partisans, which need not be a direct extrapolation from partisan identification and group membership individually. And it depends, finally, on further *combinations* of preferences, which may (or may not) establish genuine and effective cross-pressures. These are the remaining crucial elements in the mass context for issue politics, in the issue context contributed by mass political opinion. They are also the subject of Chapter 5.

5 A FRAMEWORK FOR POLITICKING

Parties, Groups, and the Issue Context

Political parties and social groups each have an evident—and evidently strong—relationship to policy preferences within the general public. Partisan identification manages to show some association with every deep factor and surface dimension and, more importantly, manifests a theoretically parallel connection across them all. Group membership offers a more diverse relationship to political opinion, one which is more idiosyncratic to the individual group but also more commensurate collectively than that with party identification. Each role, in any case, is easily strong enough that it would be unlikely to disappear if parties and groups are considered, as they exist in the real world, together.

And indeed, it is clear that parties and groups must ultimately be considered together precisely because they will always be operating that way in the real world of practical politics. In that world, individuals may still choose to subordinate group experiences to partisan attachments on any given matter. Yet they hardly cease to have had those experiences nor, presumably, to have had their perceptions shaped by them. From the other side, individuals may desert their chosen party for a key social group on matters where they find group attachments more relevant. Yet that does not alter the overarching (theoretical) alignments contributed by partisanship nor, perhaps especially, the fact that even such deviating individuals will still largely be forced to pursue their policy wishes by way of political parties.

So, partisan identification and group membership seem likely to be providing a structure to political opinion in tandem. Group membership remains more integral to the individual, in the sense of being less easily changed at will. Partisan identification remains more integral to aggregate politics, in the sense that parties, not social groups, ultimately operate governmental institutions. Conceptually, this is one more reason to ensure that each individual has some separable identification in terms of both political parties and social groups. Practically, however, both characteristics will normally be operative. Which is one more reason to go on to investigate the patterns of political opinion associated with the actual and inevitable *interplay* of partisan attachment and group membership.[1]

In the abstract, such associations can take a variety of forms. Partisanship may serve as the dominant organizing principle, the effective "first cut," for which group membership then serves as a means of elaborating and refining relationships. Alternatively, social groups may serve as the dominant organizing principle, with partisanship working, in effect, inside social groups. Or, the association between partisan identification and group membership may itself be the social characteristic which is giving either parties or groups their link with political opinion. Finally, it is worth emphasizing that this relationship (like most of the preceding relationships) need hardly be uniform from factor to factor or dimension to dimension, nor, of course, from party to party or group to group.

Political Parties and Social Groups

An understanding of the relationship among partisan attachment, group membership, and political opinion begins, again almost inevitably, with the actual relationship between political parties and social groups.[2] The specific character of this relationship will necessarily condition the general public framework for politics, and with it the strategic possibilities—and incentives—following from that framework. The lack of such an understanding, by contrast, would not just obscure the strategic import of the *simultaneous* presence of parties and groups. It might even obscure the reality of individual links between partisan attachment or group membership and policy preference: what appears to be partisanship might be covert group attachment, or vice versa.

Accordingly, Figure 5.1 divides each of the seven major social groups into Republican identifiers, Democratic identifiers, and pure independents. Even this simple initial division suggests two central facts about the contemporary relationship between political parties and social groups:

1. In modern American politics for the seven major social groups isolated here, there are three general subcategories to this relationship—obviously Republican groups, obviously Democratic groups, and overwhelmingly Democratic groups. The logically possible fourth subcategory, overwhelmingly Republican groups, does not appear.

2. Positions on the economic/welfare factor remain crucially linked to this tripartite categorization of parties-within-groups, as they did to

Figure 5.1
Partisan Factions Within Social Groups by Percent

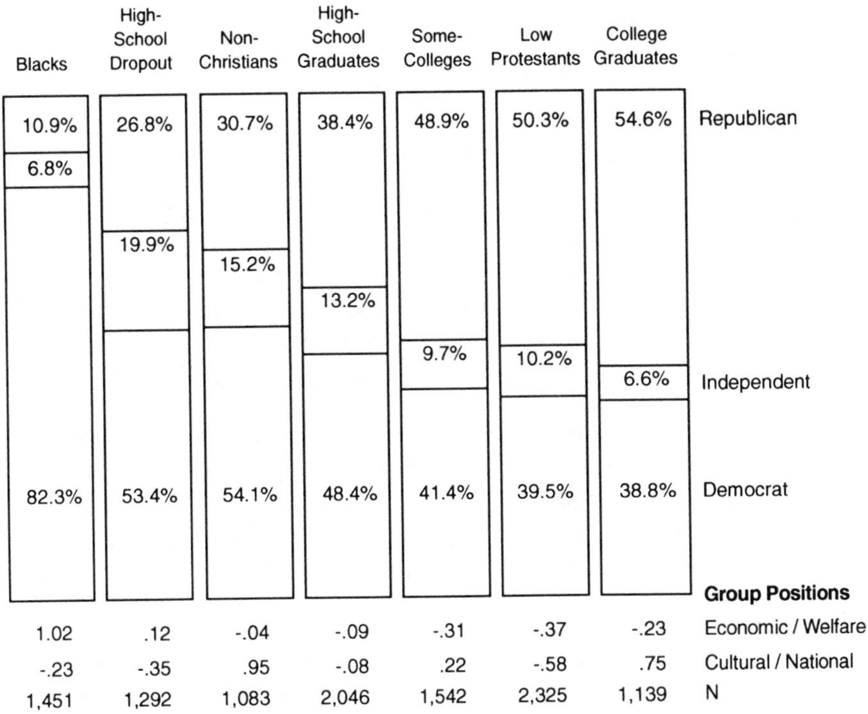

Blacks	High-School Dropout	Non-Christians	High-School Graduates	Some-Colleges	Low Protestants	College Graduates	
10.9%	26.8%	30.7%	38.4%	48.9%	50.3%	54.6%	Republican
6.8%							
	19.9%	15.2%					
			13.2%				
				9.7%	10.2%		
						6.6%	Independent
82.3%	53.4%	54.1%	48.4%	41.4%	39.5%	38.8%	Democrat
							Group Positions
1.02	.12	-.04	-.09	-.31	-.37	-.23	Economic / Welfare
-.23	-.35	.95	-.08	.22	-.58	.75	Cultural / National
1,451	1,292	1,083	2,046	1,542	2,325	1,139	N

partisanship treated alone. By contrast, positions on the cultural/national factor now appear even more completely *un*linked.

Three social groups do deserve to be categorized as Republican: the college graduates, the low Protestants, and the some-colleges. Two of these, the college graduates and low Protestants, present an actual Republican majority; the third, the some-colleges, offers only a Republican plurality. As ever, it is worth noting that these groups, even for the more homogeneous Republican party, are still constituted by very different social means, deriving from both educational and religious distinctions. Moreover, they offer further substantial ideological variety, as we shall see, just among themselves.

Likewise, three social groups deserve to be categorized as Democratic: the high-school dropouts, the non-Christians, and the high-school graduates. Again, two of these, the non-Christians and high-school dropouts, present an actual Democratic majority; again, the third, the high-school graduates, offers only a Democratic plurality. It is worth noting that the Republican minority within these Democratic groups is noticeably smaller than the Democratic minority within Republican counterparts. Otherwise, once more, the internal variety among these Democratic groups, too, remains impressive. They too are constituted from very different social bases; they too manifest not only social but ideological variation, just among themselves.

The final group is blacks, and while it shows a Democratic majority as well, this can hardly be addressed in the same terms: black Americans are overwhelmingly Democratic. Indeed, while the first three groups are clearly Republican but have a substantial Democratic minority, and while the second three are clearly Democratic but have a goodly Republican leaven, blacks as a social group are just massively Democratic. They do possess a few Republicans, and even a handful of true independents, but it would take a sample far larger than the Times Mirror survey in order to say anything reliable about them. Among blacks, as distinct from all our other major social groups, group membership is nearly an automatic indicator of partisan attachment.

Perhaps not surprisingly, given the tendency for economic/welfare concerns to be strongly associated with partisanship among individuals, the various social groups line up with the two parties in a precisely analogous way. Thus, the three social groups which deserve to be dubbed Republican overall—college graduates, low Protestants, and some-colleges—are the three groups with genuinely conservative (and clustered) preferences on economic/welfare matters. In turn, the three groups which merit a similar Democratic designation—high-school dropouts, non-Christians, and high-school graduates—are clustered together in the middle of the economic/welfare continuum. And the one group with overwhelmingly Democratic allegiance, black Americans, is the one group with wildly liberal economic/welfare preferences.

That appears to leave little room for cultural/national influences, and indeed, preferences on the cultural/national factor have no evident connection to partisan balance among social groups. Thus, the three groups with at least Republican pluralities have widely divergent preferences on cultural/national matters: +.75, −.58, and +.22 (Fig. 5.1). The three groups with at least Democratic pluralities manifest equally divergent cultural/national positions: −.35, +.95, and −.08. And the group that constitutes the far deviant extreme on internal partisan division, blacks, falls modestly below the center of the continuum on cultural/national matters, at −.23. Seen the other way around, the two social groups with the most liberal positions on this factor present one

Democratic and one Republican majority. The two groups with the most *conservative* positions offer one Democratic and one Republican majority. And the three groups with the more moderate scores comprise one Republican plurality, one Democratic plurality, and the most overwhelmingly Democratic margin of all.

There is, however, an important secondary message in this interaction of parties and groups. That message could be teased out of the partisan balance within individual groups alone, but it is more easily seen by reversing the perspective and considering the group balance within the two political parties, as in Figure 5.2. One obvious fact about partisan divisions within groups was that most groups have a significant minority identified with the other party, the party not preferred by the group as a whole. The even more obvious implication of that fact, from a group division within parties, is that both political parties still contain significant concentrations of the social groups identified with their opposite numbers.[3]

Here, nevertheless, the two parties also differ. While the comparison can be overdrawn, the Republican party *is* more socially homogeneous, in its internal group structure, and the Democratic party more socially heterogeneous. The most striking element of this is the near absence of black Americans within Republican ranks; that alone would make the Republican party less heterogeneous. But in fact, the highschool dropouts and non-Christians also contribute comparatively little to Republicanism, while the low Protestants constitute a larger share of the Republican party than does any social group for the Democrats. Only college graduates are correspondingly thin within Democratic ranks; no group bulks correspondingly large.

On the other hand, the least distinctive among these social groups in partisan terms, the high-school graduates, contribute a final balancing note. For while high-school graduates are more Democratic than Republican within the group as a whole, they are also a slightly larger *share* of the (smaller) Republican party. As such, they contribute a crucial, practical warning about the importance of groups whose overall allegiance is elsewhere: High-school graduates may be plurality Democratic, yet they constitute nearly one in five of all Republicans. Similarly, the most heavily Republican group overall, the low Protestants, still contributes fully one in six Democrats.[4]

Parties, Groups, and the Deep Factors

The interaction between political parties and social groups establishes the background for reintroducing political opinion. Given the unequal division of every social group between the two political parties, and

Figure 5.2.A
Social Factions Within Political Parties

All Republicans

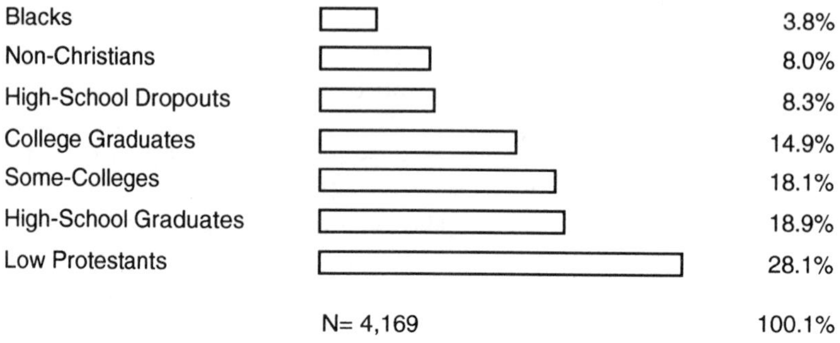

Blacks		3.8%
Non-Christians		8.0%
High-School Dropouts		8.3%
College Graduates		14.9%
Some-Colleges		18.1%
High-School Graduates		18.9%
Low Protestants		28.1%
	N= 4,169	100.1%

Figure 5.2.B
Social Factions Within Political Parties

All Democrats

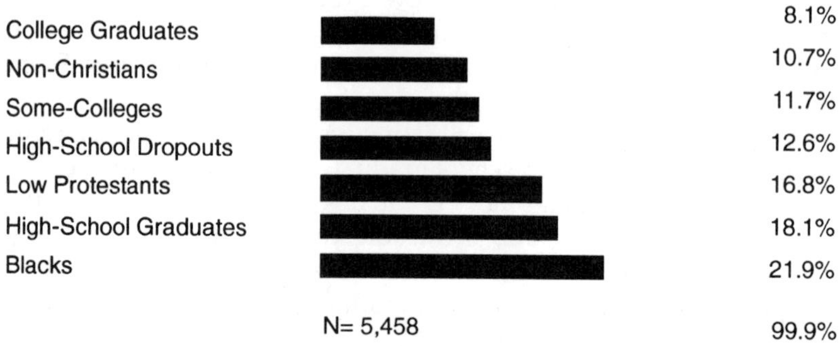

College Graduates		8.1%
Non-Christians		10.7%
Some-Colleges		11.7%
High-School Dropouts		12.6%
Low Protestants		16.8%
High-School Graduates		18.1%
Blacks		21.9%
	N= 5,458	99.9%

given the divergent composition of these two parties in terms of the seven major social groups, such a background warns against any automatic extrapolations from separate associations with political opinion. Or at least, the real nature of the interaction between political parties and social groups suggests that separate relationships with policy preferences are entitled to look very different when parties and groups are put back together.

Figure 5.3.A
Political Parties, Social Groups,
and the Deep Factors

Cultural/National Factor

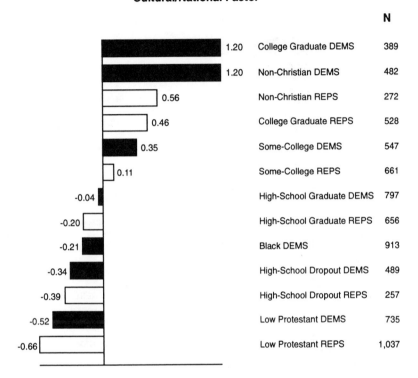

		N
1.20	College Graduate DEMS	389
1.20	Non-Christian DEMS	482
0.56	Non-Christian REPS	272
0.46	College Graduate REPS	528
0.35	Some-College DEMS	547
0.11	Some-College REPS	661
-0.04	High-School Graduate DEMS	797
-0.20	High-School Graduate REPS	656
-0.21	Black DEMS	913
-0.34	High-School Dropout DEMS	489
-0.39	High-School Dropout REPS	257
-0.52	Low Protestant DEMS	735
-0.66	Low Protestant REPS	1,037

■ = Democratic Faction
□ = Republican Faction

The most straightforward way of considering the place of parties and groups jointly is to begin with the original opinion relationships, divided this time by both party identification and group membership simultaneously. Seen one way, the product is a portrait of the social factions within each political party. Seen the other way, that product is a portrait of the partisan factions within each social group. By now, however, it is possible to allow the opinion data—the actual mean preferences for these factions—to determine which is the better way to visualize them. Figure 5.3 begins this effort.

Figure 5.3.B
Political Parties, Social Groups,
and the Deep Factors

Economic/Welfare Factor

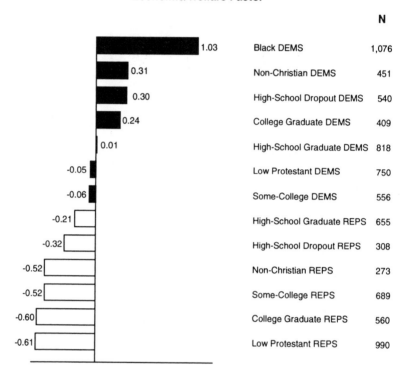

	N
Black DEMS	1,076
Non-Christian DEMS	451
High-School Dropout DEMS	540
College Graduate DEMS	409
High-School Graduate DEMS	818
Low Protestant DEMS	750
Some-College DEMS	556
High-School Graduate REPS	655
High-School Dropout REPS	308
Non-Christian REPS	273
Some-College REPS	689
College Graduate REPS	560
Low Protestant REPS	990

Figure 5.3 also reveals an immediate casualty from this way of proceeding: the share of Republican blacks, even in a large and diligently pursued sample, is just too small to permit statistical reliability, much less further internal analysis, so that black Republicans are excluded from the tables that follow.[5] With that one subtraction, however, it is now possible to put these factions and their preferences back together—back into a composite, national whole—as the mass issue framework for modern American politics.

Moreover, despite warnings about the risks in simple extrapolation from party or group portraits by themselves, the key findings from an actual joint consideration of parties, groups, and the deep factors of political opinion are ultimately an intensification—an exaggeration and "purification"—of relationships which were initially apparent when parties and groups were addressed separately, in Chapters 3 and 4:

- Issue-areas that had been most strongly associated with partisan attachment are now even more clearly partisan in their effective structure. Indeed, group relationships within them are actually weaker, suggesting that group membership was obscuring the basic partisan role.

- Issue-areas which had been most strongly associated with group membership, by contrast, are now even more clearly group-related. Here, however, partisanship still plays a reliable and regular additional role, though one confined, this time, inside social groups.

The first aspect of this, involving an augmented partisan effect, emerges from considering the economic/welfare factor in terms of partisan pieces within social groups (Fig. 5.3.B). Remarkably, such a focus reveals that *every* Democratic faction of every social group is more liberal than every Republican faction of those same social groups. As a result, the most conservative Democratic faction of any major group is still more liberal than the most liberal Republican faction within that same group universe.

That is the dominant fact about partisan factions arrayed by economic/welfare preferences. There is, however, a second aspect to this array that is of some analytic significance, involving not division between the two parties, but the *different character* of divisions within them. Put simply, the Republican party is remarkably united on economic/welfare matters. There is still some distance between factional extremes, and this will not lack strategic implications when translated into surface dimensions. Yet it pales beside the differences within the Democratic party.

There, three broad further tendencies are necessary to describe the factional situation. There are the black Democrats, on the far left by any standard. There are the non-Christian Democrats, the high-school dropout Democrats, and the college-graduate Democrats, at the center of the party but still solidly liberal within society as a whole. And there are the high-school graduate Democrats, the low-Protestant Democrats, and the some-college Democrats, on the right of the party but smack in the broad middle of American politics.

Nevertheless, the dominant fact about this factional array, despite thirteen distinctive subdivisions, remains its perfect partisan alignment. Indeed, in the case of the economic/welfare factor, dividing social groups into their partisan factions actually reduces the regularity associated with underlying group membership. Thus, college graduates may contribute the most conservative Republicans on economic/

welfare, but college-graduate *Democrats* are not particularly conservative, within the nation or even within their own party. In the same way, non-Christians make highly liberal Democrats on economic/welfare matters, but non-Christian Republicans are not particularly liberal, again either within the nation or within their own political party.

The second aspect of this joint examination, involving an augmented group relationship instead, shows up immediately upon turning back to the cultural/national factor (Fig. 5.3.A). Again, social groups and mass parties need to be considered simultaneously. And this time, a related partisan effect does not disappear: Every Republican faction of a major social group remains more conservative than its Democratic counterpart. On the other hand—and much more consequential—this effect now occurs only *inside social groups*. That is, group membership now contributes the general parameters of the relationship, within which partisanship must play its additional, lesser, refining role.

For cultural/national matters, the non-Christian and the college-graduate pieces of the Democratic *and* (more impressively) the Republican parties reside at the liberal end of the ideological spectrum. The low-Protestant and the high-school dropout pieces of the Republican and (again impressively) the Democratic parties reside at the conservative end. And the same relationship continues in between. Both partisan pieces of the some-college category are more liberal than the national average, though Democrats in this group remain more liberal than Republicans. Similarly, both partisan factions among the high-school graduates are more conservative than the national average, though again Republicans within the group remain more conservative than their Democratic fellow members.[6] As a result, group membership dominates—really overwhelms—party identification when partisan factions are arrayed by cultural/national preference.

Parties, Groups, and the Surface Dimensions

The surface dimensions of political opinion, as ever, provide elaborations and nuances to this underlying portrait (Fig. 5.4). Their most fundamental contribution is still reinforcement of the basic relationships established by the deep factors, between party identification and economic/welfare concerns or between group membership and cultural/national matters. Yet the surface dimensions also provide some noteworthy variations to this overarching relationship, variations which will prove to have major strategic implications for the choice of issues. At the same time, these surface dimensions advance the process—even more critical to subsequent strategic implications—of isolating those social pieces of the two political parties which are most out of

Figure 5.4.A
Political Parties, Social Groups,
and the Surface Dimensions

Cultural Values

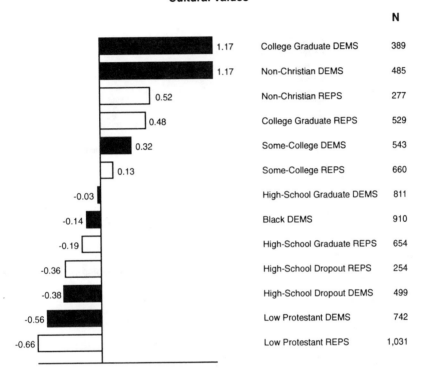

	N
College Graduate DEMS	389
Non-Christian DEMS	485
Non-Christian REPS	277
College Graduate REPS	529
Some-College DEMS	543
Some-College REPS	660
High-School Graduate DEMS	811
Black DEMS	910
High-School Graduate REPS	654
High-School Dropout REPS	254
High-School Dropout DEMS	499
Low Protestant DEMS	742
Low Protestant REPS	1,031

■ = Democratic Faction
□ = Republican Faction

alignment with their fellow partisans, and thus most likely to be the focus of strategic conflict.[7]

Among the surface dimensions associated with the economic/welfare factor, civil rights offers the most exact positional mirror of underlying factional preferences (Fig. 5.4.E). There is one Democratic faction wildly off to the left, black Democrats. There are three factions solidly liberal, both within their party and in the nation as a whole, namely, college-graduate Democrats, non-Christian Democrats, and high-school dropout Democrats. There are three Democratic factions

Figure 5.4.B
Political Parties, Social Groups,
and the Surface Dimensions

Social Welfare

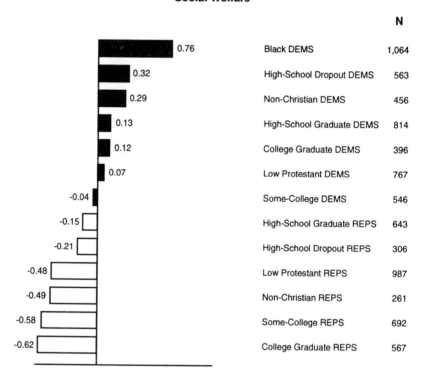

= Democratic Faction
= Republican Faction

on the right of the party but in the center of American politics, the some-college Democrats, the high-school graduate Democrats, and the low-Protestant Democrats. And the entire Republican party is once more roughly clustered and solidly conservative.

Social welfare, on the other hand, while it varies the exact policy preferences of these various factions a bit more, is actually the purest embodiment of their basic partisan associations (Fig. 5.4.B). Not only are all Democratic factions to the left of all Republican factions, as with civil rights. Now, all but one of these Democratic factions are to the left

Figure 5.4.C
Political Parties, Social Groups,
and the Surface Dimensions

Foreign Relations

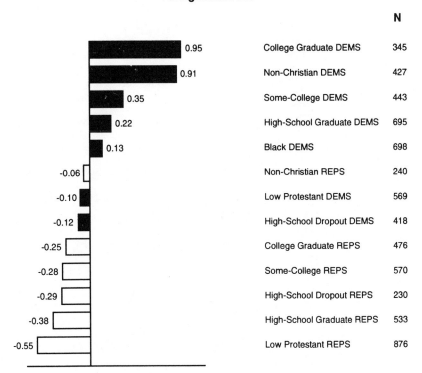

	N
College Graduate DEMS	345
Non-Christian DEMS	427
Some-College DEMS	443
High-School Graduate DEMS	695
Black DEMS	698
Non-Christian REPS	240
Low Protestant DEMS	569
High-School Dropout DEMS	418
College Graduate REPS	476
Some-College REPS	570
High-School Dropout REPS	230
High-School Graduate REPS	533
Low Protestant REPS	876

■ = Democratic Faction
□ = Republican Faction

of the national average as well, and the lone exception, the some-college Democrats, is nearly at that national midpoint. As ever, all Republican factions remain to the right of the national average.

Social insurance, the last of the economic/welfare dimensions, injects substantial group shuffling into the pattern (Fig. 5.4.D). Partisanship remains the dominant theme. But now, the line is breached in both directions: high-school dropout Republicans are not just liberal but comfortably inside the Democratic array; college-graduate Democrats are not just conservative but comfortably settled among Republican fac-

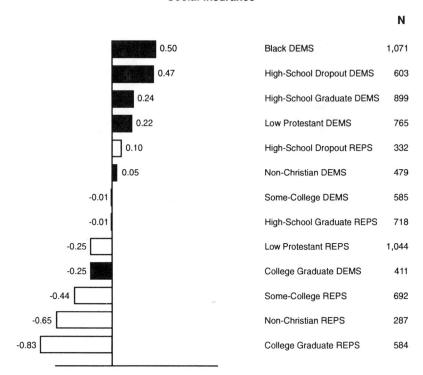

Figure 5.4.D
Political Parties, Social Groups,
and the Surface Dimensions

Social Insurance

		N
0.50	Black DEMS	1,071
0.47	High-School Dropout DEMS	603
0.24	High-School Graduate DEMS	899
0.22	Low Protestant DEMS	765
0.10	High-School Dropout REPS	332
0.05	Non-Christian DEMS	479
-0.01	Some-College DEMS	585
-0.01	High-School Graduate REPS	718
-0.25	Low Protestant REPS	1,044
-0.25	College Graduate DEMS	411
-0.44	Some-College REPS	692
-0.65	Non-Christian REPS	287
-0.83	College Graduate REPS	584

■ = Democratic Faction
□ = Republican Faction

tions. Perhaps more to the point, those Democratic factions which had been most in play on civil rights and social welfare—the some-college, high-school graduate, and low-Protestant Democrats—are each at their most liberal on social insurance. And the high-school graduate Republicans are at their most liberal, just off the national average, as well.

Among the surface dimensions associated with the cultural/national factor, in turn, cultural values offers the most direct replication of the underlying factor (Fig. 5.4.A). College graduates, non-Christians, and some-colleges, in both their Democratic and their Republican incarna-

Figure 5.4.E
Political Parties, Social Groups,
and the Surface Dimensions

Civil Rights

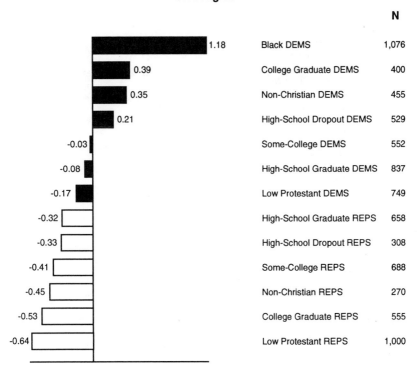

		N
1.18	Black DEMS	1,076
0.39	College Graduate DEMS	400
0.35	Non-Christian DEMS	455
0.21	High-School Dropout DEMS	529
-0.03	Some-College DEMS	552
-0.08	High-School Graduate DEMS	837
-0.17	Low Protestant DEMS	749
-0.32	High-School Graduate REPS	658
-0.33	High-School Dropout REPS	308
-0.41	Some-College REPS	688
-0.45	Non-Christian REPS	270
-0.53	College Graduate REPS	555
-0.64	Low Protestant REPS	1,000

■ = Democratic Faction
□ = Republican Faction

tions, again make up the liberal end of the continuum. Low Protestants, high-school dropouts, and high-school graduates, in both their
Republican and their Democratic variants, make up the conservative
end. Black Democrats are once more conservative as well, though
high-school graduate Democrats are really, as with the underlying factor, very close to the national average. High-school dropout Democrats
do gain the distinction, here, of being the only Democratic piece of any
social group to stand to the right of its Republican counterpart on any
measure. But otherwise, the recapitulation is exact.

Figure 5.4.F
Political Parties, Social Groups,
and the Surface Dimensions

Civil Liberties

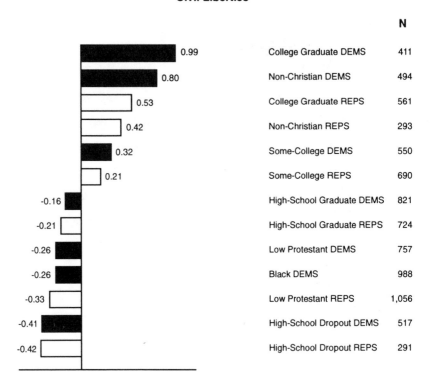

		N
0.99	College Graduate DEMS	411
0.80	Non-Christian DEMS	494
0.53	College Graduate REPS	561
0.42	Non-Christian REPS	293
0.32	Some-College DEMS	550
0.21	Some-College REPS	690
-0.16	High-School Graduate DEMS	821
-0.21	High-School Graduate REPS	724
-0.26	Low Protestant DEMS	757
-0.26	Black DEMS	988
-0.33	Low Protestant REPS	1,056
-0.41	High-School Dropout DEMS	517
-0.42	High-School Dropout REPS	291

■ = Democratic Faction
□ = Republican Faction

The ordering of these partisan factions is nearly the same on civil liberties (Fig. 5.4.F). The far right was held by the two low-Protestant factions (Republican and Democratic) for cultural values, where it is held by the two high-school dropout factions for civil liberties. But beyond that, the factional ordering remains solidly parallel. What is different, otherwise, is only the nature of the break between liberal and conservative factions. For there is really no middle ground left on civil liberties: the six liberal factions are all clearly liberal, and the seven conservative factions are clearly conservative.

The third cultural/national dimension, foreign relations, disrupts this ordering by introducing a strong partisan principle (Fig. 5.4.C). Group considerations are hardly irrelevant, since it is the low-Protestant Democrats and the high-school dropout Democrats who are most solidly drawn toward the Republicans—along with the non-Christian Republicans, this time, who are obviously drawn toward the Democrats as well. Indeed, these three factions do, in that sense, cross party lines. Yet the dominant pattern is still one of party (rather than group) attachment, such that the five most liberal factions are all Democratic, while the five most conservative are all Republican.

Strategic Implications: Events of the Day

These relationships go a long way toward clarifying the practical political structure of a contemporary issue context. And that structure proves to contain both clear implications for political strategists and intermediate projections about political outcomes. Or at least, this structure does provide many of the parameters within which political strategists must operate. It can suggest certain recurring—if conditional—patterns to the outcome, quite apart from what deliberate strategists may be doing. And it can become a tool for locating those groups whose response is likely to be a key to the success of strategic initiatives, or else an explanation for how events of the day managed to overcome conscious strategies.

The first and most evident impact of *joint* consideration of political parties and social groups, in their association with policy preferences, is to reinforce the major lesson arising from consideration of each relationship individually. To wit: joint consideration of parties and groups makes it clear that groups inside parties as well as parties inside groups were actually obscuring—weakening—relationships with policy preferences in the general public. As a result, when groups are added to the equation, preferences on the economic/welfare factor are all the more strikingly organized by partisan attachment. And when parties are added to the equation, preferences on the cultural/national factor are even more clearly anchored by group membership.

The main strategic implication of such reinforcement, in turn, is to underline the two main lessons from separate consideration of political parties and social groups. Which is to say: When the focus shifts from the relationship among groups, parties, and political opinions to the way this relationship contributes to an overarching (issue) context for political combat, there are two major and apparently ineluctable strategic corollaries. In one, *economic/welfare* concerns advance all the more as key means for activating partisanship, for encouraging individuals to support the candidates or initiatives of their established party. And in the other, cultural/national concerns advance all the more as means for *counteracting* partisanship, for minimizing partisan attachments and encouraging defections across party lines.

On the economic/welfare factor (as displayed schematically in Fig. 5.3.B), there is in fact no Democratic piece of any social group which is more conservative than any Republican piece, or vice versa. As a result, there is effectively no overlap between the central tendencies of the social factions constituting the two political parties on underlying economic/welfare concerns. On the cultural/national factor, however (as displayed with equal sharpness in Fig. 5.3.A), the specific possibilities for disrupting partisanship only multiply when social factions are distinguished inside political parties. When this is done, four out of the seven social subgroups within the Democratic party have central tendencies that actually fall on the conservative side of the national average, while three out of six measurable subgroups within the Republican coalition actually fall on the liberal side.

That is one way to describe the landscape of issue politics in the modern era, the issue context within which strategists must craft their approaches, and then succeed or fail. It is a description emphasizing strategic possibilities and strategic efforts. Because these efforts must, in practice, be made through the current party framework, and because there is a larger vehicle (the Democrats) and a smaller vehicle (the Republicans) within this two-party system, the ultimate application of this advice is additionally straightforward: Republicans should attempt to emphasize cultural/national concerns in their politicking; Democrats should attempt to emphasize economic/welfare concerns instead.

That is the leading implication from a conscious strategic approach to the current political landscape. Yet there is another way to look at this same landscape, a way much reducing the role of self-conscious strategists. This is, instead, to acknowledge that in any given contest, electoral or institutional, external events of the day may establish a priority for a given deep factor (or a given surface dimension within it) quite independently of the wishes of any or all strategic thinkers. Stated baldly, *events,* not strategists, may dictate the issue contents of practical political conflict.

Stated more precisely, events of the day may establish a need for political combat to be conducted within the cultural/national or economic/welfare factors, thereby imposing all the associated partisan or apartisan implications and constraints. When current public concerns dictate a focus on economic/welfare concerns, then Democrats should be advantaged—and Republicans should be confined to looking for ways to minimize the benefits. Conversely, when events of the day dictate a focus on cultural/national concerns, Republicans should benefit, and Democrats be confined to minimizing the damage.

By extension, in both cases, events of the day will simultaneously establish the *social terrain* upon which conflict should be—and normally will be—pitched. In this, certain groups are just much closer to the mean position of the other party, and thus presumably much more amenable to issue blandishments from it. Failure to locate them implies failing either to maximize advantages or minimize losses. By further extension, a shift out of one deep factor and into the other—whether that shift is deliberate or enforced, a product of internal strategy or just external events—means that the groups at the center of conflict will shift as well. And again, these are the groups whose response is likely to determine the outcome.

Thus, when events move the economic/welfare factor to the center of politics, Figure 5.3.B suggests that there are three factions which are best able to go with either party, and which thereby merit attention from both: high-school graduate Democrats, low-Protestant Democrats, and some-college Democrats. These are all, obviously, Democratic fac-·tions, and that fact has two further implications, one powerfully and effectively familiar, the other contrary to stereotypical perceptions.

For the latter, this particular partisan array means that there are Republican prospects even on this most party-related, pro-Democratic dimension. Indeed, addressed optimally by both parties, the risks all run in a *pro-Republican* direction: while it is unlikely that any Republican factions would flirt seriously with the Democrats, three Democratic factions can be drawn to the Republicans. On the other hand, this still means that both active and successful Republican wooing is necessary to realize these prospects. Otherwise, and normally, Democrats should prevail. The weight of inertia, even before any strategic reinforcement, rests with the Democratic party here; practical operatives—and scholarly analysts—will not be surprised.

Conversely, when events (and not politicians) dictate that the cultural/national factor move to the center of politics, Figure 5.3.A spotlights four factions which are most out of line with the preferences of their fellow partisans: low-Protestant Democrats, high-school dropout Democrats, non-Christian Republicans, and college-graduate Republicans. Here, however, the practical strategic import of this array will prove dependent on two further, issue-based relationships: (1) on specific links with the surface dimensions which help operationalize the underlying (cultural/national) situation, and (2) especially on the way these four factions themselves *join* cultural/national concerns with economic/welfare matters.

Strategic Implications: Inherent Cross-Pressures

All of this implies that shifting the essence of any given conflict from one deep factor to the other should shift the factions central to its resolution (with the noteworthy exception of low-Protestant Democrats, who figure centrally in both arrays). Yet because individual identification with political parties tends to be long-lasting, and individual membership in most social groups even more so, it is possible to treat this linkage between policy preferences and factional membership as a more fundamental element of the political landscape. As such, this link should make its own, presumably recurring, inherent demands and thus its own contributions to the established character of politics.

In other words, if particularly apt strategies or peculiarly powerful events can produce distinctive outcomes from an array of partisan factions holding distinguishable opinions, that situation can just as logically be viewed from the other side: this array ought just as logically to command regularized patterns of attention, recurring patterns of conflict, and most especially, recognizable and recurring outcomes. Political tacticians, or political journalists, have good reason to concentrate on immediate adaptations to an issue context—and on the result. Analysts with a longer perspective, however, might more reasonably look at what the continuing structure of a particular issue context contributes to (and demands from) political actors over time.

The key to such an approach remains those longer-lasting party factions which proved useful even in interpreting outcomes of the moment. Yet with a longer perspective, there is likely to be a crucial further distinction among these factions. Some, the ones with more extreme and more consistently partisan views, ought to serve more as a *base* for overall party strategies, establishing the bounds beyond which such strategies cannot practicably go, while simultaneously providing a floor below which party fortunes should not normally fall. Others, those which might possibly be shifted between the parties, ought to serve more as the crucial *increment,* not just for a given contest but for a succession of contests over time.

A concern for the way in which strategists and candidates decide what to do in response to these two types of party faction is disproportionately a matter of elite politics, the focus of Chapters 6 and 7. But a concern with the distinction itself, and especially with identifying those potentially crucial factions which could in principle be attracted by either party, is the final element in the mass public framework for contemporary politicking. This final element is very much a matter of mass policy preferences, of the way political opinions are tied to factional membership within the general public. And while these crucial factions are, by definition, more likely to determine specific outcomes, they are also likely to be more consequential in shaping strategic behavior over the longer run.

So far, the analysis putting political parties and social groups together, in the search for these potentially critical party factions, has treated the two deep factors of political opinion (and their associated surface dimensions) in isolation. Sometimes, this is surely appropriate, when powerful currents or successful campaigns manage to create precisely this (separate) situation. Yet such opinions do not in fact exist separately in the preferences of most partisans, so that most individuals could presumably, again in principle, be addressed on both grounds. Indeed, an essential element of political strategy, when events permit, is precisely to exploit one cluster of issues and avoid the other, so as to maximize partisan loyalty or partisan defection.

Said differently, when the two deep factors to political opinion are considered jointly, it becomes possible to search for the partisan factions—the specific social groups within each party coalition—that seem most likely to reward issue-based attention from the opposite party. Any faction that is "misidentified" on both deep factors, offering preferences closer to the mean position of the opposite party on both, would, of course, head this list. Yet any faction that is, in effect, cross-pressured[8]—sharing preferences with one party on one deep factor but with the other party on the other—would also provide a promising social target.

Many factions, of course, are superficially cross-pressured, in the sense of offering liberal values on one deep factor and conservative values on the other. The two deep factors *are* essentially independent, so that it would be surprising if a number of partisan factions were not cross-pressured in this limited sense, as Figure 5.3 has already suggested that they are. Yet in strategic terms, this apparently large set of cross-pressured groups is both more limited with respect to the appeals which might move its members and, more importantly, much reduced in its practical contents by the operational demands of an *effective* cross-party appeal.

The first limitation is, by now, well established. No partisan subgroup has economic/welfare preferences fundamentally out of alignment with those of its political party; all Republican factions are more conservative than all Democratic factions. As a result, effective cross-party appeals, by way of an issue-based cross-pressure, must ordinarily consist of conservative cultural/national blandishments aimed at Democratic factions, or liberal cultural/national appeals aimed at Republican counterparts. Unless the opposition party is willing to help by moving even farther off its normal economic/welfare positions (to the right for the Republicans, to the left for Democrats), the potential for activating a cross-pressure on economic/welfare grounds would appear limited.

But beyond this—and much more constraining for the possibility of activating incipient defections—there is no reason for any group to *feel* cross-pressured, at least to the point of deserting its habitual political party, unless its cultural/national preferences are not only discordant with those of its party as a whole but also *stronger* than its preferences on economic/welfare matters. Said differently, a strategically effective cross-pressure requires not only the presence of ideologically divergent positions for the partisan faction in question on the two deep factors of American political opinion. It also requires stronger preferences on the factor that countervails normal partisanship, which in American politics means the cultural/national factor.

Absent such a situation, ongoing partisan identifications, as reinforced (powerfully) by economic/welfare preferences, have every right to govern political outcomes. Black Democrats can be used to make the point most concretely. Their mean positions on the two deep factors—+1.03 on economic/welfare and −.21 on cultural/national—constitute a superficial cross-pressure, in a party system where one party is uniformly liberal, the other uniformly conservative. Yet these positions also suggest that economic/welfare issues *matter* far more to the group than do cultural/national concerns, working to keep it firmly in the Democratic camp. Research on the voting record of blacks is certainly consistent with such a predisposition.[9]

Black Democrats, then, represent most starkly the type of partisan faction for which an abstractly intriguing, issue-based cross-pressure might well prove ultimately disappointing in practice—where the sophisticated political strategist ought not to expect to convert a hypothetical opportunity into an actual defection. On the other hand, the same criterion for real, issue-based cross-pressures should also push such a strategist toward precisely those partisan factions where such an expectation might be rewarded instead, where a discordant partisan preference on cultural/national matters is actually stronger than a consistent partisan preference on economic/welfare concerns.

Such a standard (applied to Fig. 5.3) does in fact produce four incipiently but inherently cross-pressured party factions. Collectively, these four promise especially suggestive contributions to the continuing pattern of partisan outcomes in the United States—and to their explanation. Yet they also differ individually among themselves, and these differences too are likely to have further major strategic consequences:

- One of these factions is not so much cross-pressured as simply misidentified. The *low-Protestant Democrats,* in fact, are modestly more conservative than the national average on economic/welfare matters (at −.05), much more conservative on cultural/national affairs (at −.52).[10]

- The most full-blown cross-pressure in the stereotypical sense is thus apparently reserved for the next factional product. The *non-Christian Republicans* are militantly conservative on economic/welfare matters (−.50), slightly more militantly liberal on cultural/national affairs (+.56).[11]

- A scaled-down but equally clear version of the same pattern runs in the opposite partisan direction. The *high-school dropout Democrats* are solidly liberal on economic/welfare matters (+.30), even more solidly conservative on cultural/national affairs (−.34).[12]

- That leaves a faction which is as much compulsively centrist as it is stereotypically cross-pressured. The *high-school graduate Democrats,* at +.01 on economic/welfare matters and −.04 on cultural/national affairs, really just continue their compulsive moderation, adding a very modest issue cross-pressure to their opposite but modest edge in party identification.[13]

Further Implications: Issue Options and Party Fortunes

The same sort of analysis could be built around the surface dimensions, highlighting both the further impact of events of the day and the elaborated role of inherent cross-pressures. In this, it would be possible to compare those factions which should be most central when social welfare is the focus of political conflict, for example, with those which should be most central when cultural values is the focus instead. Likewise, it would be possible to see who is inherently cross-pressured when any given *pair* of surface dimensions (e.g., social insurance and foreign relations) dominates the political landscape.

Both approaches will appear intermittently in the remaining chapters. At this point, however, two larger strategic implications need to be introduced, or at least emphasized. The first involves the further choice of surface dimensions to help harvest (or countervail) advantages implicit in the deep factors. And the second involves the real, net partisan balance implicit in the continuing cross-pressures which characterize this general issue environment. The first produces a further hierarchy of partisan advantages within the six surface dimensions.

The second then imparts a much more sophisticated—and conditional—gloss to the background balance in party identification.

For the first of these further implications, arraying the surface dimensions of political opinion by the policy preferences of thirteen major partisan factions does reveal incipient partisan advantages for each of these individual dimensions as well. The propensity of economic/welfare matters to favor Democrats and of cultural/national concerns to favor Republicans is, if anything, additionally affirmed. But now, a further patterning of partisan advantages *within* each cluster also appears. From one side, this should color the choice among surface dimensions for political conflict, whenever party strategists have that choice. From the other side, this patterning should help explain the outcome, whatever strategists manage to do. Figure 5.4 provides the basic data for both effects.

Seen this way, for the surface dimensions associated with the economic/welfare factor, it is *social welfare* that most directly reflects the inherent partisan impact of the underlying factor (Fig. 5.4.B). Party lines remain clearly drawn. The some-college Democrats, being more conservative than the national average, offer the leading opportunity for Republicans, though the low-Protestant Democrats are not all that far behind. Yet the high-school graduate Republicans and high-school dropout Republicans are not really out of reach of the Democrats either, so that the normal partisan trade-off might be expected to be a wash—and a clear Democratic benefit.

That potential benefit is reduced with a shift toward civil rights, increased with a shift toward social insurance. Even in the case of civil rights, party lines remain intact (Fig. 5.4.E). Yet here, *three* Democratic factions fall below the national average, the low Protestants notably so. Moreover, none of the Republican factions are remotely drawn toward Democratic positions. Civil rights is thus a "swing" surface dimension. From a Democratic viewpoint, it still appears preferable to any cultural/national dimension. From a Republican viewpoint, it appears to be the best option within the economic/welfare factor.

Social insurance is sharply different, taking Democratic assets to their zenith, Republican assets to their nadir (Fig. 5.4.D). Party lines do break, in both directions. But in a world where Republicans must crack the Democratic coalition in order to win, those Democratic factions which were most in question on social welfare or civil rights are at their most liberal on social insurance. Indeed, the high-school dropout Republicans are now well inside the Democratic party as well, and high-school graduate Republicans are obviously "at risk." In such an environment, the Republican gain among college-graduate Democrats is meager compensation.

Seen the same way, for the surface dimensions associated with the cultural/national factor, it is *cultural values* that most directly reflect the incipient partisan impact of the underlying factor. Here, for the party that must crack the opposite coalition, the Republicans obviously acquire a powerful draw for low-Protestant and high-school dropout Democrats, and high-school graduate Democrats are at least potentially in play (Fig. 5.4.A). The party does suffer counterpart stresses, especially among its non-Christian and college-graduate identifiers. But if it cannot get this trade-off right, it should not expect to do better on any of the economic/welfare dimensions, so that a major opportunity—for the minority party—is at least present.

Civil liberties exaggerates this opportunity, taking Republican prospects to their zenith and Democratic prospects in the opposite direction. Republican stresses remain as they were (Fig. 5.4.F). Yet now, *all* the Democratic factions which were potentially within reach on cultural values are comfortably within Republican ranks, including those high-school graduate Democrats. And the Democratic party acquires no fresh advantage in return.

Foreign affairs, finally, takes the balance back—well back—in the other direction. Most Democratic factions are reunited with the bulk of their own party (Fig. 5.4.C). Two still are not, the low-Protestants and high-school dropouts. But this time, the non-Christian *Republicans* stand to the left of both these factions, so that they are potentially amenable to a counterappeal. As a result, foreign relations becomes the other main "swing" dimension: its three critical factions are all still more conservative than the national average, suggesting that foreign relations remains more potentially beneficial to the Republicans than any economic/welfare dimension. Yet it is simultaneously the best of the cultural/national dimensions for Democrats.

In the same way, it is now possible to take the four factions which emerged from an analysis of cross-pressures using the deep factors of political opinion—the low-Protestant Democrats, the non-Christian Republicans, the high-school dropout Democrats, and the high-school graduate Democrats—and look at their preferences on the surface dimensions as well (Fig. 5.5). Such a portrait gives a different, and much more concrete, focus to the search for a partisan ordering among these dimensions. Yet what it really does, at bottom, is to reinforce the sense of comparative partisan advantage gained by looking at whole issue-areas, rather than just key factions:

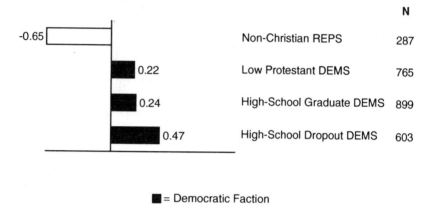

Figure 5.5.A
Policy Preferences of
Cross-Pressured Factions

Social Insurance

		N
Non-Christian REPS		287
Low Protestant DEMS		765
High-School Graduate DEMS		899
High-School Dropout DEMS		603

■ = Democratic Faction
□ = Republican Faction

Figure 5.5.B
Policy Preferences of
Cross-Pressured Factions

Social Welfare

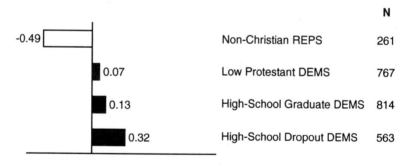

		N
Non-Christian REPS		261
Low Protestant DEMS		767
High-School Graduate DEMS		814
High-School Dropout DEMS		563

■ = Democratic Faction
□ = Republican Faction

Figure 5.5.C
Policy Preferences of
Cross-Pressured Factions

Civil Rights

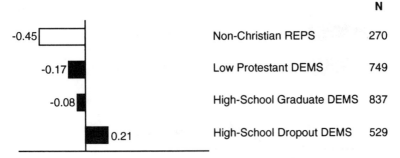

		N
-0.45	Non-Christian REPS	270
-0.17	Low Protestant DEMS	749
-0.08	High-School Graduate DEMS	837
0.21	High-School Dropout DEMS	529

■ = Democratic Faction
□ = Republican Faction

Figure 5.5.D
Policy Preferences of
Cross-Pressured Factions

Foreign Relations

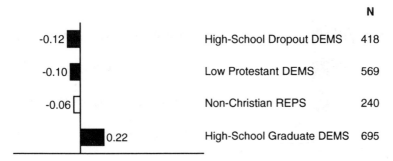

		N
-0.12	High-School Dropout DEMS	418
-0.10	Low Protestant DEMS	569
-0.06	Non-Christian REPS	240
0.22	High-School Graduate DEMS	695

■ = Democratic Faction
□ = Republican Faction

Figure 5.5.E
Policy Preferences of
Cross-Pressured Factions

Cultural Values

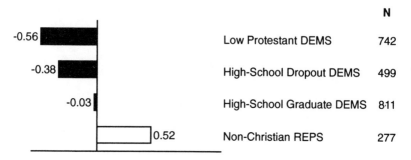

		N
-0.56	Low Protestant DEMS	742
-0.38	High-School Dropout DEMS	499
-0.03	High-School Graduate DEMS	811
0.52	Non-Christian REPS	277

■ = Democratic Faction
□ = Republican Faction

Figure 5.5.F
Policy Preferences of
Cross-Pressured Factions

Civil Liberties

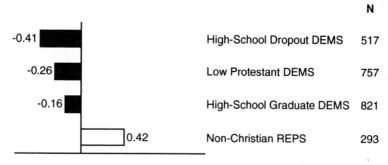

		N
-0.41	High-School Dropout DEMS	517
-0.26	Low Protestant DEMS	757
-0.16	High-School Graduate DEMS	821
0.42	Non-Christian REPS	293

■ = Democratic Faction
□ = Republican Faction

- Social insurance, the most strongly Democratic composite dimension, actually shows the three key Democratic factions at their most liberal and the central Republican faction at its most conservative (Fig. 5.5.A). Such a situation is, of course, the optimal partisan reinforcement, and partisan reinforcement contributes the maximum Democratic bias.

- All four factions are more moderate on social welfare, making its impact less pronounced (Fig. 5.5.B). Yet ordering and basic ideological preference are otherwise identical, retaining a clear (if somewhat reduced) Democratic edge.

- Only civil rights makes the balance problematic (Fig. 5.5.C). The four key factions still remain in precisely the same order. But this time, the high-school graduate and low-Protestant Democrats are more conservative than the national average, while the non-Christian Republicans are not notably more liberal. Good Democratic strategy could certainly rescue such a situation; good Republican strategy, however, might harvest it instead.

- At the other extreme, once again, is civil liberties (Fig. 5.5.F). By comparison to the social-insurance dimension, all the cross-pressured factions have actually reversed their basic ideological preferences. All three Democratic factions are now clearly conservative; the central Republican faction is strongly liberal. By extension, a Democratic maximum on social insurance has been converted to an incipient Republican maximum on civil liberties.

- Cultural values shows the same basic pattern, with one modest—and moderating—exception (Fig. 5.5.E). High-school graduate Democrats, while still conservative, are now nearly back to the national average, making cultural values a less overwhelming (though still evidently important) Republican asset.

- That leaves foreign relations to introduce a more complicated balance, which it certainly does (Fig. 5.5.D). One key Democratic faction, the high-school graduates, is clearly back within the Democratic fold; the two others are not, but the low-Protestant and high-school dropout Democrats are only modestly conservative, and the non-Christian Republicans are even more moderately so. As a result, Republicans should still enjoy an advantage in this dimension, though far less of one than with civil liberties or cultural values. Nevertheless, this issue-area does markedly expand the room for strategic initiatives—and strategic error.

Yet a different way to view the contribution of these four factions, in turn, is to go looking for their *aggregate* impact. Moreover, this is a hunt with a major side-benefit: these key, cross-pressured factions contribute a much more sophisticated gloss to strategic implications drawn from the basic partisan balance. For they remind us that while there are still substantially more Democrats than Republicans overall, a greater

Figure 5.6.A

The Sophisticated Strategic Balance of Party Identification

Background Division of Party Identifiers

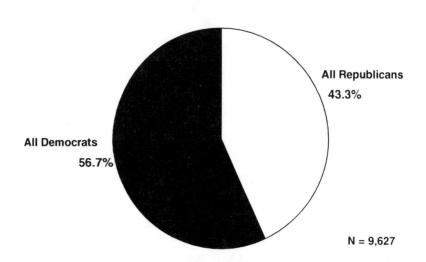

share of the former are less solidly rooted by their policy preferences. It is, of course, this (more sophisticated) partisan landscape upon which political conflict actually occurs.

The fact of three Democratic factions but only one Republican counterpart under sustained, issue-based cross-pressure does by itself suggest a further Democratic problem, and a further Republican opportunity. And that is before noting that the Republican faction in question, the non-Christian Republicans, is also the *smallest* of the four, at 3.5% of the total, versus 10.3% for the high-school graduate Democrats, 9.5% for the low-Protestant Democrats, and 7.2% for the high-school dropout Democrats.

Figure 5.6 reassembles these facts for maximum strategic import. In this, the overall encompassing balance does not disappear, nor should it (Fig. 5.6.A). There are still more—far more—self-identified Democrats than Republicans. Nevertheless, the strategic reality becomes more complex, and not so one-sided, when associated cross-pressures are added to the equation (Fig. 5.6.B). In that light, the largest single cluster of party loyalists consists not of Democratic factions at all, but of

Figure 5.6.B

The Sophisticated Strategic Balance of Party Identification

Partisan Distribution of Cross-Pressured Factions

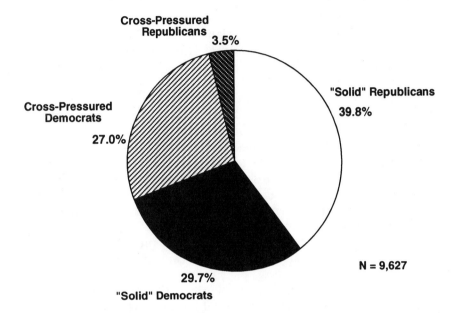

Cross-Pressured
Republicans
3.5%

"Solid" Republicans
39.8%

Cross-Pressured
Democrats
27.0%

N = 9,627

29.7%
"Solid" Democrats

Republican factions that are not cross-pressured. They are, admittedly, followed by Democratic factions that are not cross-pressured, but these are only slightly larger than the cluster of Democratic factions that *are* cross-pressured. And cross-pressured Republican factions bring up a very inconsequential rear.

The larger strategic world in which these factions seem particularly crucial is thus easily summarized. Again on the one hand, there are more Democratic than Republican identifiers in the aggregate. The balance may be closing in our time, but the edge remains undeniable. Accordingly, whenever normal partisan identifications are paramount, whenever economic/welfare concerns are central to the campaign and handled reasonably by both parties, *or* whenever cultural/national concerns are central but are not handled effectively, Democrats should go on to defeat Republicans.

On the other hand, the largest partisan piece of this aggregate consists of Republican factions which are not even incipiently cross-pressured, followed by Democratic factions which are not cross-pressured, followed by Democratic factions which *are* potentially under stress, with Republican counterparts which are numerically inconsequential. In such an environment, if any significant part of the problematic Democratic piece defects—the low-Protestant and high-school dropout Democrats, for example, without even worrying about the high-school *graduate* Democrats—such defection is more than enough to shift the underlying partisan balance. Accordingly, whenever Republicans can apply cultural/national issues efficiently, in order to split this crucial cross-pressured partisan piece, they seem entitled to defeat Democratic opponents.

The picture could be further elaborated with particularistic twists and turns for individual surface dimensions, treated individually. Yet at that point, a different sort of consideration probably becomes dominant. For whether political parties can use any of these apparent prospects to their advantage is, of course, a matter of more than particular positions, or even inherent cross-pressures. Low-Protestant Democrats, after all, along with their high-school dropout brethren, are still Democrats by habitual attachment and can be expected to vote Democratic in the absence of countervailing pressures. Which is to say: The other side of an intrinsic receptiveness to cross-party pressures is the provision of issue blandishments which might capitalize upon that receptiveness.

Providing these blandishments is principally the concern of opposition-party candidates and, indeed, of all those party activists who shape opposition offerings, with the latter perhaps playing a more crucial *continuing* role than the candidates themselves. But it is also a concern of own-party elites, who can obviously provide attractive and reinforcing—or, in fact, repellent—policy promises to their own supporters. Chapter 6 begins consideration of the likelihood that these key actors will seek to provide such stimuli, by considering what it is that active partisans want. Chapter 7 then addresses some elements of how they come to want it—as well as what the ultimate impact of their preferences should be.

6 THE SHAPE OF POLICY OPTIONS

Activists, Followers, and Political Preferences

Chapters 2 to 5 provide the general public framework for contemporary substantive politics, the mass base for practical issue politicking. This begins with a set of underlying policy concerns (Chapter 2). These acquire a structure by way of political parties and social groups (Chapters 3 and 4). That structure then envelops—"organizes"—much of ongoing political life (Chapter 5). From one side, such a framework encourages some initiatives and discourages others. From the other side, it goes a long way toward determining the outcome for all, in the process establishing the issue context for modern American politics.

Yet that cannot be the end of the story. For what such a structure also implies is that what is reliably on offer—the choices which the general public actually faces—can itself be a central aspect of a continuing issue context. Here, however, the character of the mass framework for issue politicking runs into another, equally stubborn structural fact: not all citizens are effectively equal. At a minimum, some are much more active in pursuit of their policy preferences, and presumably this matters. In the very nature of democratic politics, candidates must be recruited, campaigns must be organized, public officials must be contacted, and policies must be fostered. Probably, such tasks could not be shared equally. In practice, in any case, they are not.[1]

And therein lies the importance of the policy preferences—the "sample" of political opinion—within that influential segment of the general public that actually manages these tasks. For in their persons, those who undertake these crucial labors inevitably *transmute*, while translating, an issue context. This is not to deny that their activities are both integral and essential to democratic politics, to connecting less active citizens to their candidates and public officials. It is just to note that the politically active inevitably have their own values and interests, and that these are often integral to motivating them to do the work of practical politics. These preferences are thus destined, on the average and over time, to be of greater consequence than those of any similarly sized sample of more passive citizens.

As a result, the relationship between activists' preferences and those of their putative rank and file can be a crucial element of the modern political landscape, adding, in effect, an elite aspect to the mass framework for contemporary politicking.[2] The first part of this aspect involves its simple representational character, how the wishes of these key elites relate to the wishes of their putative followers within the institutional framework of the two political parties. That is the subject of Chapter 6. The second part is then the struggle *among* these activists to shape what is on offer, along with the impact of various possible outcomes to that struggle upon their rank and file. That is the subject of Chapter 7.

Activist Opinions in Earlier Eras

The more active participants in politics inevitably "stand in for" the less active public, in the process bearing some (crucial) relationship to that public—representing it well or badly, or more likely, better in some areas and worse in others. Some part of the resulting "representation" is more or less automatic, as when most members of a society share implicit premises about policy and politics. At the other extreme, some part has become so specialized that it must be "hired out," in our time, to technical experts whose *job* is to interpret public wishes—or at least, to suggest what the general public will and will not tolerate.[3]

Yet much of the broad middle of active politicking consists of motivating behavior from the incipient participants, who reliably have their own views of what should be on offer and, indeed, are motivated largely by these views. This seems more true than ever in our time, and that fact makes these activists an especially logical target of inquiry. On the other hand, while the breadth and social identity of this stratum has varied immensely, over time and across nations as well, the problem inherent in their representational role is an old and familiar one. Indeed, early efforts at a self-conscious social science took the problem of elite identity and behavior to be one of those at the center of the democratic prospect. These early studies took one of three general viewpoints.

The most pessimistic argued that because specialized political actors were largely self-selected and yet inescapably integral to the organization of any political activity—nothing could happen without specialized elites with distinctive characteristics—the goal of a government controlled by public opinion was a hopeless, bootless, and chimerical aspiration.[4] A second camp argued that while elites might be structurally integral to any mass impact on politics, this did not mean that they could not mobilize a general public to effect political change: indeed, history provided numerous examples to the contrary. This possibility did not, however, eliminate the prospect that such elites would have partially separable wishes that would grow more dominant (and separate) as time passed.[5] Still others, finally, accepted the reality of the functional need for political specialists, a need for elites to operationalize policy choice for the mass public, but argued that a focus on practical distinctions among such elites—their social backgrounds, of course, but especially their attitudinal representativeness and their practical responsiveness—was more nearly the crucial question.[6]

The coming of scientific survey samples during the Depression and the Second World War, and then the focus by social scientists upon this potential research tool in the immediate postwar years, reinvigorated the classical debate. By the 1950s, it was possible to inquire directly into relationships between the general public and the politically active. One major line of the resulting research (the subject of Chapters 3 to 5) centered on the social shaping of political attitudes within the mass public. Yet there was to be a second major line of inquiry as well, centered on the representational links—and hence the value transmissions—between the general public and more specialized political actors. And there were to be two further subthemes within this second line of inquiry.

The first of these, spurred most generally by the experience of the Second World War and more pointedly by the rise of the fascist states at its center, concerned support for democratic values in the general public and among specialized political actors.[7] This was probably the more topical, and surely the more emotionally freighted, of the two substrands. The second then concerned the distinctions among and between crucial segments of political activists and the general public— between partisan activists and partisan identifiers—on specific policy preferences and on the broader ideological identifications (if any) which united them.[8] This work has probably had a more constant influence on subsequent research.

Both strands, under the joint stimulus of events of the time and of new tools of inquiry, attracted an array of scholars. Yet these approaches can be well exemplified—well capsulized as a scholarly method but also, especially, well considered for their theoretical contributions—in a seminal set of articles by Herbert McClosky and colleagues. Two of these in particular—"Issue Conflict and Consensus among Party Leaders and Followers" and "Consensus and Ideology in American Politics" —were to establish the contours of a field, as well as to suggest the contours of practical politics implied by the data of the 1950s.[9]

McClosky sought explicitly to focus on relationships involving "those people who occupy themselves with public affairs to an unusual degree."[10] While his data provide a rich and internally varied picture of public preferences and mass-elite relationships in the 1950s, his overall conclusions can be straightforwardly summarized. In the matter of support for democratic values, McClosky found that political activists, both Democratic and Republican, tended to be more like each other than like their fellow party identifiers, in "their stronger approval of democratic ideas, their greater tolerance and regard for proper procedures and citizen rights, their superior understanding and acceptance of the 'rules of the game,' and their more affirmative attitudes toward the political system in general." In fact, "the evidence suggests that it is the articulate classes rather than the public who serve as the major repositories of the public conscience and as the carriers of the Creed. Responsibility for keeping the system going, hence, falls most heavily upon them." McClosky found that the activists' greater support for democratic values "plainly has to do with the differences in their political activity, involvement, and articulateness."[11]

By contrast, when the question was not the "rules of the game" but specific policies and programs, political activists stood in a very different relationship to each other and to the general public. Here, on the alternative postures of one or another elected governments, partisan activists tended to differ more sharply from each other—Republicans versus Democrats—than did their partisan rank and file. Active partisans were thus reliably more extreme than their putative followers, who differed more modestly, and sometimes not at all:

1. Although it has received wide currency, especially among Europeans, the belief that the two American parties are identical in principle and doctrine has little foundation in fact. Examination of the opinions of Democratic and Republican leaders shows them to be distinct communities of co-believers who diverge sharply on many important issues . . .

2. Republican and Democratic leaders stand farthest apart on the issues that grow out of their group identification and support—out of the managerial, proprietary, and high-status connections of the one, and the labor, minority, low-status, and intellectual connections of the other . . .

3. Whereas the leaders of the two parties diverge strongly, their followers differ only moderately in their attitudes toward issues . . . Republicans followers, in fact, disagree far more with their own leaders than with the leaders of the Democratic party. Little support was found for the belief that deep cleavages exist among the electorate but are ignored by the leaders. One might, indeed, more accurately assert the contrary, to

wit: that the natural cleavages between the leaders are largely ignored by the voters.[12]

Activists, Followers, and the Deep Factors

The main routes to political activism still run through the two major political parties. All electoral campaigns of consequence, with the rarest of exceptions, are partisan campaigns. All the resulting elected officials, with even fewer exceptions, are partisan products. And almost all the higher elective governmental institutions are then organized by party. This does not imply, either in principle or, as it develops, in practice, that all activists are stereotypical partisans. But it does mean, because both electoral and institutional politicking is channeled by political parties, that they constitute the obvious place to begin the search for—and then to register—elite contributions to an issue context.

On the other hand, the activities which could serve to mark an active participant off from the general public are effectively legion, considering that every facet of electoral politics, and then every facet of the institutional politicking which follows, requires (an array of) supporting tasks. No survey is likely to—or could—ask about all of these, and even the notion of an accurate "sample" is ambiguous and problematic.[13] The Times Mirror survey that provides our measure of policy preferences did, however, ask about seven of these potential activities, and they range from displaying public endorsements to attending political events to contributing money for a variety of purposes (Fig. 6.1.A).

As a result, respondents can be ranked according to the number of these activities which they themselves have undertaken within the last four-year election cycle (Fig. 6.1.B). Not surprisingly, they stretch out across the full range of possibilities. More surprisingly, this progression is perfectly linear: the larger the number of activities, the smaller the share of participants. Such a distribution should make the relationship between activism and political opinion easy to follow, in principle. In practice, what is still required is some defensible means of dividing this distribution into more and less active populations, since many of these individual levels of activism contain too few participants to be analyzed by themselves.

A sense that the activist stratum (and hence the statistical cut) should be as "exclusive" as possible can be gained from the best observational work on the movers and shakers of American politics.[14] Fortunately, there is some related theoretical work which contains further, rough hypotheses about where the appropriate cut should come. Or at

Figure 6.1
Participation in Various Political Activities

A. Checklist of Political Activities

Which of the following things, if any, have you done
in the last four years or so?

1. Wore a campaign button, put a campaign sticker on your car, or placed a sign in your window or in front of your house?

2. Went to any political meetings, rallies, speeches, or dinners in support of a particular candidate?

3. Worked for a political party or a candidate running for office?

4. Checked off the option on your federal income tax return applying one dollar of your taxes to the campaign fund?

5. Contributed money to an individual candidate running for public office?

6. Contributed money to a political party organization?

7. Contributed money to political action groups such as groups sponsored by a union, or a business, or any other issue groups that supported or opposed particular candidates in an election?

B. Distribution of Political Activists

	Number of Activities	Percent of Sample	
Active Partisans (19.3%)	Seven	1.0%	**True Activists (6.2%)**
	Six	2.1%	
	Five	3.1%	
	Four	5.0%	**Rank and File (93.8%)**
	Three	8.1%	
Rank and File (81.7%)	Two	12.1%	
	One	21.4%	
	None	47.1%	

N = 10,346

least, this work suggests that there is a further natural division among the politically active, creating a much more specialized (and narrower) population that undertakes even more specialized and demanding tasks.[15] Two examples of this work, with otherwise quite different orientations, can indicate its thrust.

Perhaps the most fully developed gloss on the overarching argument, in a work actually focused on political sophistication, comes from W. Russell Neuman, whose conclusion might serve as a reasonable summary statement here too:

> Although political sophistication is defined and measured as a continuous variable, the curve has two inflection points which generate the theory of three publics. There is no clear and unmistakable dividing line between these publics, but their different patterns of behavior suggest that the distinctions are important . . .
>
> A much smaller stratum, perhaps less than 5 percent of the population, contains the political activists. Members of this higher stratum of political sophistication exhibit uniquely high levels of political involvement. Previous research has derived similar figures.[16]

In a different enterprise, focused more explicitly on political participation, Sidney Verba and Norman H. Nie make the same basic point:

> The complete activists engage in all types of activity with great frequency. How active they are becomes clear when they are compared to the communalists and campaigners. Not only do they combine both campaign and communal participation but they are considerably more active on each mode than either of the groups that specialize in the respective acts. About one in ten Americans falls in this most active segment.[17]

Using the outside limits set by Neuman and Verba/Nie, it seems appropriate initially to reclassify all those who engaged in *five or more* of the seven benchmarks on our continuum of political activities (Fig. 6.1.A) as the "true activist" population. The "rank-and-file" population then becomes those who have engaged in four or fewer. This in effect isolates the most active 6% of our sample, whom we now dub the truly active, the "hyperactivists." The right-hand side of Figure 6.1.B presents this initial division. From there, it is but a small step to compare the preferences of these hyperactivists with those of their less active fellow partisans.

Figure 6.2 separates the rank and file from the true activists in both the Republican and the Democratic parties, so that the policy preferences of all four subgroups can be compared.[18] When this is done, recognizable previous findings (re)appear, both as regards the policy preferences which distinguished the total memberships of the two

Figure 6.2.A
"True Activists" and Their Rank and File
on the Deep Factors of Political Opinion

Cultural/National

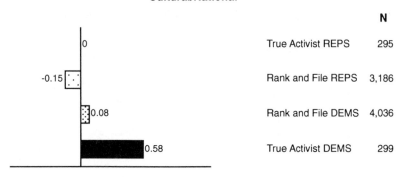

		N
True Activist REPS		295
Rank and File REPS		3,186
Rank and File DEMS		4,036
True Activist DEMS		299

Figure 6.2.B
"True Activists" and Their Rank and File
on the Deep Factors of Political Opinion

Economic/Welfare

		N
True Activist REPS		297
Rank and File REPS		3,278
Rank and File DEMS		4,239
True Activist DEMS		301

contemporary parties from each other and as regards the policy differences which had distinguished activists from their (putative) followers
in an earlier era. Nevertheless, there are further elite-mass distinctions
that do *not* so obviously extend previous findings, and these not only
seem much the more impressive in terms of elaborating an issue context; they promise additional strategic implications as well.

Indeed, in the case of the cultural/national factor, any shadows of
preceding research pale beside the current, stark empirical outline.
(Fig. 6.2.A). In this, the Republican rank and file contribute a modest

right wing; Republican activists sit just at the national average; the Democratic rank and file are very modestly more liberal; and Democratic activists contribute the far—the truly distant—liberal extreme. What the specifics of these positions imply, in addition, is that Republican activists are actually closer to both Republican *and Democratic* followers. Mean preferences for all three groups effectively cluster. Democratic activists, by comparison, stand wildly off to the left—not just of Republicans, elite or mass, but of the Democratic mass as well!

Such a summary does mask some lesser continuities with preceding research. Thus, the Democratic rank and file remain more liberal than their Republican counterparts, as has been the case at every point in our analysis. Moreover, activists within both parties remain more liberal than their respective partisan followers on these cultural/national concerns, as they apparently were in the postwar years.[19] Yet the more striking finding, even on its own terms, is the subgroup array: Republican activists, Republican followers, and Democratic followers together, with Democratic activists far off to their (collective) left.

The economic/welfare factor, by contrast, largely elaborates findings associated with analysis of contemporary parties-in-the-electorate *or* of elite-mass relationships in an earlier era (Fig. 6.2.B). Thus, even without their respective partisan activists, Republican and Democratic followers remain sharply distinct. Republican and Democratic activists are then only more so, flanking their rank and file to the right and to the left. Finally, active Republicans are additionally—massively—farther off to the right of their putative followers than are active Democrats off to the left of theirs, a positioning which would not have been historically unfamiliar but which is destined to acquire additional strategic implications in the modern era.

Hyperactivists, Active Partisans, and the Rank and File

The preceding is a genuinely stark portrait of policy preferences by level of political activity, and thus of elite-mass relations within the two political parties. This portrait also appears to promise major strategic implications when reimmersed in the rest of the analysis. Yet such a portrait does have one huge associated problem: activist populations defined and isolated this way, for all their theoretical defensibility and all their dramatic substantive product, are simply too small for some critical further analyses. Their size would at least interfere, for example, with looking at their social background. Likewise, it would eliminate the possibility of looking at struggles *among* activists over the proper content of party offerings.

The obvious solution is to seek some second, broader definition of the politically active. Such a definition could be designed to isolate a numerically larger population, as long as it does not produce a population whose views are notably different from those deriving from a more theoretically appropriate definition of activism. In truth, there *is* a further, obvious, practical divide within the continuum of available political activities. The only question is whether its product would violate the substantive logic of all the preceding. For in fact, one of the activities in this roster (Fig. 6.1.A) involves nothing more than utilizing a tax check-off on the federal income tax, and this would hardly qualify a respondent as politically active in any operational sense.

So, a *minimum* standard for distinguishing active participants from their more passive rank and file would surely demand more than one political activity beyond utilizing the tax check-off. That implies a population of political activists who have engaged in at least three— three or more—of the seven available activities, and the left-hand side of Figure 6.1.B, accordingly, presents this division. This is now a quite modest definition of activism. Yet it is a further cut with substantive justification, and it does lead immediately to the question of the policy preferences of those "active partisans" versus *their* rank and file.

What results is only a somewhat more modest and restrained— though in our view, still quite striking—version of the original elite-mass portrait (Fig. 6.3). On cultural/national matters, there is a clustering of the same three subgroups—active Republicans, rank and file Republicans, *and* rank and file Democrats—with active Democrats far off to their left (Fig. 6.3.A). The position of the latter is now not quite as extreme, yet it is also true that the Democratic rank and file are now even closer to Republican activists. On economic/welfare issues, both active extremes have pulled in a bit (Fig. 6.3.B). While this represents a larger move by active Republicans, of course, they remain massively farther away both from the national average *and from their own rank and file* than do active Democrats.

Moreover, defining the politically active in this way—as active partisans rather than hyperactivists—provides some added confidence for a few additional observations. Thus, on cultural/national issues, regardless of the situation in the immediate postwar years, even the current American elite-mass portrait is clearly *not* the situation suggested by an examination of the two parties as undifferentiated aggregates today (as from Fig. 3.1.A onward). The Republican party, in truth, still offers relatively minor internal differences between elite and mass identifiers, so that its composite portrait is refined only modestly. But the Democratic party now features a huge internal divide. Seen one way, there are now only two basic clusters to cultural/national opin-

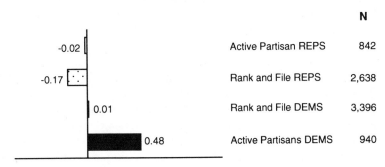

Figure 6.3.A
Active Partisans and Their Rank and File
on the Deep Factors of Political Opinion

Cultural/National

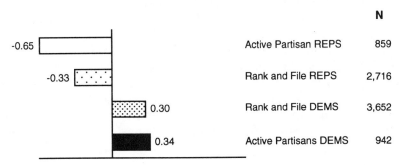

Figure 6.3.B
Active Partisans and Their Rank and File
on the Deep Factors of Political Opinion

Economic/Welfare

ion, since the Democratic rank and file effectively join the entire Republican party. Seen another way, the apparent liberalism of the Democratic party as a whole on these issues proves to be overwhelmingly a product of its active elite; rank-and-file Democrats stand almost exactly at the national average.

With economic/welfare issues, by contrast, what is in some sense most remarkable is the *continuity* of (two pairs of) internal party portraits, from the immediate postwar years through today. Now, with active partisans as the defining cut, the rank and file of the two parties are still sharply divided on these matters; active partisans themselves are even more divided; but active Republicans then stand additionally off to the right—as much as, or more than, they did in the 1950s. Moreover, by these standards, there is now very little difference at all (of an overall elite-mass sort) among Democrats. As a result, there are really three subgroups on economic/welfare matters rather than four: active Republicans, the Republican rank and file, and the entire Democratic party!

Despite these elaborations, the key fact about this new cut, between more and less active party identifiers, is that it only moderates the basic findings from a more restrictive—and theoretically more defensible—definition of activism. This suggests that it is reasonable to go on and examine the further preferences of both these active partisans and their rank and file on the surface dimensions of political opinion in the remainder of this chapter. It suggests that it is also reasonable to examine any further differences *within* these populations, as we do in Chapter 7. It will, of course, still be possible to bring back the hyperactivists when internal divisions are not the focus, and indeed, they play a very suggestive role again at the end of the next chapter.

In the meantime, the active partisans seem an entirely appropriate body for further analysis. The resulting figures (and the data on which they are based) would still not satisfy those who have a more specific subgroup in mind when they conjure with the notion of "activist." Those who are thinking of state party or campaign chairs, for example, could not isolate them through such a sample. Neither could those who are thinking of truly giant financial operatives.[20] Yet within the limits inherent in a national sample, and with these deep factors and surface dimensions as the focus, a comparison of the hyperactivists with these active partisans does not warn against going on to analyze the latter as reasonably representative of the active parties.[21]

Activists, Followers, and the Surface Dimensions

A shift from relationships between active partisans and their putative rank and file on the deep factors of political opinion to those same relationships on the surface dimensions is the obvious next step in any elite-mass inquiry. When the focus was on political parties in the electorate (as in Chapter 3) or on social factions within those parties (as in Chapter 5), these surface dimensions reflected the deep factors in very straightforward ways. Cultural values and civil liberties reflected the underlying cultural/national factor more or less directly, while foreign relations was colored by a more strongly partisan influence. Similarly, social welfare and civil liberties reflected the underlying economic/ welfare factor in a more or less straightforward fashion, while social insurance was colored by a more explicitly group-related shuffling.

When the focus shifts to activists and followers, however, and to distinctions between and among them, the situation is different. Or, at least, the relationship between the deep factors and the surface dimensions of political opinion is noticeably looser—more elaborate and more nuanced. Which is to say, a shift in focus to the elite-mass distinction makes the reflection of the deep factors by the surface dimensions appear much less straightforward and automatic. Continuities which had seemed fundamental do, in fact, appear. But they are joined by further differentiations of some potential consequence.

Among the cultural/national dimensions, it is cultural values, this time, that most directly mirrors elite-mass relations on the underlying factor (Fig. 6.4.A). Republican activists again sit *between* the mass of Republican and Democratic identifiers. These three subgroups again form, in effect, one social cluster, with very little difference in preferences among them. And Democratic activists again stand well off to the left. Moreover, the minority of politically active identifiers are once more pulling both of their respective parties in the same—the liberal— direction.

In this, Republican party activists now stand revealed as moderating the aggregate party position slightly, though that position (at Fig. 3.2.A) was not really masking a major elite-mass difference. For the Democrats, by contrast, almost every bit of the apparent liberalism of the party as a whole on issues of cultural values can now be seen to have been contributed by party activists. When these individuals are removed from the total, the vast majority of party members—its effective rank and file—sit almost exactly at the national average, and the party is seen to be hugely divided along elite-mass lines. All of this, nevertheless, is still directly recognizable from the situation on the underlying factor.

Civil liberties, too, could still be described in language appropriate to the underlying factor, with Republican activists again closer to both the Republican and the Democratic rank and file, and Democratic activists again well off to the left (Fig. 6.4.F). Now, however, such a description would obscure the more accurate summary. For in fact, with preferences on civil liberties divided by party attachment and by level of political activity, both sets of activists are in effect pitted against their collective rank and file. Both sets of partisan activists are not just more liberal than their fellow partisans but are actually more liberal than the national average on matters of civil liberties. Moreover, both

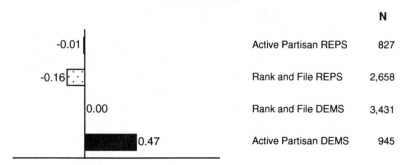

Figure 6.4.A
Active Partisans and Their Rank and File
on the Surface Dimensions of Political Opinion

Cultural Values

		N
-0.01	Active Partisan REPS	827
-0.16	Rank and File REPS	2,658
0.00	Rank and File DEMS	3,431
0.47	Active Partisan DEMS	945

Figure 6.4.B
Active Partisans and Their Rank and File
on the Surface Dimensions of Political Opinion

Social Welfare

		N
-0.65	Active Partisan REPS	858
-0.29	Rank and File REPS	2,699
0.28	Rank and File DEMS	3,646
0.26	Active Partisan DEMS	949

sets of partisan followers are not only more conservative than the national average. They are also, now, essentially indistinguishable as between themselves.

Civil liberties is thus the classic example of how lumping activists with their rank and file will often mask underlying preferences, thereby obscuring the related strategic considerations as well. For here, these activists were almost solely resonsible for the apparent difference *between* the two parties (Fig. 3.2.F). Moreover, both sets of activists are still so much more liberal than their less active fellow partisans that

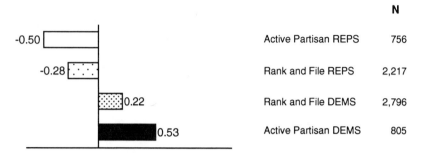

Figure 6.4.C
Active Partisans and Their Rank and File
on the Surface Dimensions of Political Opinion

Foreign Relations

		N
-0.50	Active Partisan REPS	756
-0.28	Rank and File REPS	2,217
0.22	Rank and File DEMS	2,796
0.53	Active Partisan DEMS	805

Figure 6.4.D
Active Partisans and Their Rank and File
on the Surface Dimensions of Political Opinion

Social Insurance

		N
-0.51	Active Partisan REPS	883
-0.24	Rank and File REPS	2,867
0.27	Rank and File DEMS	3,824
0.00	Active Partisan DEMS	951

they can be seen to have been creating a further, impressive surface confusion about party positioning: With activists included but submerged, Republicans appeared, as ever, to be more conservative than the national average, and Democrats more liberal. With activists isolated, Republican identifiers look somewhat more conservative—but Democratic identifiers prove to be conservative, too![22]

All of which makes foreign relations look even more distinctive than usual. Now, the familiar addition of a thoroughgoing partisan principle serves to break up the internal elite-mass clustering characteristic of cultural values and civil liberties. Traces remain—for exam-

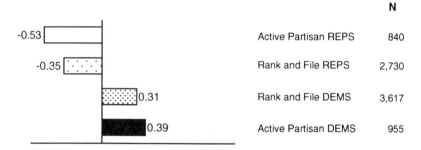

Figure 6.4.E
Active Partisans and Their Rank and File
on the Surface Dimensions of Political Opinion

Civil Rights

		N
-0.53	Active Partisan REPS	840
-0.35	Rank and File REPS	2,730
0.31	Rank and File DEMS	3,617
0.39	Active Partisan DEMS	955

Figure 6.4.F
Active Partisans and Their Rank and File
on the Surface Dimensions of Political Opinion

Civil Liberties

		N
0.16	Active Partisan REPS	912
-0.08	Rank and-File REPS	2,765
-0.07	Rank and File DEMS	3,564
0.48	Active Partisan DEMS	962

ple, in the fact that Democratic activists are still (nominally) farthest from the national average (Fig. 6.4.C). But these are overwhelmed by the return of a strong partisan division *between* the two rank and files, and of an even stronger one between the two activist populations. Indeed, foreign relations actually offers the purest embodiment of a partisan conflict, in the sense of being both the most clear-cut and the most symmetric. Said differently, here more than anywhere else, active partisans are apparently working to reinforce a classic two-party confrontation, rather than to skew it in any number of available ways.

Economic/welfare dimensions, too, become even more varied when levels of activity are added to basic party identification. From an elite-mass perspective, civil rights now comes closest to mirroring the situation on the underlying factor, with all its hallmark characteristics: the Republican and Democratic rank and files are themselves sharply divided; Republican and Democratic activists are more sharply divided still; and Republican activists pull additionally off to the right (Fig. 6.4.E). As a result, the elite-mass relations capsulized in the economic/welfare factor are apparently, in our time, best captured by the surface dimension of civil rights.

Social welfare then skews this basic alignment in a further and distinctive fashion (Fig. 6.4.B). *Most* of the fundamental pattern—the template—can still be discerned, with the rank and file of the two parties standing well apart, and Republican activists plunging additionally to the right. But here, Democratic activists fall back to the same mean preference as their rank and file, so that they are collectively indistinguishable. On social welfare matters, then, active Democrats exaggerate their effective unity with party followers, while from the other side, active Republicans simultaneously exaggerate *their* propensity to pull away to the right. Social welfare is actually the high-water mark of both tendencies.

The final economic/welfare dimension, social insurance, sees Democratic activists shift once again. In the process, the dimension itself takes on some of the group-related patterning more characteristic of cultural/national affairs, albeit with a major twist (Fig. 6.4.D). On the one hand, social insurance effectively replicates the situation on *cultural values*, where Republican activists stood between the two parties' rank and files. On the other hand, this effect now runs in exactly the opposite direction. For here, it is Democratic activists who stand between the Democratic and Republican rank and files, with Republican activists farther off to the right. On no other dimension are active Democrats so close to the Republican rank and file. On no other dimension do they flank their own rank and file so dramatically *to the right.*

Perhaps not surprisingly, social insurance is thus also a case (like cultural values and civil liberties) where activist preferences were blurring the internal character of the parties as a whole. Without these activists, the Democratic rank and file is actually *more liberal* than it was when analysis focused on the two composite parties-in-the-electorate (Fig. 3.2.D). Without them, the distance between mean positions for the two rank and files is actually greater than it was when active partisans were included in the totals!

Seen the other way around, social insurance is the only dimension where party activists were actually suppressing the difference between rank-and-file Republicans and rank-and-file Democrats. (See Table 6.1 and its analysis, below.) On every other dimension, party activists were exaggerating this difference. On civil liberties, and to a great degree on cultural values, they were effectively creating it. On social insurance, by contrast, the party rank and file were—and are—sharply distinctive. It is party activists who were reducing the apparent policy differences between the two parties, and this impact really traces to Democratic activists, with their position at the national average.

Strategic Implications: The Basics, Revisited

Despite all these analytic twists and turns—these findings, these elaborations, and their nuances—the single strongest piece of recurring strategic advice from the modern issue context remains intact. Even after party identifiers have been divided into their more and less active participants, so that activists can be isolated from their rank and file, partisanship is best reinforced through economic/welfare issues, best disrupted through cultural/national concerns. As before, the Democratic party, in its candidates and its initiatives, is the obvious beneficiary of partisan reinforcement, just as the Republican party is the evident beneficiary of its disruption—in fact, now more than ever.

When the two parties were considered as simple aggregates (in Chapter 3), economic/welfare matters were far more closely tied to party identification than were cultural/national concerns. When the two parties are *dis*aggregated according to internal levels of activity, the same basic relationship holds, for all the resulting pieces as well as for the newly complex parties as a whole (Table 6.1). The politically active, by themselves, reflect the differential partisanship of the two deep factors, with a range of .99 on economic/welfare issues versus .50 on cultural/national concerns and an eta of .46 versus .23. Yet the *less* politically active testify to the same basic situation, with ranges of .63 on economic/welfare against .18 on cultural/national and etas of .32 against .09.[23]

The lessons of this underlying partisan attachment—whether they are conscious lessons, in the sense of helping to make strategic decisions, or only environmental lessons, when effectively imposed by the issues of the day—get their most obvious and impressive support, however, from the internal structure of each deep factor. Now, in the case of the economic/welfare factor, it is clear not just that the two sets of rank-and-file identifiers stand well apart (Figs. 6.2.B and 6.3.B). It is also clear that their fellow activists contribute, in effect, to sharpening this division. Which is to say, party activists prefer an even greater

Table 6.1
Partisanship and Policy Preferences

Issue	Rank and File	Parties-in-the-Electorate	Activists Only
	A. Distance between Partisan Means (range)		
Deep Factor			
Cultural/National	.18	.25	.50
Economic/Welfare	.63	.73	.99
Surface Dimension			
Civil Liberties	.01	.07	.32
Cultural Values	.16	.23	.48
Foreign Relations	.50	.62	1.03
Civil Rights	.66	.73	.92
Social Welfare	.57	.66	.91
Social Insurance	.51	.52	.51
Average N	6,152	7,930	1,778
	B. Strength of Association (eta)		
Deep Factor			
Cultural/National	.09	.12	.23
Economic/Welfare	.32	.34	.46
Surface Dimension			
Civil Liberties	.01	.04	.16
Cultural Values	.08	.11	.23
Foreign Relations	.26	.29	.46
Civil Rights	.33	.34	.44
Social Welfare	.29	.31	.44
Social Insurance	.26	.25	.23
Average N	6,152	7,930	1,778

separation, in the process making it additionally difficult for their rank and file to cross party lines.

Indeed, in a further and potentially critical extension, Republican activists—already possessing the minority party identification, of course—actually prefer pulling their party even farther away from the national average on these issues, thereby presumably making Democratic defections even more difficult. Were it not for the situation on the cultural/national factor, this fact might be decisive in and of itself, at least whenever politics partakes of the issue context of its era. To wit: The Democrats are already the majority party; when party offerings then encourage a net advantage in defections, that ought to be sufficient to determine the outcome.

Yet the internal situation on cultural/national matters *is* different, strikingly different—so different as to offer at least the promise of regaining (or surrendering) strategic ground. In the analytic sense, the cultural/national factor is the stereotypical realm in which activists create most of the apparent partisan difference, such that the rank and file of the two parties are hardly differentiated at all (Figs. 6.2.A and 6.3.A). But in the strategic sense, the crucial further fact is that all of this partisan difference is contributed by *Democratic* activists this time, by active Democrats pulling away from the national average, on their own and without any compensating move by active Republicans.

As a result, the preferences of rank-and-file Democrats are closer (much closer) to those of active Republicans, while the preferences of active Democrats stand well off from the entire rest of American society. As a further result, cultural/national concerns gain an even greater ability to play a disruptive role in partisan politics, thanks almost entirely to Democratic party activists. In the process, the fundamental logic for partisan strategists is only affirmed: partisanship is best reinforced by economic/welfare matters, best disrupted by cultural/national concerns.

Revisiting the surface dimensions of political opinion with these strategic implications in mind largely repeats the same lessons, though it does provide some added explanation for previously deviant dimensions. Civil rights and social welfare still reflect the underlying economic/welfare situation more or less directly, with strong differences between the composite parties, reflecting strong differences even among the rank and file, and still stronger differences among their activists (Table 6.1). And civil liberties and cultural values still mirror the underlying cultural/national situation, with minimal differences between the composite parties, masking modest differences among partisan actives, and nearly none at all among party rank and files.

It is not unusual for social insurance and foreign relations to differ additionally from the economic/welfare and cultural/national factors, respectively. Yet now, with the addition of an elite-mass division, part of the reason for their recurring deviation comes into focus. Previously and consistently, social insurance has appeared less partisan than history might have suggested, just as foreign relations has appeared more partisan. Now, the preferences of partisan actives go some way toward explaining this anomaly.

Admittedly, part of the explanation may well be simple social change: social insurance has become less partisan in American society as the central programs of the New Deal (and hence the welfare state) have become more consensual. By contrast, foreign relations has probably become more conflictual as a bipartisan operating consensus in international affairs has deteriorated across the postwar years. Yet the introduction of an elite-mass distinction suggests a further explanation as well: party activists have actually been suppressing the rank-and-file partisan difference on social insurance, just as they have been—notably—magnifying this difference on foreign relations.

As a result, when active partisans are removed from the analysis (as they can be in the bottom half of Fig. 6.1, col. 1), social insurance becomes the sole dimension to feature a *greater* partisan association among the rank and file than among active partisans, while foreign relations, at the other extreme, opens the greatest gap between mass and elite partisanship. Said differently, the three economic/welfare dimensions are now arguably the most partisan among the rank and file, going from civil rights, to social welfare, to social insurance. Yet foreign relations—a cultural/national dimension—turns out to be the most partisan among activists; for them, social insurance is only marginally more partisan than cultural values. We shall return to these facts at the end of Chapter 7, when activist priorities come into question.

Further Implications: Issue Options and Party Fortunes

In the meantime, the *patterning* of elite-mass divisions on the deep factors of political opinion provides another way to measure partisan advantage and to rank the surface dimensions as tools for operationalizing basic strategy. To do this, it is necessary merely to reset the midpoint of policy preferences, not at the national average as in previous tables, but at a point halfway between the mean preferences of the two sets of party activists. Theoretically, this reflects the view that the politically active are likely to be disproportionately influential in shaping the options available to rank-and-file identifiers. Mechanically, anyone who is closer to Democratic activists becomes "liberal," anyone who is closer to Republican activists becomes "conservative," and their precise position is determined by where they stand with regard to the midpoint between the two activist populations.

Recasting the situation on the deep factors in these terms (from Fig. 6.3) shows a familiar situation in a different light. Now, on the cultural/national factor, *both* rank and file populations show up as conservative, with the Republicans at −.40 and the Democrats at −.22, *clearly* conservative in both cases (Fig. 6.5.A).[24] The economic/welfare factor is not as immediately striking, though its strategic import is every bit as great (Fig. 6.5.B) Here, the two rank and files still stand on opposite sides of the ideological divide, with the Republicans at −.18 and the Democrats at +.45. Now, however, it is the comparative balance

Figure 6.5.A
Rank and File Identifiers on the Deep Factors:
Preferences Relative to the Active Parties

Cultural/National

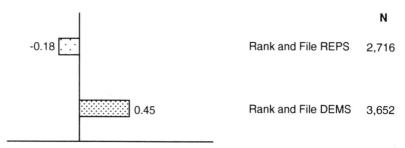

Figure 6.5.B
Rank and File Identifiers on the Deep Factors:
Preferences Relative to the Active Parties

Economic/Welfare

on potential issue-based defections that is highlighted—as a disproportionate advantage to the Democrats, given that it would be much
more difficult to draw the Democratic rank and file to the Republican
activist mean than vice versa.

Presenting the surface dimensions of political opinion in the same
fashion has additional advantages (Fig. 6.6). As before, this measure
(with its visual display) highlights the situation which activist preferences create for the rank and file. Yet now, such a presentation also creates a new way of ranking surface dimensions, according to their incipient partisan advantages. This was done at the end of Chapter 5
using factional preferences, both their ideological scores and their comparative positions. Now, it can be done with elite-mass preferences as

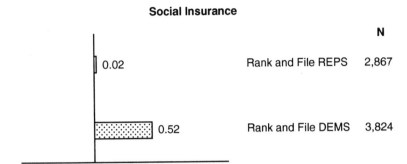

Figure 6.6.A
Rank and File Identifiers on the Surface Dimensions:
Preferences Relative to the Active Parties

Social Insurance

	N
Rank and File REPS	2,867
Rank and File DEMS	3,824

0.02

0.52

Figure 6.6.B
Rank and File Identifiers on the Surface Dimensions:
Preferences Relative to the Active Parties

Social Welfare

	N
Rank and File REPS	2,699
Rank and File DEMS	3,646

-0.09

0.48

well—a very different measure—and the outcome is exactly the same, as follows:

- In these terms, the obvious Democratic bonanza is social insurance, where *both* rank and file populations are closer to Democratic activists (+.02 and +.52), and where it is hard to conceive of anything other than disproportionate Republican defections (Fig. 6.6.A).

- Social welfare, too, is a clear Democratic benefit, though much in the manner of the underlying factor (Fig. 6.6.B). The two rank and files are now ideologically divided. But the Democratic rank and file (at +.48) should be much harder to pull to the Republican side of the aisle than the Republican rank and file (at only –.09) to the Democratic side.

Figure 6.6.C
Rank and File Identifiers on the Surface Dimensions:
Preferences Relative to the Active Parties

Civil Rights

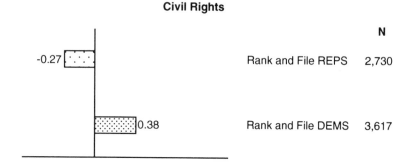

		N
Rank and File REPS	2,730
Rank and File DEMS	3,617

Figure 6.6.D
Rank and File Identifiers on the Surface Dimensions:
Preferences Relative to the Active Parties

Foreign Relations

		N
Rank and File REPS	2,217
Rank and File DEMS	2,796

- Civil rights is the least clear-cut of the economic/welfare dimensions in this regard (Fig. 6.6.C). On the one hand, the two rank and files do stand well apart here, with Republicans at –.27 and Democrats at +.38, so that the edge remains Democratic. On the other hand, the size of this edge is sharply reduced, so that strategic possibilities are correspondingly enhanced.

- Foreign relations then appears, once again, the most closely balanced of all the surface dimensions (Fig. 6.6.D). It is also the first (and weakest) with a Republican edge. With Republicans at –.29 and Democrats at +.20, strategy is again at a premium, though good strategy should still, this time, narrowly benefit Republicans.

Figure 6.6.E
Rank and File Identifiers on the Surface Dimensions:
Preferences Relative to the Active Parties

Cultural Values

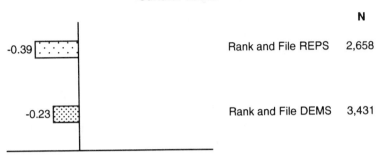

	N
Rank and File REPS	2,658
Rank and File DEMS	3,431

Figure 6.6.F
Rank and File Identifiers on the Surface Dimensions:
Preferences Relative to the Active Parties

Civil Liberties

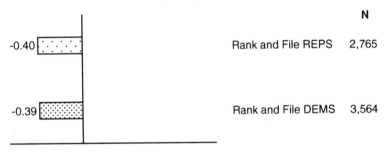

	N
Rank and File REPS	2,765
Rank and File DEMS	3,564

- Those Republicans ought to need less skill on cultural values (Fig. 6.6.E). Here, as with social insurance but in the opposite direction, both rank and files are much closer to Republican activists (at –.39 and –.23). In such a world, defections ought to run disproportionately in one (pro-Republican) direction.

- This is all the more true of civil liberties, the ultimate Republican asset (Fig. 6.6.F). The two party rank and files are both very conservative and indistinguishable in their conservatism (–.40 and –.39).

Such a portrait (along with its rankings) is a good way to empha-size the importance of activist contributions to the issue context of modern American politics. Mass contributions are also always important, and often determinative. The various factions do stand in a clear and differentiated relationship to each other, and that relationship does shape their probable response to any given deep factor or surface dimension, especially the likelihood that they might defect from their normal partisan moorings. Yet that likelihood is also always affected by the precise nature of the offerings on these factors and dimensions. The innate preferences of rank-and-file factions constrain this powerfully over the long run; they do not determine it.

Which is to say: What is actually on offer in response to those preferences is always some mix of implicit demands from the rank and file and of the wishes—and influence—of those who do the actual work of politicking. Without the activists, electoral campaigns are not mounted; without them, policy initiatives are not sustained. Nevertheless, they have values—strong values, ordinarily—of their own. As a result, it should logically be the *interplay* between a background issue context and its social structure, on the one hand, and the specific content of policy options, on the other, that actually determines political outcomes. And this policy content—the question of what is effectively on offer—will be shaped by struggles among the active minority, and not just by the preferences of a larger but unfocused majority. These struggles are the subject of Chapter 7.

7 THE SHAPE OF POLICY OPTIONS

The War inside the Parties

There are essential tasks to the pursuit of politics, and these almost demand different levels of activity within the general public. Yet the ability or willingness to undertake these tasks can itself hardly be a neutral phenomenon. From one side, the support of those who do undertake such tasks is simply worth more to electoral candidates and to elected officials than is the support of those who do not. From the other side, those who provide the practical labor of politics have their own values—strong, motivating values, in most cases—which they would prefer to realize in the course of their participation.

Initially, this magnifies the importance to the modern issue context of any specific differences in policy preference between the politically active and their rank and file. In Chapter 6 we looked for such differences and found them in abundance. On their own terms, these distinctions constitute a crucial further differentiation to the political landscape, adding an elite element to the mass framework for contemporary politicking. Yet their very existence (even leaving aside the possibility that the elites in this divide will possess disproportionate practical influence) leads immediately to a second set of questions. Or at least, these policy differences and their potential political consequences raise, inescapably, the possibility of a recurring struggle over available policy options, perhaps even with recurring resolutions and recurring reactions to them.

The first aspect of any such regular struggle involves the possibility of policy differences within the two party elites. Here, the question is whether the simple fact of being highly active (within the Republican versus the Democratic parties) is the social fact of greatest consequence, or whether different factions among the active partisans seek to have their party present significantly different options. And the second aspect of such a potentially regular struggle, completing the description of an issue context for political conflict, involves the impact of recurring outcomes from this internal war. Said differently, this is the question of what happens when the politically active are successful, and thus of what the general public (or, as ever, key factions within it) does in response to their success.

Active Parties in the Modern Era

The difference in influence between the active partisans and their rank and file, and thus the importance of the situation inside the active parties, can still be overstated. On many matters, the existence of a clear majority view within the general public (or a clear majority within the party rank and file) means that neither aspiring candidates nor incumbent officials are likely to ignore that view, at least to the point of confrontation. Explicitly confronting the activists of one's own party, when they differ from this view, might always produce an internal challenge. But explicitly confronting the *electorate* of one's own party might well produce defeat and retirement.

On the other hand, over time, the potential for the politically active to acquire a regular (and disproportionate) influence with these same candidates and public officials remains large. Active partisans are, after all, still the individuals whose support most clearly facilitates securing (and then retaining) public office. Moreover, they are still the individuals with whom such officials are likely to "touch base," to see where active party opinion lies and to make sure that their personal bases of support are intact. Finally—and this is the important point— there is good reason, both theoretical and empirical, to believe that the importance of those active partisans who *are* motivated by their own policy preferences has increased over time, perhaps dramatically so in the modern era.

Indeed, most contemporary analysts would argue, theoretically, that the older incentives of direct pecuniary reward or extended social solidarity have declined as motives for doing the work of political parties.[1] Most analysts would also argue that various ideational concerns, in the form of attachment to causes, issues, or ideologies, have increased as at least a partial replacement for those older incentives. Empirically, there is even more work suggesting that an older model of political parties, as disciplined hierarchies of loyal operatives, has been displaced in practice by a newer model of political parties as formal frameworks where issue-oriented volunteers shift in and out.

The change between models came most forcibly to scholarly attention through the explicit reform struggles over Democratic party structure in the late 1960s and early 1970s. But such developments had been proceeding apace in both parties for a much longer time, and the

Republican party may actually have reached the status of a contemporary, activist-based organization first. What has resulted, in any case, is a voluntaristic party system, built around precisely the sorts of intense policy preferences that characterize our partisan activists.[2] This is well and succinctly summarized by Leon Epstein, with his notion of American political parties as "public utilities":

> The progressive reaction is an understandable American phenomenon, and now so fully institutionalized that, as I shall explain at length, it poses obstacles for even newer-style party organizations. The direct primary, the chief institutional monument of progressivism, fits a political culture in which voters choose individuals, not merely parties, to represent them in executive and legislative offices. Party organizations, as I shall emphasize, are surely less effective as a result, but their accommodation to progressivism has not been entirely unsuccessful.
>
> That accommodation is an important part of the more general long-term adaptation that American parties have made to their adverse circumstances. The adaptation takes the form of an institutionalized porousness. Each major party is porous, or permeable, in the sense that it is readily entered by individuals and groups who want its electoral label. Party membership is loosely defined, often by state law that allows access without dues or organizational commitments. Parties so constructed are less meaningful than parties elsewhere, but they fit our circumstances. At the least, they provide labels that candidates seek and that officeholders use for certain collaborative purposes. Remarkably, the labels are the same, Republican and Democratic, in every state as in the nation, and still more remarkably, they have been the same, with only minor or transient exceptions, for over 130 years.[3]

Such "utilities"—formal party frameworks, staffed and operated by party activists—are not incompatible with newer forms of technical support services, as a partial substitute for the old hierarchies of party regulars; indeed, they facilitate such substitution. Even more self-evidently, they are the perfect vehicle for a "war inside the parties," for a struggle among active partisans over the policy options that electoral candidates and public officials will ultimately offer to the general public.[4] The fact of socially diverse parties suggests the importance of internal party politicking. The fact of increasingly participatory—voluntaristic—parties suggests the key role of activists within this struggle.

The obvious starting point for an investigation of that struggle is thus the established array of social factions within the active parties. Originally, the total population could be divided, in its policy preferences, into a small set of distinctive social groups (Chapter 4). When these were further divided into Republican and Democratic party identifiers (Chapter 5), these groups proved robust; that is, they retained their policy identities and differed reliably within the larger party. So, the obvious starting point for a more immediate struggle over the shaping of substantive party appeals is the counterpart array of factions within the activist stratum.

Such factions might not, of course, *matter* at the elite level. If similar policy preferences motivate activism within each of the parties, then activist preferences may not vary by social group. Or, if individuals from all social factions tend to adopt dominant party preferences when they become more active in party affairs, social background might quickly *become* secondary. Yet both party identification and group membership registered powerfully at the mass level. They are at least the obvious starting points at the elite level, too.

Statistically, their analysis does present a problem, in that some party factions are so underrepresented at the activist level as not to have sufficient numbers, in a national sample, for separate examination. Conceptually, on the other hand, the underlying purpose of the analysis provides a way around this problem. Or at least, for purposes of examining conflict over policy preferences within the active party, the focus is necessarily on those groups which either (*a*) constitute a disproportionate share of party activists, whatever their representational status, or which (*b*) fare significantly better at the elite as opposed to the mass level, so that simple overrepresentation becomes potentially important.[5]

Viewed in these terms, what emerges in the case of the Republicans is a party that looks notably different—socially and factionally—at the elite as opposed to the mass level (Fig. 7.1.A). The largest party faction, the low Protestants, is actually represented in nearly proportionate terms at both levels. But two factions—the college graduates and the some-colleges—are noticeably overrepresented among the activists, the college graduates especially so. That leaves every other faction to be underrepresented, several (as with the high-school dropouts and blacks) severely.

This result, in turn, gives the Republican party a significantly different social configuration at the activist level (Fig. 7.1.C). For the college graduates and the some-colleges, this configuration constitutes a clear gain; factions that previously contributed less than 30% of the total party now contribute more than 45% of partisan actives. For the low Protestants, the social shift from mass to elite, by itself, is a matter of indifference. And for the other groups—the four factions that constituted over 40% of the rank and file—it is a serious diminution; these

Figure 7.1.A
Partisan Actives vs. the Rank and File
as a Percentage of Party Identifiers

Republican Party

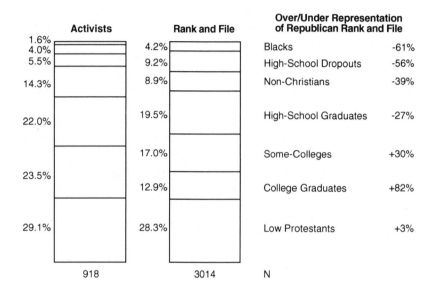

Activists	Rank and File	Over/Under Representation of Republican Rank and File	
1.6%	4.2%	Blacks	-61%
4.0%			
5.5%	9.2%	High-School Dropouts	-56%
14.3%	8.9%	Non-Christians	-39%
22.0%	19.5%	High-School Graduates	-27%
	17.0%	Some-Colleges	+30%
23.5%	12.9%	College Graduates	+82%
29.1%	28.3%	Low Protestants	+3%
918	3014	N	

factions, previously the same size as the college graduates and the some-colleges *together*, are now nearly matched by either one.

The elite Democratic party is different in its details, but its recomposition is no less striking (Fig. 7.1.B). Again, the largest faction, black Democrats, achieves roughly proportionate representation. Yet this time, three factions are clearly overrepresented at the elite level: the some-colleges, the non-Christians, and especially the college graduates. This leaves three others to shrink in the transition from mass to elite: high-school graduates, the low Protestants, and, again especially, the high-school dropouts—once providers of the stereotypical Democrat.

Proportionately, then, the Democratic party, too, has three great subclusters at the elite level (Fig. 7.1.C). The winners in this transition, those social groups which are better represented among active partisans than within the rank and file, move up sharply, from slightly more than a quarter to slightly less than a half. One great faction (black Democrats) prospers equally at both levels in narrow social—though

Figure 7.1.B
Partisan Actives vs. the Rank and File
as a Percentage of Party Identifiers

Democratic Party

Activists	Rank and File	Over/Under Representation of Democratic Rank and File	
6.3%	14.6%	High-School Dropouts	-57%
12.1%			
14.1%	18.0%	Low Protestants	-33%
13.5%	18.9%	High-School Graduates	-26%
14.4%	11.2%	Some-Colleges	+21%
17.5%	9.7%	Non-Christians	+48%
	5.9%	College Graduates	+198%
22.1%	21.7%	Blacks	+2%
1017	4151	N	

not, as we shall see, in ideological—terms. And the three factions that lose in this transition manage to lose in a major way; once a clear majority, they now are slightly less than a third.

The two parties do differ, then, in the *social* relationship between their rank and file and its active partisans. Given that they differed originally in their social compositions, such a further difference may seem unsurprising. Yet a composite look at the two parties together does reveal some interesting additional twists. In both cases, for example, the largest single faction within the party—low Protestants for the Republicans and blacks for the Democrats—manage to be represented in roughly proportional terms at the elite level. Moreover, in both cases, religious and racial groups which were notably underrepresented in one party—low Protestants for Democrats; non-Christians and especially blacks for Republicans—are even more underrepresented in active party circles within that party.

And in both cases, finally, groups based on social class fare roughly

Figure 7.1.C
Factional Groupings by Representational Status

Representational Status	Change	Activists	Rank and File
Republican Party			
Overrepresented (college graduates, some-colleges)	+52%	45.5%	29.9%
Proportionate (low Protestants)	+3%	29.1%	28.3%
Underrepresented (all others)	-39%	25.4%	41.8%
Democratic Party			
Overrepresented (college graduates, some-colleges, non-Christians)	+69%	45.4%	26.8%
Proportionate (blacks)	+2%	22.1%	21.7%
Underrepresented (high-school graduates, low Protestants, high-school dropouts)	-37%	32.5%	51.5%

the same in the transition from rank and file to active partisan. Which is to say: Some-colleges and college graduates are overrepresented, while high-school graduates and high-school dropouts are underrepresented, *in both parties.* The most extraordinary element of this, however, involves the college-graduate Democrats. College graduates as a social group are, of course, Republican (Fig. 5.1). College-graduate Democrats, as a social faction, are the smallest faction within the Democratic party—less than 6% of the party rank and file (Fig. 7.1.B). Yet college graduates nearly triple their share of the party at the activist level, to become the second largest faction there.

The Roots of Republican Policy Offerings

What this differential representation means, of course, depends on the actual distribution of policy preferences within the active parties—that is, on whether these preferences differ among activist factions within the same party, and on how such differences are linked to the policy preferences of their respective rank and files. At one extreme, activism may be so powerfully and tightly tied to policy views that the differential representation of party factions among the politically active will not matter. At the other extreme, what appears to be an elite-mass distinction may prove to be merely a by-product of the over-representation of some rank and file factions (and the consequent underrepresentation of others) among the politically active.

More probably, some mix of both considerations will characterize any given issue realm within each political party.[6] In any case, it is easy enough to compare policy preferences among active partisans, as well as between partisan activists and their putative rank and file, for the main factional clusters from Fig. 7.1.C. Some individual factions do not generate sufficient activists within the Times Mirror survey to allow reliable further analysis, but all of these factional groupings do. Two partisan portraits emerge:

- For the Republicans, the dynamics of activism itself appear to be the main explanation of elite-mass differences, though this does imply a convergence in cultural/national issues and a consistently augmented conservatism in economic/welfare matters.

- For the Democrats, a *mix* of activism and sampling leads party activists to track their factions closely on economic/welfare matters, but to divide deeply on cultural/national concerns, dragging the active party leftward while they do.

To take the internal issue landscape of the Republican party first: The Republican party as a whole, the party-in-the-electorate, was sharply divided on cultural/national matters (see Chapter 5, especially Fig. 5.3.A). This remains true among its rank and file when active partisans are removed from their number, just as it remains true among these activists when they are apportioned to factional groupings. (Fig. 7.2.A). Yet among the activists, two other facts about policy preferences are now added to the equation.

The first of these leads directly to modest elite convergence on cultural/national matters. Here, activists from the two factional groupings which were more conservative among the rank and file prove to be more liberal than their followers, and this moderation is greatest for the grouping which was most conservative. Simultaneously, activists from the factional grouping which was most liberal among the rank and file prove to be slightly more *conservative* than their followers. The result is a consistent if mild convergence toward the party mean, which

Figure 7.2.A
Factional Activists and their Rank and File
within the Republican Party

Cultural/National

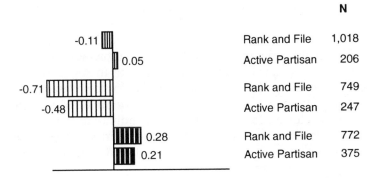

	N
Rank and File	1,018
Active Partisan	206
Rank and File	749
Active Partisan	247
Rank and File	772
Active Partisan	375

Underrepresented Factions (Blacks, High-School Dropouts, Non-Christians, and High-School Graduates)

Proportionate Factions (Low Protestants)

Overrepresented Factions (College Graduates and Some-Colleges)

largely explains why activist opinion is so similar to rank-and-file opinion on these matters within the party as a whole.

The picture is then fine-tuned by a second, lesser fact about elite politics. The more liberal factions among the party rank and file (the some-colleges and especially the college graduates) are still overrepresented at the elite level. As a result, even though their activists do move in a more conservative direction, this shift is not enough to bring them all the way back to the overall party mean. Consequently, the elite of the Republican party remain a trifle more liberal than the party's rank and file, though the dominant fact about the party on cultural/national matters is still that it is powerfully unified, as between the entirety of its rank and file and the entirety of its active partisans.

A different kind of ideological drift, characterizing the party elite as a whole but *not* unifying it with the rank and file, is presented by economic/welfare concerns (Fig. 7.2.B) Here, the dominant fact is that

Figure 7.2.B
Factional Activists and their Rank and File
within the Republican Party

Economic/Welfare

N

		N
-0.11	Rank and File	1,057
-0.34	Active Partisan	213
-0.50	Rank and File	714
-0.92	Active Partisan	234
-0.53	Rank and File	822
-0.64	Active Partisan	383

Underrepresented Factions (Blacks, High-School Dropouts, Non-Christians, and High-School Graduates)

Proportionate Factions (Low Protestants)

Overrepresented Factions (College Graduates and Some-Colleges)

activists from each factional grouping (under-, over-, and proportion-ately represented) stand in a more conservative position than their respective rank and file. It may be that active participation in Republi-can politics increases economic/welfare conservatism; it may well be that ideologically conservative members are more drawn to participate in party affairs. Either way (or both ways), all activist groupings con-tribute to the tendency of the Republican elite to move off to the right on economic/welfare matters.

There is, nevertheless, some further differentiation among active party groupings, with some modest further consequences. The most conservative grouping at the rank-and-file level (comprising the some-colleges and the college graduates) moves the least at the elite level. In turn, the most moderate of the rank-and-file groupings (comprised of four party factions) contributes an impressively larger rightward move-ment, though it still retains the most moderate partisan activists. But the serious rightward move on economic/welfare matters—really a plunge—belongs to the remaining group, the low Protestants. Their rank and file was already very conservative; their activists become extremely so. If the latter merely confined themselves to a less severe elite conservatism, the rightward lurch of the entire activist party would, of course, be similarly moderated.

The internal Republican party which emerges, overall, from such a portrait is easily described. It features modest elite convergence on cultural/national matters, consistent conservative drift on economic/ welfare concerns (Fig. 7.2). These developments suggest that it is the nature of activism itself—the values motivating activists and/or acquired by them—which is the central fact of internal Republican party politicking. The additional fact of over- or underrepresentation of some factions, despite its dramatic scale, is just much less consequential— and the pivotal role of the great proportionately represented faction, the low Protestants, only serves to underline that fact.

The Roots of Democratic Policy Offerings

Matters are not so simple—or so simply summarized—within the Democratic party. Like the Republicans, the Democrats were sharply divided on cultural/national matters within the party as a whole (Fig. 5.3.A). There, however, the similarity ends. For the Republicans, elite preferences actually reduced this division, while moving the party toward the center—both of itself and of the nation (Fig. 7.2.A). For the Democrats, by contrast, elite preferences manage to *expand* the range of internal divisions, while moving the party off to the left (Fig. 7.3.A). And in this, elite-mass differences within each of the three main groupings, as well as sharp differences across the groupings, both have a role to play.

Both main aspects of a separable elite influence—activist ideology and activist sampling—are important here. In the case of simple sampling, the most underrepresented factions are also the most conservative, while the most overrepresented are the most liberal. The very large underrepresented segment of the party actually secures highly accurate policy representation from its more active members on cultural/national issues (−.29 among the rank and file, −.27 among the activists). It is just that there are comparatively few of the latter. Conversely, the most overrepresented segment of the party begins with strongly liberal preferences at the level of the rank and file (+.75), and these become all the more liberal at the (strongly overrepresented) level of active partisans (+1.06).

The picture is then completed by the remaining major faction, black Democrats. Rank-and-file blacks are proportionately represented at the elite level, so that their contribution to the active party is purely a reflection of activist values. On the other hand, the shift in these

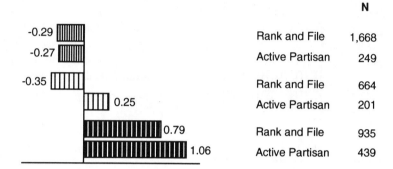

Figure 7.3.A
Factional Activists and their Rank and File
within the Democratic Party

Cultural/National

			N
-0.29		Rank and File	1,668
-0.27		Active Partisan	249
-0.35		Rank and File	664
	0.25	Active Partisan	201
	0.79	Rank and File	935
	1.06	Active Partisan	439

▥ Underrepresented Factions (Low Protestants, High-School Dropouts and High-School Graduates)

▯ Proportionate Factions (Blacks)

▮ Overrepresented Factions (Non-Christians, Some-College, and College Graduates)

values is so extreme as to complete the explanation of how the Democratic party, whose rank and file collectively sits right at the national average on cultural/national concerns, can end up wildly liberal on the elite level. For the black faction actually possesses the body of activists who stand farthest off from their putative followers—off to the left.

In this, the black rank and file would have contributed the most *conservative* of these three factional groupings on cultural/national matters (−.35). By any measure, then, the extent to which black activists (+.25) desert their rank and file is impressive. The distance between the rank and file and their putative leadership is not just the largest in absolute terms of the three factional groupings. Nor is it just the largest in relative terms, though it is both. Rather, it is the largest such move in either party. Moreover, this shift within the black Democratic faction actually features a move from a rank and file with a mean preference patently more conservative than the national average to an activist population with a mean preference evidently more liberal.

Figure 7.3.B
Factional Activists and their Rank and File
within the Democratic Party

Economic/Welfare

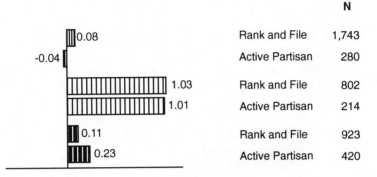

	N
Rank and File	1,743
Active Partisan	280
Rank and File	802
Active Partisan	214
Rank and File	923
Active Partisan	420

Underrepresented Factions (Low Protestants, High-School Dropouts and High-School Graduates)

Proportionate Factions (Blacks)

Overrepresented Factions (Non-Christians, Some-College, and College Graduates)

In one sense, the absence of such drama is what appears, by now, most noteworthy about the relationship between the Democratic rank and file and Democratic activists on economic/welfare matters (Fig. 7.3.B). Said differently, the element of distinction in these relations within the Democratic party is that this is the one realm, within either party, where the mean policy preferences of factional elites most closely (and hence accurately) represent the mean preferences of factional groupings within their rank and file. This implies, of course, that the potential for conflict over economic/welfare concerns is merely transferred to the elite level, since both the black elite and the black mass would prefer far more liberal positions here than would the rest of the party.

On the other hand, the dominant fact for elite-mass comparisons is how closely partisan activists within the Democratic party, on economic/welfare matters only, do track the preferences of their respective rank and files. The propensity of Democratic activists as a whole to be modestly more liberal on these matters is, in turn, due principally to the situation within the overrepresented segment. While these factions, too, are reasonably representative of their rank and file, they do show the largest move at the elite level—leftward, in their case. Moreover, because they are the most overrepresented at that level, this liberal shift is sufficient to move the activist mean moderately leftward.

The internal Democratic party that emerges from such a portrait thus differs in its elite-mass relations as between the two deep factors, while it also requires a focus on both elite ideology and elite (over- and under-) representation—on the nature of activism itself *and* on simple activist sampling—in order to explain these different opinion patterns.[7] In this, the party, already sharply divided on cultural/national issues among the rank and file, manages to exaggerate its division among active partisans. This is all the more striking because on economic/welfare matters, the party merely transfers its (previously large) divisions—accurately—to the activist stratum.

Simple over- and underrepresentation is especially critical to the first outcome. In the cultural/national realm, differential sampling moves the party sharply to the left; in the economic/welfare realm, such sampling contributes only a modest (albeit liberal) bias. At the same time, however, an *elite shift* in policy preferences—the values associated with activism itself—occurs in the cultural/national but not in the economic/welfare realm, causing a vastly augmented leftward move on the former. And here, the great proportionately represented faction, black Democrats, provides the strongest embodiment of the effect: black activists simply desert the preferences of their rank and file on cultural/national issues, by any measure, simultaneously pulling the active party well to the left of where it would otherwise be.

Strategic Implications: Events of the Day and Inherent Cross-Pressures

There is, then, an incipient internal politics to the mean preferences of the active party. In Chapter 6, the overall substance of these preferences emerged from an initial division of each party into active partisans and their rank and file. In this chapter, those preferences have acquired an additional differentiation, *within* the active parties, tied to elite factional groupings. Their content has also acquired some modest further explanation, by way of the differing contributions associated with activism itself or with the differing propensities of various factions to produce activists. Regardless, such preferences represent, at the very least, what these most active and influential participants would prefer to see as dominant policy options.

What we have not yet examined is the potential impact of the preferences of these elite factional groupings on specific party factions—

and this is the crucial missing element in the strategic context for contemporary politics. Party activists are not, of course, always successful in getting the parties to stand behind their preferences, so that this impact is not unfailingly crucial. A given primary campaign or a given legislative coalition may in fact frustrate them completely. On the other hand, it is not just that these preferences are the positions which party activists would prefer to realize. It is also that these individuals are, by definition, more active in seeking to realize them, and that American politics is actually structured to provide numerous advantages for the politically active, in everything from institutional devices like the primary election through social facts like the essentially voluntary character of much political labor.

In either case, however—and this is the important point—the simplest way to see the drift of these particular strategic impacts is merely to set party positions on the two deep factors according to the aggregate preferences of party activists. When activists collectively are unsuccessful, such impacts will presumably be reduced. Conversely, when individual factions within the activist population are even more successful, such impacts should be exaggerated.[8] In both cases, regardless, an analysis which disregards the preferences of these activists, or which fails to give them extra weighting, yields obviously unreasonable—not to mention understated—implications. These preferences must be allowed to play an augmented role in the analysis, if it is admitted that these activists are more likely to participate and may well be disproportionately influential in shaping the available options. When they are given such a role, the strategic landscape changes noticeably.

The simplest way to grasp the import of this change is to contrast policy options on the two deep factors when the parties-in-the-electorate determine them, as opposed to the options when active partisans get to determine them instead. If the total party aggregate gets to set party policy, then the mean positions will be −.14 for the Republicans and +.11 for the Democrats on cultural/national matters, and −.41 for the Republicans and +.32 for the Democrats on economic/welfare concerns (as at Fig. 3.1). Conversely, if active partisans get to determine party policy instead, then on cultural/national affairs the Republicans will stand at −.02 and the Democrats at +.48, with the Republicans at −.65 on economic/welfare matters and the Democrats at +.34 (as at Fig. 6.3). An individual voter confronting the difference between a Democratic position of +.11 versus +.48 on cultural/national issues, for example, or even that same voter confronting a Republican position of −.41 versus −.65 on economic/welfare concerns, is entitled to respond very differently.

Not surprisingly, if the rank and file are "rescaled" with regard to these activist positions, the strategic analysis looks notably different, too. To do this, it is necessary merely to set the overall midpoint, not at the national average, but at the average of preferences for the two sets of active partisans, the same procedure used at the end of Chapter 6. Each faction is then placed not at its absolute position (based on a national average of zero) but at its *relative* position, relative to the midpoint between the two sets of party activists. This appears to be a considerably more realistic scale. Or at least, a voter who is left of the national average on cultural/national issues but still closer to the active Republican party remains predisposed to vote Republican, just as a voter who is right of the national average on economic/welfare issues but still closer to the active Democratic party is positionally predisposed to vote Democratic.

Two simple examples may help clarify this. On cultural/national issues, the some-college Republicans stand left of the national average, with a mean preference of +.11 (Fig. 5.3). Yet because the active Republican party stands at −.02 and the active Democratic party at +.48, some-college Republicans remain much closer to the Republican party. In a rescaling to reflect this, the new midpoint becomes +.23 (the midpoint between −.02 and +.48). The some-college Republicans, in turn, now stand at −.12, reflecting their closer position to the active Republican party (Fig. 7.4.A). Likewise, on economic/welfare issues, the low-Protestant Democrats stand to the right of the national average, with a mean preference of −.05 (Fig. 5.3). Yet because the active Republican party stands at −.65 while the active Democratic party is at +.34, low-Protestant Democrats are still closer to the active Democratic party. In rescaling, the new midpoint becomes −.15 (midway between −.65 and +.34), so that low-Protestant Democrats now stand at +.10 (Fig. 7.4.B).

The resulting newer and more accurate scales should add clarity—not to mention reality—to previous strategic analyses. As indeed they do. Now, under these conditions, the shift in economic/welfare implications becomes profound (Fig. 7.4.B). *Every* Democratic faction is liberal—which is to say, closer to Democratic than to Republican activists. Even the low-Protestant Democrats, who had been listing conservative with respect to the nation as a whole, are back on the liberal side of the active parties. Obviously, this is a world where the dominant party identification is reinforced, perfectly in every sense, by the economic/welfare factor. It is not just that all Democratic factions are to the left and all Republican factions to the right. All Democratic factions are now liberal (and all Republican factions conservative) as well.

Figure 7.4.A
Party Factions and the Deep Factors:
Relative Preferences

Cultural/National

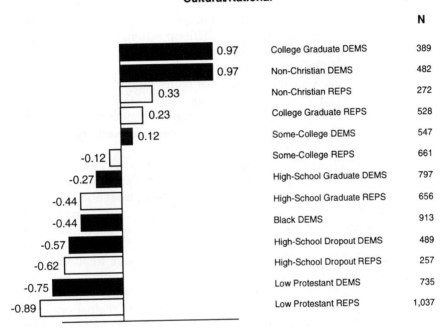

	N
College Graduate DEMS	389
Non-Christian DEMS	482
Non-Christian REPS	272
College Graduate REPS	528
Some-College DEMS	547
Some-College REPS	661
High-School Graduate DEMS	797
High-School Graduate REPS	656
Black DEMS	913
High-School Dropout DEMS	489
High-School Dropout REPS	257
Low Protestant DEMS	735
Low Protestant REPS	1,037

■ = Democratic Faction
□ = Republican Faction

This is also a world, as a result, which appears to throw away every incipient Republican asset on this factor. Originally (at Fig. 5.3 and following), if the minority party was in the minority position on economic/welfare issues too, it was also true that (a) the Republican party was at least more unified on these issues, and (b) the key factions which formed the middle ground—the battleground—were all Democratic. Now, with active partisans in charge, all these Democratic factions have been drawn (really pushed) back inside their own party. Indeed, the party faction closest to the partisan midpoint is actually high-school graduate *Republicans!*

A related but profoundly opposite drama awaits in the case of cultural/national matters, already the source of dire predictions for

Figure 7.4.B
Party Factions and the Deep Factors:
Relative Preferences

Economic/Welfare

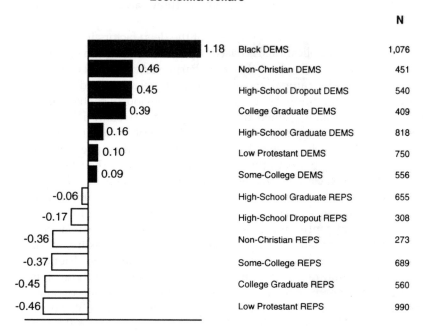

		N
1.18	Black DEMS	1,076
0.46	Non-Christian DEMS	451
0.45	High-School Dropout DEMS	540
0.39	College Graduate DEMS	409
0.16	High-School Graduate DEMS	818
0.10	Low Protestant DEMS	750
0.09	Some-College DEMS	556
-0.06	High-School Graduate REPS	655
-0.17	High-School Dropout REPS	308
-0.36	Non-Christian REPS	273
-0.37	Some-College REPS	689
-0.45	College Graduate REPS	560
-0.46	Low Protestant REPS	990

■ = Democratic Faction
□ = Republican Faction

Democrats, fond hopes for Republicans. Now, with the preferences of the active parties anchoring the full array, *most* factions slip to the conservative side of the spectrum—closer, in effect, to the active Republican party (Fig. 7.4.A). Before, the college-graduate, non-Christian, and some-college factions of both parties had lodged on the liberal side, with the high-school graduate Democrats not far off center. Now, with party activists calling the shots, the some-college Republicans fall back to the conservative side; the high-school-graduate Democrats are solidly conservative; and no one has moved left in compensation.

As a result, this time, it is the *majority* party which risks a massive and disproportionate outflow. Before, all this majority party had to do, being the majority and being reinforced by economic/welfare matters, was to guard its flank on cultural/national affairs. Now, if Republican and Democratic activists—and especially Democratic activists, here—manage to have their way, the active parties sharply alter the ideological landscape. In the process, they evidently restore the possibilities which activists—especially Republican activists—threw away on economic/welfare grounds.[9]

Such an approach, examining each of the deep factors individually for their strategic implications, is based on the view that much of day-to-day politics will in fact occur this way. Particularly forceful events, or especially successful campaign gambits, will propel an individual issue-cluster to public attention. When they do, they obviously contribute one (stark) strategic context when these are economic/welfare issues, another (equally stark) context when they are cultural/national issues instead. Yet over time, because individuals do not hold their relevant preferences on these two great opinion-clusters in isolation, their *linkage* is likely to become a crucial shaping element of the strategic landscape.

That, of course, suggests looking at the two realms simultaneously. And from there, once again, it is but a short step to looking for apparently strong and continuing cross-pressures and for the party factions which experience them. The test of an effective cross-pressure, in this new activist-influenced political world, remains the same. Factional preferences on cultural/national matters must be opposite to those of the majority of their own party *and* stronger than preferences on economic/welfare issues. (See the final section of Chapter 5.) For Republican factions, this means a cultural/national *liberalism* greater than their economic/welfare conservatism. For Democratic factions, it means the reverse: a cultural/national conservatism greater than their economic/welfare liberalism.

In any case, in a world where active partisans (which is not even to mention the true "hyperactivists") get to shape policy options disproportionately, the mathematics of cross-pressure have shifted additionally. When we examined the situation in which the full composite parties set party policy (at the end of Chapter 5), there were four cross-pressured factions, one Republican and three Democratic. Now, there are no longer any Republican factions that are effectively cross-pressured (Fig. 7.4). The non-Christian Republicans, subject to a stereotypical cross-pressure when the total parties set party policy, are now back within Republican ranks. They are Republican identifiers, after all, and their economic/welfare conservatism now outweighs their cultural/national liberalism as well, though it must be noted that their Republican reversion is largely a product of the sharp leftward movement on cultural/national matters by *Democratic* party activists.

On the other hand (still at Fig. 7.4), there remain three large Democratic factions that are incipiently cross-pressured. The degree of cross-pressure is actually exacerbated for each. And together, they still claim almost half of the total Democratic party (at 47.6%):

- When the focus was parties in the electorate (at the end of Chapter 5), the low-Protestant Democrats were actually misidentified, rather than cross-pressured. Now, they are classically cross-pressured instead, at +.10 on economic/welfare and –.75 on cultural/national, thanks to the rightward shift of the active Republican party on economic/welfare issues.

- With parties in the electorate, the high-school dropout Democrats had been stereotypically cross-pressured. Facing the active parties, standing at +.45 on economic/welfare and –.57 on cultural/national, the pressure is exaggerated, thanks to rightward Republican moves on the former and leftward Democratic moves on the latter.

- Finally, the high-school graduate Democrats, who had been compulsively moderate when faced with the policy preferences of the two composite parties, can no longer sustain that motivation in the face of the two active parties instead. At +.16 on economic/welfare and –.27 on cultural/ national, they are now simply cross-pressured as well.

Strategic Implications: Elite-Mass Tensions and Party Fortunes.

The strategic possibilities intrinsic to the surface dimensions of political opinion have already acquired an implicit partisan character—even an implicit partisan ordering—both within and across the deep factors. Yet now, the strategic possibilities in these surface dimensions (and thus their differential strategic uses) become even clearer. Which is to say: Given the apparent power (and stark implications) of recasting the deep factors with regard to activist preferences on them, the same treatment seems justified, methodologically, for the surface dimensions. Figure 7.5 applies that treatment, and the result is, again, substantively illuminating.

Indeed, the resulting potential impacts—and differences among them—are so striking that it is perhaps time to stop and note that this is really a quite modest and understated way of searching for such impacts. From the elite side, it would be entirely reasonable to use the preferences of the *hyperactivists* to set party policy, on the theory that these are really the individuals who mount electoral campaigns or institutional initiatives. Likewise, from the mass side, it would be easily practicable to *isolate* the rank and file, so as to focus on the impact of activist preferences on less active partisans, uncontaminated by the simultaneous presence of those activists themselves.[10]

Nevertheless, the resulting picture is severe enough. In this, social in-

Figure 7.5.A
Party Factions and the Surface Dimensions:
Relative Preferences

Cultural Values

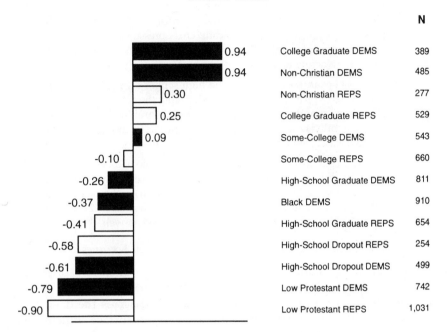

		N
0.94	College Graduate DEMS	389
0.94	Non-Christian DEMS	485
0.30	Non-Christian REPS	277
0.25	College Graduate REPS	529
0.09	Some-College DEMS	543
-0.10	Some-College REPS	660
-0.26	High-School Graduate DEMS	811
-0.37	Black DEMS	910
-0.41	High-School Graduate REPS	654
-0.58	High-School Dropout REPS	254
-0.61	High-School Dropout DEMS	499
-0.79	Low Protestant DEMS	742
-0.90	Low Protestant REPS	1,031

■ = Democratic Faction
□ = Republican Faction

surance had already appeared as the extreme embodiment of economic/ welfare influence and, thus, as the extreme pro-Democratic contribution from any issue dimension. Now, when active partisans are assigned a crucial, shaping role, these effects reach truly gigantic proportions (Fig. 7.5.D). Only three factions remain closer to the active Republican party; the other *ten* lean Democratic. Two among these, it is true, the low-Protestant Republicans and the college-graduate Democrats, are positionally on dead center. Yet they are themselves a partisan balance, and even if both should go Republican, every other Democratic faction would be aligned with its party—as would two Republican factions, the high-school dropouts and the high-school graduates.[11]

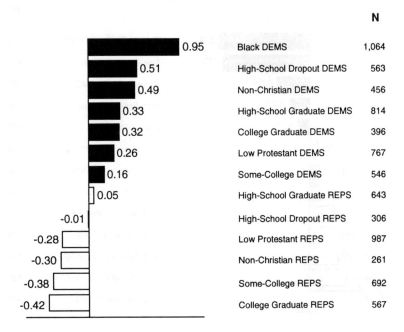

Figure 7.5.B
Party Factions and the Surface Dimensions:
Relative Preferences

Social Welfare

		N
0.95	Black DEMS	1,064
0.51	High-School Dropout DEMS	563
0.49	Non-Christian DEMS	456
0.33	High-School Graduate DEMS	814
0.32	College Graduate DEMS	396
0.26	Low Protestant DEMS	767
0.16	Some-College DEMS	546
0.05	High-School Graduate REPS	643
-0.01	High-School Dropout REPS	306
-0.28	Low Protestant REPS	987
-0.30	Non-Christian REPS	261
-0.38	Some-College REPS	692
-0.42	College Graduate REPS	567

■ = Democratic Faction
□ = Republican Faction

Social welfare is then more modestly Democratic, albeit still disastrous for Republicans (Fig. 7.5.B). *All* Democratic factions are now clearly liberal; none are easily tempted by the active Republican party. Moreover, the high-school graduate Republicans remain liberal as well, and the swing faction—the one that could most easily go in either direction—is *Republican* high-school dropouts. The active Republican party thus holds more of its natural constituency, but this is still only a portion of its own membership, and includes no Democratic factions at all.

That leaves civil rights as the lone Republican economic/welfare hope (Fig. 7.5.E). The internal factional alignment is still perfectly partisan, with all Democratic factions to the left of all Republican factions. But now, two Democratic factions are modestly closer to the active

Figure 7.5.C
Party Factions and the Surface Dimensions:
Relative Preferences

Foreign Relations

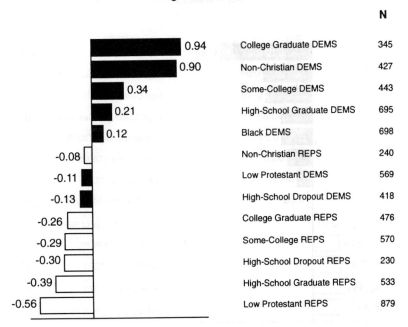

		N
0.94	College Graduate DEMS	345
0.90	Non-Christian DEMS	427
0.34	Some-College DEMS	443
0.21	High-School Graduate DEMS	695
0.12	Black DEMS	698
-0.08	Non-Christian REPS	240
-0.11	Low Protestant DEMS	569
-0.13	High-School Dropout DEMS	418
-0.26	College Graduate REPS	476
-0.29	Some-College REPS	570
-0.30	High-School Dropout REPS	230
-0.39	High-School Graduate REPS	533
-0.56	Low Protestant REPS	879

■ = Democratic Faction
□ = Republican Faction

Republican party—the high-school graduate and low-Protestant Democrats—so that active Republicans might plausibly appeal to them, while the some-college Democrats are not all that far away. The Republican party, by contrast, is strongly conservative and obviously unified, so that civil rights is once again the leading battleground—the swing dimension—on economic/welfare matters.

The swing dimension on cultural/national matters, and the great competitive issue-area of our time, is foreign relations (Fig. 7.5.C). Five Democratic factions are liberal and line up to the left; five Republican factions are reliably conservative and line up to the right. Three factions, accordingly, sit in the middle: high-school dropout Democrats, low-Protestant Democrats, and non-Christian Republicans. On the one

Figure 7.5.D
Party Factions and the Surface Dimensions:
Relative Preferences

Social Insurance

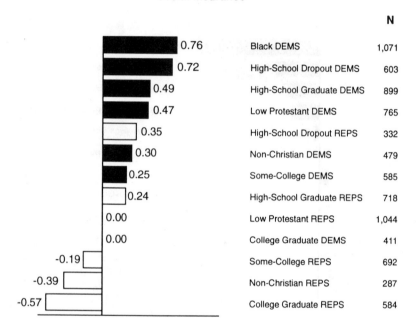

		N
0.76	Black DEMS	1,071
0.72	High-School Dropout DEMS	603
0.49	High-School Graduate DEMS	899
0.47	Low Protestant DEMS	765
0.35	High-School Dropout REPS	332
0.30	Non-Christian DEMS	479
0.25	Some-College DEMS	585
0.24	High-School Graduate REPS	718
0.00	Low Protestant REPS	1,044
0.00	College Graduate DEMS	411
-0.19	Some-College REPS	692
-0.39	Non-Christian REPS	287
-0.57	College Graduate REPS	584

■ = Democratic Faction
□ = Republican Faction

hand, such an array does hold out the prospect that the Democratic party can compensate for any losses among its high-school dropouts and low Protestants by appealing to non-Christian Republicans. On the other hand, all three factions remain closer to the active Republican party. Ambiguous party prospects thus suggest that both parties will have occasion to turn to deliberate partisan conflict on foreign relations.

With the arrival of cultural values, on the other hand, this ambiguity largely disappears (Fig. 7.5.A). Cultural values had already established itself as one of two dimensions which contribute an extreme embodiment of cultural/national influence, and of the pro-Republican bias which goes along with that. Now, when active partisans take their crucial shaping role, there are still Republican factions that are drawn

Figure 7.5.E
Party Factions and the Surface Dimensions:
Relative Preferences

Civil Rights

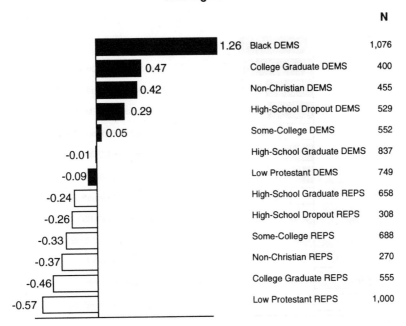

	N
Black DEMS	1,076
College Graduate DEMS	400
Non-Christian DEMS	455
High-School Dropout DEMS	529
Some-College DEMS	552
High-School Graduate DEMS	837
Low Protestant DEMS	749
High-School Graduate REPS	658
High-School Dropout REPS	308
Some-College REPS	688
Non-Christian REPS	270
College Graduate REPS	555
Low Protestant REPS	1,000

■ = Democratic Faction
□ = Republican Faction

toward the Democrats. There are not many of them, however, and at the same time, most of the Democratic party is drawn toward the active Republicans. Moreover, not only are the factions closest to the activist midpoint, the some-college Democrats and some-college Republicans, themselves a partisan balance, but Republicans could *concede* their some-college faction and still have the overwhelming factional majority.

Civil liberties, finally, removes even these last strategic considerations (Fig. 7.5.F). The some-college Republicans are safely within Republican ranks; even the some-college Democrats have pulled away from their party; and on one has joined it. There is no evident Democratic strategy within the constraints of the underlying activist preferences, except perhaps avoidance.

Figure 7.5.F
Party Factions and the Surface Dimensions:
Relative Preferences

Civil Liberties

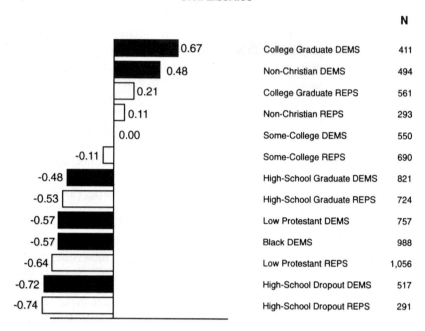

N

College Graduate DEMS	411
Non-Christian DEMS	494
College Graduate REPS	561
Non-Christian REPS	293
Some-College DEMS	550
Some-College REPS	690
High-School Graduate DEMS	821
High-School Graduate REPS	724
Low Protestant DEMS	757
Black DEMS	988
Low Protestant REPS	1,056
High-School Dropout DEMS	517
High-School Dropout REPS	291

■ = Democratic Faction
□ = Republican Faction

Further Implications: A Party for the Rich and a Party for the Deviant?

The role of party activists is thus so potentially critical in shaping policy options for their respective parties, and activist preferences do add such strong additional contours to the political landscape, that it seems worth closing by inquiring into the continuing *priorities* of these activists themselves. At bottom, if factions within the rank and file have continuing predispositions, and if the nature of policy options activates these in evident ways, *and* if partisan actives have disproportionate influence over these options, then the question of their continuing preferences acquires serious potential consequence. But more to the point, we already know that the preferences of Republican activists on economic/welfare matters, and/or of Democratic activists on cultural/national matters, present extreme strategic difficulties—potentially of great practical injury—to precisely the parties to which these activists are attached.

So, the question of how much emphasis these active partisans place on those "difficult" policy preferences is one of great potential consequence. One immediate caveat to any answer is that anything that can be adduced about these continuing preferences must be adduced with caution. Even when elite preferences can be tied to the factional composition of the activist stratum, activists themselves are especially well equipped, thanks to their greater attention to politics, merely to change their minds. On the other hand, research focused on elite political participants has reliably found that they possess better-formed, better-connected, and hence more stable opinions and preferences.[12] That fact will never be a substitute for the collection of data specifically focused on priorities in their own right. Nevertheless, even in just our own preceding analysis, there is a wide variety of elements which can be tapped for hints about these preferences and emphases.

The first of these derives from a simple reconsideration of the original elite-mass analysis (in Chapter 6), with the question of elite priorities now the focus. A second derives from reconsidering the analysis (from Chapter 7) of influential factors *inside* each party elite, especially those involving activism itself. And a third, requiring some genuinely new calculations, follows on from earlier inquiries (again in Chapter 6) about preferences at various *levels* of activism. Because the results of all three types of analysis prove congruent, they provide at least strong and consistent suggestions about continuing activist priorities.

Consider just the difference between active partisans and their rank and file, that is, the aggregate difference before party factions were introduced. With a different interpretive focus, this was the substance of Figure 6.3. Now, if more extreme positions are assumed to reflect more intense preferences, Figure 6.3 yields an obvious further message. Three of its four groupings—Republican activists, Republican followers, and Democratic followers—have their highest values (and apparent priorities) on the economic/welfare factor. Only one grouping, Democratic activists, favors the cultural/national factor instead. Yet seen from the perspective of a continuing activist contribution to politics, such an array produces two powerfully ironic implications.

The more obvious of these involves Democratic party activists, the sole group whose stronger preferences are on cultural/national issues. These are, of course, precisely the issues which, for the rank and file alone, created major potential strains within the Democratic coalition. Yet Democratic activists not only have their stronger preferences on them, but hold these preferences in the direction most evidently calculated to *increase* such strains. Remarkably, the situation on the Republican side of the aisle manages to provide a less visible but equally ironic counterpart. For while Republican activists do share an apparent priority with the Republican and Democratic rank and files, what they do *not* share is preferences on it: active Republicans throw away any advantage in this shared priority by rejecting the preferences of—by locating themselves far away from—Democratic followers and, in truth, their own rank and file.

Summarizing provocatively: If these preferences really do reflect the priorities of party activists, then activists from each party are most concerned with the realm in which their party is most likely to lose! Left to themselves, what they would do, in effect, is to create a party for the rich (the Republicans) and a party for the deviant (the Democrats). On the other hand, it is not really necessary to assume that a higher score indicates a stronger emphasis in order to come to precisely the same conclusion. To that end, consider not the inherent substance of the policy preferences of activists but only the contribution which activism as a process (rather than simple over- or underrepresentation) makes to the distinctiveness of these preferences. With different interpretive goals, this was the subject of Figures 7.2 and 7.3.

The theme for the Republicans at the more active level was very much the power of activism itself, which is to say, the power of the values which seemed integral to greater party activity (Fig. 7.2). On the cultural/national factor, these produced a modest convergence toward the center, while on economic/welfare, they produced a striving toward the extremes—on a factor which was already a problem for the party. Yet now, the key point is that this latter extremism was not principally the product of oversampling the more conservative factions; it was just an integral aspect of activity within the party. It was, in other words, what being an active Republican was most distinctively about.

The Democrats were not so easily characterized because both the values associated with activism and the differential representation of various factions within the activist stratum appeared central to elite placement (Fig. 7.3). At that stage in the analysis, the key fact was that both these influences kept the party close to its rank and file on economic/welfare issues, while shifting it radically (in the strategically wrong direction) on cultural/national affairs. Now, the key fact is instead that where the activist impulse really mattered for the Democrats was on cultural/national affairs, not on economic/welfare issues. Among Democrats, in other words, cultural/national liberalism was what party activism was most distinctively about.

Once again, summarized provocatively, what distinguished activists from their fellow partisans was precisely the wrong values when viewed strategically—economic/welfare conservatism for active Republicans, cultural/national liberalism for active Democrats—yet these nevertheless appeared to be the values most central to activism within their respective parties.[13] Finally, while all of this follows merely from reconsidering previous analyses, there is some new evidence—or at least, new extensions of evidence—which also points in the same direction. Moreover, this evidence requires neither any assumption about issue priorities nor any role for differential motivating influences within the activist stratum. Instead, the analyst simply asks for the *preference profiles* of party activists on the surface dimensions.

In this, the profile for the hyperactivists, those most committed of Republican and Democratic partisans, proves particularly helpful. The preferences of these hyperactivists were previously used (on the deep factors at Fig. 6.2) to guarantee that further elite analysis based on the views of the active partisans would not be misleading. That comparison did produce some modest further—even curious—distinctions as one moved up the activism scale, but these were not worthy of attention when the question was gross elite-mass differences. Now, however, the overall views of the hyperactivists on the surface dimensions, along with any further drift by comparison to the active partisans, can provide an additional comment on activist priorities, especially because this reinforces the hints given by other measures.

In this regard, the Republican profile is once again striking (Fig. 7.6.A). Republican hyperactivists are, of course, generally conservative across the surface dimensions. Yet they do offer an exception, on civil liberties, where greater activism is clearly associated with greater liberalism in the Republican party. Beyond that, they offer a second realm, cultural values, where they not only sit to the left of their rank and file, but where they are only marginally conservative—essentially at the national average. This suggests that while any given cultural gambit might not be opposed by these hyperactivists, it would have no private attractiveness for them.

What does attract these partisans, then—the apparent "red meat" of internal Republican politics—comes from four other dimensions, where the hyperactivists are just unrelievedly conservative. Moreover, three of these dimensions are in fact economic/welfare dimensions: social welfare (−.79), civil rights (−.60), and social insurance (−.58). They

Figure 7.6.A
Hyperactivist Preference on the Surface Dimensions

Republican Party

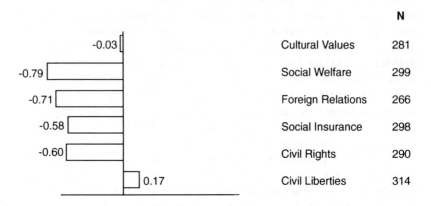

	N
Cultural Values	281
Social Welfare	299
Foreign Relations	266
Social Insurance	298
Civil Rights	290
Civil Liberties	314

Figure 7.6.B
Hyperactivist Preference on the Surface Dimensions

Democratic Party

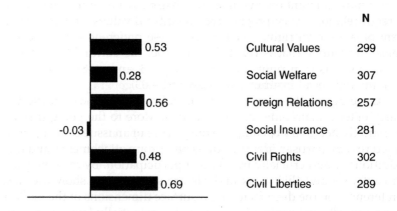

	N
Cultural Values	299
Social Welfare	307
Foreign Relations	257
Social Insurance	281
Civil Rights	302
Civil Liberties	289

are joined by foreign relations (–.71), so that, substantively, Republican hyperactivists are militantly hostile to orthodox welfare, strongly un-enthusiastic about public policies targeted by race, firmly committed to reining in the existing welfare state, and extremely nationalistic on foreign relations. But if this is not also a picture of priorities (–.79, –.71,

−.60, and −.58 versus −.03 and +.17), it is hard to know what such a picture would look like.

Democratic hyperactivists are different, though not in a mirror-image fashion (Fig. 7.6.B). They are the reverse of their opponents in the most general sense, offering four dimensions of militant liberalism and one where they are actually conservative, to contrast with four dimensions of militant conservatism and one of actual liberalism for the Republicans. But thereafter, everything is additionally different. Indeed, the identity of their deviant conservative preference is surely surprising as well: *social insurance*, the dimension of most widespread benefit to the Democratic party with the general public, has no apparent private attraction to these individuals. Their preferences are not just substantially closer to those of the Republican rank and file than to those of their own, but actually shade to the right of the national average!

As if to emphasize this situation, the other dimension on which Democratic hyperactivists do not have rampantly liberal preferences is social welfare, the other self-evident economic/welfare dimension. They are still clearly liberal here, and their mean preference brings no hint of opposition to social-welfare initiatives. Yet their outstanding liberalism obviously resides elsewhere. Specifically, a galloping liberalism characterizes all three of the cultural/national dimensions: civil liberties (+.69), foreign relations (+.56), and cultural values (+.53). When civil rights is added to these (+.48), Democratic hyperactivists prove, substantively, to be wildly tolerant on civil liberties, extremely accommodationist on foreign relations, very progressive on cultural values, and very interventionist on civil rights. As a whole, these preferences, too, create a sense of priority that is difficult to escape: the cultural/national dimensions plus civil rights (at +.69, +.56, +.53, and +.48) versus social welfare and social insurance (at +.28 and −.03).

Once again, these indications of policy priority within the two party elites remain only that: indications. More to the point, they are not strictly necessary to complete the picture of an issue context, structured first by partisan identifications and group attachments, and then additionally and crucially by levels of participation. By the time partisan activists and their rank and file are separated to showcase their preferences on the deep factors and surface dimensions of the modern issue context, that context has acquired a potentially large, and stark, contribution to the modern political *era*. It remains, then, only to go back and say something about how that context undergirds the modern era in American politics, how this era apparently differed from the earlier years of postwar politics, and how its context could have shaped key individual incidents within both.

8 AN ISSUE CONTEXT FOR
CONTEMPORARY POLITICS

The Two Majorities and Partisan Conflict

There is an immediate logic, both structural and strategic, to the policy differences between Democrats and Republicans, and between the activists of each party and their rank and file. In this logic, if the active Republican party merely anchors itself at its preferred position on economic/welfare issues, it ought to lose. Or, if the active Democratic party merely stands for its own preferences on cultural/national issues, it ought, as the majority party, at least to be in danger of losing. By the same token, if *events* push economic/welfare concerns to the fore, the Republican party ought to be in danger of truly serious reversals, for what is already, after all, the minority party. Just as if events push cultural/national concerns to the fore, the Democratic party ought to be painfully exposed.

Yet because this effect has *social and institutional roots*, it can be given a more extended interpretation. In this longer run, policy preferences are clearly tied to fundamental social groups, and while the distribution and intensity of group attachments do change, they also change only slowly. Policy preferences then find an evident and distinctive attachment to political parties; and while parties in the American mold tolerate a great deal of internal diversity, party identifications, too, change only slowly in practice. Finally, when active partisans, the more consequential players in the political game, prove to have additionally distinguishing (and apparently recurring) preferences, a continuing structure is in place to buttress a continuing issue context—and to delineate an extended political era.

What remains for such an analysis, then, is to turn the focus around, so as to sketch the character of the modern political *era*, the one which ought logically to follow from this issue context. In doing so, it will be helpful to look back to the beginning of the postwar period, the (extended) political era before our own. Likewise, it will be helpful to patch all of the postwar presidential contests into the resulting frame-work, in at least a thumbnail fashion.[1] And it should be possible to close by addressing the problems inherent in looking toward the political era(s) that will follow our own. Such an exercise will inevitably establish limits on the influence of even a thoroughly institutionalized issue context. Ideally, it will underline its power, an enveloping power, as well.

An Issue Context for the Late New Deal Era

There is a curious but ultimately reassuring consensus on the under-lying issue structure of the late New Deal era, roughly the years from 1948 to 1968. Historians working from the orthodox archival record, along with social scientists working from public opinion surveys, have generally seen the same two policy realms as central to practical politics over all those years. The vocabulary changes, by discipline and by focus, but the concerns remain overwhelmingly consistent and central.

The great and traumatic event which launched the political era preceding our own was, of course, the Great Depression. One major public response was the election of Democrats to control both the presidency and Congress in 1932. One major result of that was the New Deal, which brought an extended array of social-welfare pro-grams to the United States and which gave its name to a political era stretching out for the next thirty-five years. Survey data are thin and problematic for the early part of this era, but it is hard to argue that the politics of the 1930s was organized by anything to rival the institu-tionalization of the welfare state. The 1940s intruded on this with the Second World War, a war of total mobilization, so that practical politics came to be characterized by issues of foreign relations as well, joining but not supplanting economic/welfare concerns.[2]

There was no guarantee that these inescapably central concerns of the "early" New Deal era would come to represent a continuing issue context (and political era) after the Second World War. But in fact, the struggle to implement the welfare state was followed by the struggle to implement a "full employment state," with many continuing substan-tive concerns—the minimum wage, unemployment insurance, farm price supports, positive fiscal policy, and so forth. Moreover, prosecu-tion of the Second World War was supplanted, in a remarkably short time, by prosecution of a "Cold War," with things like creation of the Marshall Plan, formation of NATO, pursuit of the Korean War, and pursuit of the Vietnam War to give it ongoing definition. If none of these grand successor concerns was to have the consuming intensity of their predecessors, they *were* to be the logical inheritors, and they were to provide a string of major events sufficient to sustain an existing issue context.[3]

Indeed, by the 1960s, those doing public opinion research—both social scientists and private pollsters—were discovering a precisely analogous structure to public opinion: continuing concern with social welfare, continuing concern with foreign affairs, but a large and evident priority for the former. The authors of *The American Voter*, that path-breaking study, found the predominance of social-welfare concerns to be initially surprising (see Chapter 2). Thirty years later, careful and comprehensive analysts still come to the same conclusion about this period, as witness William G. Mayer in *The Changing American Mind:*

> The point that needs emphasizing here is that the New Deal, in both political and policy terms, was almost entirely an *economic* phenomenon. The programs that we instinctively associate with the New Deal—the AAA, NRA, TVA, and WPA, the Wagner Act and social security—were all designed to revitalize and restructure the American economy. Similarly, the groups and interests that came together in the New Deal coalition were attracted by economic promises and rewards: subsidies and price supports for farmers, the NLRB and wages and hours legislation for unions, jobs and relief for the poor and the working class, expanded federal aid for the big cities . . .
>
> But the New Deal had little or nothing to say about social and cultural affairs or, until the late 1930s, about foreign policy. Roosevelt did preside over the ending of Prohibition. But with that major exception, the New Deal made no concerted attempt to get involved in race relations, crime, sexual mores, religion, civil liberties, drugs, or the role of women . . .
>
> From the 1940s to the early 1960s, American liberalism continued to operate within the basic guidelines set down by Roosevelt and the New Dealers.[4]

In our terms, in a vocabulary drawn from the contemporary issue context, we would say the same thing slightly differently. It was not just that the economic/welfare factor dominated the cultural/national factor in the politics of the time. It was also—and more importantly—that the underlying economic/welfare factor received its translation into practical politics almost entirely through the surface dimension of *social insurance*, while the (underlying) cultural/national factor received its practical translation almost entirely through the surface dimension of *foreign relations*—and that the former was, again, predominant.

A simple portrait of the postwar environment for policy conflict can thus be developed by taking public preferences on the same two

Figure 8.1.A
Issue Dimensions for the
Late New Deal Era

Social Insurance

N

0.76	Black DEMS	1,071
0.72	High-School Dropout DEMS	603
0.49	High-School Graduate DEMS	899
0.47	Low Protestant DEMS	765
0.35	High-School Dropout REPS	332
0.30	Non-Christian DEMS	479
0.25	Some-College DEMS	585
0.24	High-School Graduate REPS	718
0.00	Low Protestant REPS	1,044
0.00	College Graduate DEMS	411
-0.19	Some-College REPS	692
-0.39	Non-Christian REPS	287
-0.57	College Graduate REPS	584

■ = Democratic Faction
□ = Republican Faction

dimensions (from Fig. 7.4) and setting them side by side. There is, of course, substantial risk—at the very least, a number of assumptions—in applying research on the issue context of our time to the politics of those earlier years. But there is also some justification in the self-consciously *positional* logic of the particular approach used here; there are clear substantive gains to be achieved through its careful application; and there are even ways to gauge the general scope and direction of any misestimates. Ultimately, of course, the real defense of such an approach lies in the further explanations—here, historical explanations—which it can contribute.

An issue context portrayed in terms of these two surface dimensions does have a distinctive strategic character (Fig. 8.1). Or at least,

Figure 8.1.B
Issue Dimensions for the
Late New Deal Era

Foreign Relations

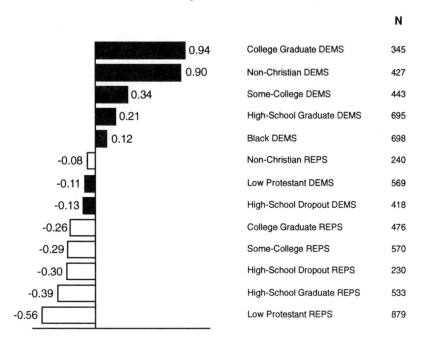

	N
College Graduate DEMS	345
Non-Christian DEMS	427
Some-College DEMS	443
High-School Graduate DEMS	695
Black DEMS	698
Non-Christian REPS	240
Low Protestant DEMS	569
High-School Dropout DEMS	418
College Graduate REPS	476
Some-College REPS	570
High-School Dropout REPS	230
High-School Graduate REPS	533
Low Protestant REPS	879

■ = Democratic Faction
□ = Republican Faction

social insurance certainly appears to be the single most beneficial Democratic issue dimension. It was social insurance that helped create a Democratic partisan majority in the country as a whole; it is social insurance that continues, most easily, to mobilize that majority. And the weight of partisan factions that sit on the liberal side of the national average on these matters, both Democratic *and Republican* factions, remains overwhelming (Fig. 8.1.A).

Foreign relations is more problematic, and thus more comparatively beneficial for Republicans. Moreover, there are strong indications that this has been true, with only a few short exceptions, over the entire duration of the postwar years. Or at least, when asked which party can better handle foreign affairs, the general public has almost always said, "the Republicans."[5] At a minimum, in our different but complementary data, foreign relations does jumble the alignments which formed around social insurance (Fig. 8.1.B). The partisan balance to this realignment is not overwhelming, but—and this is the important historical point—our data suggest that foreign relations can be treated as an inherently Republican asset.

Fundamentally, however, the overarching point is that an issue context developed in this way is still conducive to Democratic dominance, from top to bottom. It does contain the possibility of Republican interludes; foreign relations can guarantee that chance. But it does not suggest the possibility of sustained Republican successes; the situation on social insurance is just too severe for that. There is, again, some risk in visualizing the issue context of the late New Deal era in this way, in terms of current opinion data projected backwards. Yet there is also evidence that such a portrait *understates* the implications of these two surface dimensions in an earlier day. For in fact, those factions (from Fig. 8.1.A) leaning liberal on social insurance were proportionately larger at the end of the Second World War than they are today, while those factions leaning conservative were correspondingly smaller.

Practical Outcomes under the Old Issue Context

Indeed, the strategic imbalance was probably more serious even than we have implied. For if social insurance and foreign relations were central to the issue context of the immediate postwar years, with a clear priority for the former, then it is possible to apply our cross-pressure test to that era as well. This test looks for discordant factional preferences on cultural/national versus economic/welfare concerns, where the stronger preference leads away from the chosen party. (See the final sections of Chapters 5 and 7.)

This time, with social insurance and foreign relations contributing the issue context, there is only one such faction. Yet its stronger, discordant preference—the one where it is most out of step with its ostensible party—is actually on economic/welfare matters. Moreover, this time, that one faction is actually Republican! In the perspective of such a test, not only do all Democratic factions (for the larger party) lack an incipient cross-pressure, but the fact that the high-school dropout Republicans are the ones to be cross-pressured suggests that the underlying Democratic majority can easily be larger than it appears.

That is, then, the issue-based strategic framework, along with its most pressing partisan implication, that results when current opinion measures are adapted in light of historical accounts to generate a *historical* issue context. From there, it is possible to turn back to the actual historical record and to engage the outline facts about specific presidential contests in the immediate postwar era. At a minimum, these facts ought to be consistent with this putative issue context. Ideally, that context will provide not just a way of interpreting each electoral outcome individually, but a way of *connecting* these outcomes across the extended period when this particular issue context was dominant.

Thumbnail sketches of the presidential-year elections in this period do suggest obvious applications. And the biggest surprise among these, to observers at the time, was surely the first, in 1948. Democrat Harry Truman emphasized protection of social-insurance gains from the Roosevelt years, along with a "tough"—a sufficiently conservative— posture on foreign relations. That proved sufficient, given the overarching issue context, to maintain the presidency and capture Congress, in the face of low personal ratings, economic dislocation, and an actual party split. In the process, it confirmed that the New Deal era was not going to end merely with the demise of Franklin Roosevelt.[6]

Democratic dominance of the presidency did end in 1952, but only when the Republicans fielded what was to be their absolutely optimal strategy within the dominant issue context. Their nominee, Dwight Eisenhower, was none other than the victorious leader of the Allied forces in the Second World War, taking foreign relations to its maximum emphasis in his very person. Yet he was also the champion of a promising (if vague) "modern Republicanism" that signified a willingness at least to come to terms with the welfare state. That combination brought Eisenhower the presidency and brought Republican majorities to Congress with him.[7]

This Republican Congress, on the other hand, was peopled by new party elites with a commitment to the old—the basic and continuing— activist Republican position on economic/welfare concerns, even on social insurance. Figure 8.1.A would suggest little hope for such an approach, and the Republican majority was indeed swept out of Congress at the next available opportunity, in 1954. Eisenhower himself was reelected in 1956—he had in fact ended the war in Korea while continuing to assert his personal moderation on social insurance—but he could no longer bring a Republican Congress back with him. The result was a forerunner of the partisan pattern destined to become diagnostic a dozen years later. It also ended the last unified Republican control of national government, to date, in American history.[8]

The contests of 1960 then restored the orthodox late New Deal pattern, with Congress and the presidency united under Democratic control. Democrat John Kennedy emphasized protection and cautious expansion of social-insurance programs, the moderate liberal position, while his opponent, Republican Richard Nixon, emphasized an ability to hold the line on these programs while administering them less expensively, the moderate Republican alternative. The two candidates also dueled extensively on foreign relations, where Kennedy again took the "tough"—the Trumanesque conservative—position, arguably managing to get to the right of Nixon on this dimension.[9]

No one could have known that 1964 was to bring both the culmination and the practical exhaustion of the late New Deal era. Democrat Lyndon Johnson did benefit from a backwash of public sentiment after the death of John Kennedy. But he also benefitted from a Republican opponent, Barry Goldwater, who was willing to talk about making major social-insurance programs voluntary, and who was willing to move sharply right on foreign relations as well, against an incumbent who was already prosecuting a war against Communism in Vietnam. President Lyndon Johnson was the result, along with an overwhelmingly Democratic Congress, the high-water mark of unified Democratic government in the postwar years.[10]

An Issue Context for the Era of Divided Government

The elections of 1968 brought this political era to an end and inaugurated a new one in its place. The immediate result, split partisan control of national government with a Republican president and a Democratic Congress, was to be repeated often enough to contribute a name for the new political era, an extended period of "divided government." Yet what changed was not so much the partisan pattern as the issue context behind it. Indeed, the *two* common partisan outcomes in the era of divided government—Republican presidencies with Democratic Congresses, or else unified Democratic control—were arguably the partisan outcomes of the late New Deal era as well, reshuffled in their frequency but otherwise recognizable. On the other hand, both the complexity and the priority of the issue context associated with these outcomes were different. And that combination was the important change.

In truth, the elements of this change had been building for some time, so that 1968 did not so much produce them as merely register their (coordinate) arrival. The very success of Lyndon Johnson and his "Great Society," in expanding the welfare state but especially in fostering genuine redistribution to the disadvantaged, was critical in giving social welfare a boost, as a major and separate expression of the economic/

Figure 8.2.A
Surface Dimensions for the Era of Divided Government:
The Economic/Welfare Factor

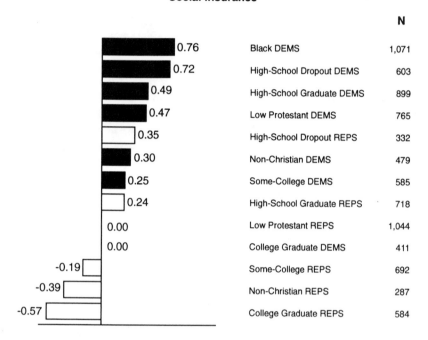

Social Insurance

	N
Black DEMS	1,071
High-School Dropout DEMS	603
High-School Graduate DEMS	899
Low Protestant DEMS	765
High-School Dropout REPS	332
Non-Christian DEMS	479
Some-College DEMS	585
High-School Graduate REPS	718
Low Protestant REPS	1,044
College Graduate DEMS	411
Some-College REPS	692
Non-Christian REPS	287
College Graduate REPS	584

■ = Democratic Faction
□ = Republican Faction

welfare factor. But so was the evolution of the civil rights movement, to the point where it had a major claim on national politics and on national public attention. Civil rights as an issue area had gained momentum from the mid-1950s onward, thanks to a series of desegregation decisions from the U.S. Supreme Court; this had already produced several major and historic legislative acts as well, during the late 1950s and early 1960s.

The larger product, in any case, was not just a far greater complexity to surface expressions of the underlying economic/welfare factor. The larger product was also a clear partisan hierarchy for the impact of economic/welfare concerns. Social insurance remained little changed,

Figure 8.2.B
Surface Dimensions for the Era of Divided Government:
The Economic/Welfare Factor

Social Welfare

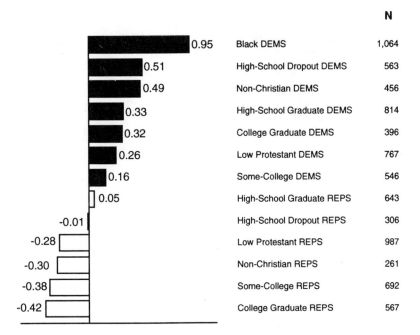

	N
Black DEMS	1,064
High-School Dropout DEMS	563
Non-Christian DEMS	456
High-School Graduate DEMS	814
College Graduate DEMS	396
Low Protestant DEMS	767
Some-College DEMS	546
High-School Graduate REPS	643
High-School Dropout REPS	306
Low Protestant REPS	987
Non-Christian REPS	261
Some-College REPS	692
College Graduate REPS	567

■ = Democratic Faction
☐ = Republican Faction

in associated factional alignments and hence in its propensity to bene-fit Democrats in a major way (Fig. 8.2.A). Social welfare, however, be-came the more direct embodiment of the underlying factor, and while it still offered potential advantages to the Democrats, when handled correctly, it was sufficiently balanced to dissipate those advantages when handled wrongly (Fig. 8.2.B). Finally, civil rights—in some sense the strangest embodiment of the underlying factor—offered the optimal *Republican* alternative among economic/welfare concerns (Fig. 8.2.C).

The position of civil rights within this hierarchy calls for additional comment. Its practical balance was clear enough: few partisan factions were enthusiastic about the position of the active Democratic party,

Figure 8.2.C
Surface Dimensions for the Era of Divided Government:
The Economic/Welfare Factor

Civil Rights

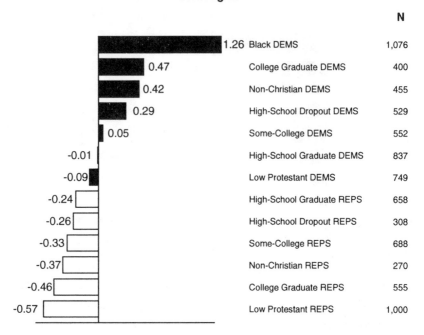

	N
Black DEMS	1,076
College Graduate DEMS	400
Non-Christian DEMS	455
High-School Dropout DEMS	529
Some-College DEMS	552
High-School Graduate DEMS	837
Low Protestant DEMS	749
High-School Graduate REPS	658
High-School Dropout REPS	308
Some-College REPS	688
Non-Christian REPS	270
College Graduate REPS	555
Low Protestant REPS	1,000

■ = Democratic Faction
□ = Republican Faction

and significant portions of its rank and file were obviously amenable to Republican arguments. This may have reflected the evolution of the policy content of this dimension, beyond an affirmation of fundamental American rights and values, and over into issues of compensation and preferment. Or it may just have reflected the fact that any tangible products from racial policy had a clearly (and narrowly) targeted set of beneficiaries. In either case, the public viewed civil rights not as a cultural/national matter, but as an economic/welfare concern.

The evolution of the cultural/national factor in an incipiently new political era was to be similar in some regards, very different in others. The shift toward complexity was equally reflected here: where the underlying factor once received its dominant expression through one

Figure 8.2.D
Surface Dimensions for the Era of Divided Government:
The Cultural/National Factor

Foreign Relations

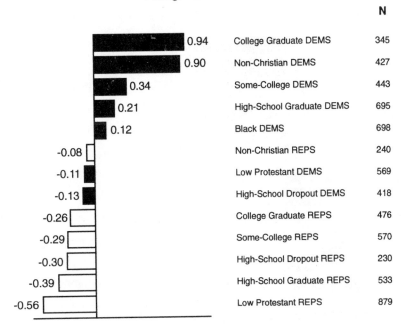

		N
0.94	College Graduate DEMS	345
0.90	Non-Christian DEMS	427
0.34	Some-College DEMS	443
0.21	High-School Graduate DEMS	695
0.12	Black DEMS	698
-0.08	Non-Christian REPS	240
-0.11	Low Protestant DEMS	569
-0.13	High-School Dropout DEMS	418
-0.26	College Graduate REPS	476
-0.29	Some-College REPS	570
-0.30	High-School Dropout REPS	230
-0.39	High-School Graduate REPS	533
-0.56	Low Protestant REPS	879

■ = Democratic Faction
□ = Republican Faction

main surface dimension, it would now receive that expression through three clearly separable dimensions instead. Inevitably, these offered their own (revised) hierarchy for partisan strategies, and if the overall range of these was reminiscent of that on the economic/welfare factor, this range nevertheless began (and ended) at a very different point. Finally, and perhaps most crucially of all, the applied *priority* of cultural/national issues as a body, by comparison to economic/welfare concerns, was to rise significantly during the era of divided government.

The role of the United States in the outside world did not diminish in the years after 1968, so that foreign relations hardly went away as a dimension for incipient political conflict. On the other hand, social, technological, and regulatory change, and, crucially, relevant interven-

Figure 8.2.E
Surface Dimensions for the Era of Divided Government:
The Cultural/National Factor

Cultural Values

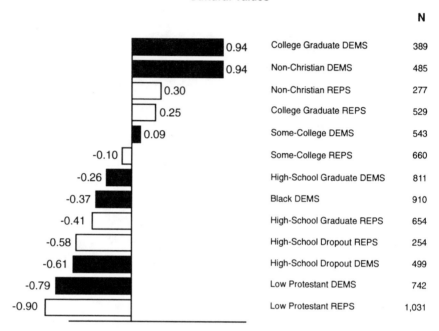

		N
0.94	College Graduate DEMS	389
0.94	Non-Christian DEMS	485
0.30	Non-Christian REPS	277
0.25	College Graduate REPS	529
0.09	Some-College DEMS	543
-0.10	Some-College REPS	660
-0.26	High-School Graduate DEMS	811
-0.37	Black DEMS	910
-0.41	High-School Graduate REPS	654
-0.58	High-School Dropout REPS	254
-0.61	High-School Dropout DEMS	499
-0.79	Low Protestant DEMS	742
-0.90	Low Protestant REPS	1,031

■ = Democratic Faction
□ = Republican Faction

tions from the U.S. Supreme Court, all created powerful added emphases on the dimension of cultural values. When the active parties then
diverged sharply on these matters, the latter were destined to assume
a much larger role in national politics. Moreover, in an emphasis even
more strongly reflecting the priorities of the Court, but also reflecting a
shift from elite to mass influences in politicking, civil liberties became
an explicit dimension of political conflict, and thus of conflict in public
preferences.

Foreign relations remained a modestly Republican dimension, as
it had been throughout the late New Deal era (Fig. 8.2.D). The factional
situation still favored the Republican party on balance, though strate-

Figure 8.2.F
Surface Dimensions for the Era of Divided Government:
The Cultural/National Factor

Civil Liberties

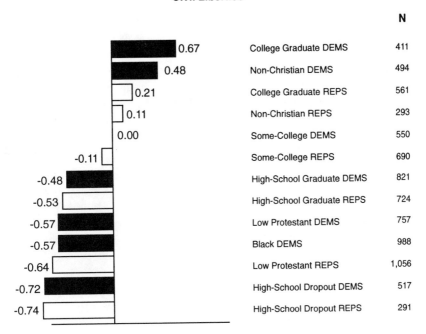

		N
0.67	College Graduate DEMS	411
0.48	Non-Christian DEMS	494
0.21	College Graduate REPS	561
0.11	Non-Christian REPS	293
0.00	Some-College DEMS	550
-0.11	Some-College REPS	690
-0.48	High-School Graduate DEMS	821
-0.53	High-School Graduate REPS	724
-0.57	Low Protestant DEMS	757
-0.57	Black DEMS	988
-0.64	Low Protestant REPS	1,056
-0.72	High-School Dropout DEMS	517
-0.74	High-School Dropout REPS	291

■ = Democratic Faction
□ = Republican Faction

gic miscues by either party could shift that balance in either direction. On the other hand, cultural values was to displace foreign relations as the most direct embodiment of the underlying factor, and the mathematics of cultural values was to be less equivocal—and more Republican (Fig. 8.2.E). Very few factions (all of them Democratic) shared any real enthusiasm for the preferences of the active Democratic party, while there were major Democratic factions actually standing to the right of Republican activists. On civil liberties, finally, this partisan drift reached its ultimate extension (Fig. 8.2.F). Most of the Democratic party was more comfortable with the preferences characterizing the *Republican* party. If cultural values nevertheless continued to receive more emphasis in practical politics, this may have been because Republican activists themselves disliked the positions necessary to harvest civil liberties.

Political Dynamics for a New Issue Context

The simplest way to summarize—and visualize—this changed situation, and to apply it to the elections after 1964, is to turn back to the underlying factors. These have already been addressed at Figure 7.4, which treats the active party as critical to shaping policy options, and the total party as then critical to choosing among them. Accordingly, Figure 8.3 merely repeats Figure 7.4. That figure is striking in its own right, and its two main findings bear repeating. In the era of divided government,

- The economic/welfare factor remains an evident asset to the active Democratic party, holding every Democratic faction on the liberal side of the partisan divide and leaving a Republican faction, the high-school graduate Republicans, marginally closest to that divide as well (Fig. 8.3.B).

- On the other hand, the cultural/national factor is even more an asset in the disruption of these patterns, with four Democratic factions solidly joining the active Republicans, while only two Republican factions go Democratic, and mildly so at that (Fig. 8.3.A).

Yet two other things are now powerfully evident about the structure of public preferences in the modern era, by contrast to their apparent structure in the immediate postwar years. Both suggest a change, and both are best seen by comparing the two surface dimensions that were once predominant in expressing the underlying factors (at Fig. 8.1) with the full factors themselves (at Fig. 8.3). The comparison is not ideal, in that these surface dimensions have to be separated from the same (current) deep factors. But if the historical logic associated with them is correct—and there is much superficial evidence to that effect—they can at least be powerfully suggestive.

The first of these further implications involves the evolution of the deep factors individually. Part of the old order, the part involving economic/welfare issues, is in fact hardened and clarified in the modern era (Fig. 8.1.A versus 8.3.B). Social insurance by itself jumbled the two parties somewhat, putting two Republican factions comfortably inside the Democratic factional array. On balance, that represents a decisive edge for the Democrats. The underlying economic/welfare factor draws party lines much more cleanly and thus jumbles the parties much less, putting every Democratic faction on the liberal side but luring no Republican factions across that line. The net Democratic edge

Figure 8.3.A
Dominant Dimensions for the Era
of Divided Government

Cultural/National

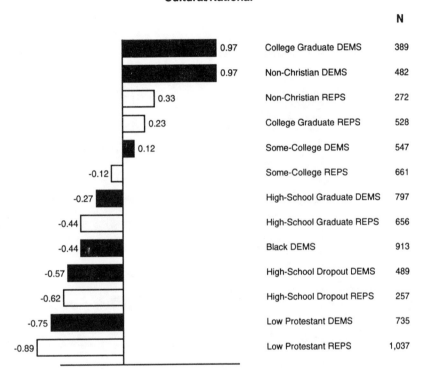

		N
0.97	College Graduate DEMS	389
0.97	Non-Christian DEMS	482
0.33	Non-Christian REPS	272
0.23	College Graduate REPS	528
0.12	Some-College DEMS	547
-0.12	Some-College REPS	661
-0.27	High-School Graduate DEMS	797
-0.44	High-School Graduate REPS	656
-0.44	Black DEMS	913
-0.57	High-School Dropout DEMS	489
-0.62	High-School Dropout REPS	257
-0.75	Low Protestant DEMS	735
-0.89	Low Protestant REPS	1,037

■ = Democratic Faction
□ = Republican Faction

thus drops a bit in the modern era, though there is some compensation not just in the clarity of party lines but also in the distance—the policy gap—between the two most moderate party factions.

On the other hand, part of the old order becomes far more fluid, and thus of tremendously increased strategic import, in the modern era. This vastly increased fluidity—and presumably, strategic possibility—comes, of course, with the cultural/national factor (Fig. 8.1.B versus 8.3.A). Foreign relations, as a surrogate for the situation in the late New Deal era, actually drew party lines rather cleanly as well,

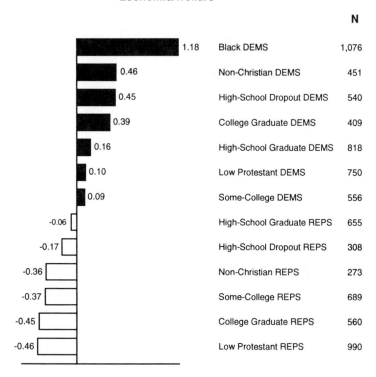

Figure 8.3.B
Dominant Dimensions for the Era
of Divided Government

Economic/Welfare

		N
1.18	Black DEMS	1,076
0.46	Non-Christian DEMS	451
0.45	High-School Dropout DEMS	540
0.39	College Graduate DEMS	409
0.16	High-School Graduate DEMS	818
0.10	Low Protestant DEMS	750
0.09	Some-College DEMS	556
-0.06	High-School Graduate REPS	655
-0.17	High-School Dropout REPS	308
-0.36	Non-Christian REPS	273
-0.37	Some-College REPS	689
-0.45	College Graduate REPS	560
-0.46	Low Protestant REPS	990

■ = Democratic Faction
□ = Republican Faction

with a slight edge to the Republicans this time. Two Democratic factions moved to their side; one Republican faction was drawn to the left of these; and the resulting balance, while not overwhelming, ranged from marginally to evidently Republican. The underlying cultural/national factor, however, blasts any such partisan consistency, exhibiting the classic group-dominated pattern instead. Moreover, it actually draws a majority of Democratic factions solidly toward the active Republican party, while shifting only two Republican factions, much more hesitantly, toward the active Democratic party.

The era of divided government, then, could be argued to represent a world shifting clearly in a Republican direction, marginally on the economic/welfare factor, much more reliably on the cultural/national factor. On the other hand, this change on the economic/welfare factor is hardly enough to encourage hopes of a Republican majority there; and when continuing Democratic majorities in partisan attachment are reinforced by economic/welfare concerns, the Republican party has not come close to a new position of partisan dominance. What results instead, from a proper comparison of Figures 8.1 and 8.3, is a sense of widened possibility. This can be capsulized most concretely by examining the associated shift in the pressures (really the *cross*-pressures) falling upon various factions, as one era gives way to another. That widened possibility is then reinforced by resurrecting the "lost" faction in our analysis.

To take the shift in cross-pressures first: When the two deep factors to political opinion are focused principally through social insurance and foreign relations, as we believe that they were in the late New Deal era, the only faction in either party which meets our test of an effective cross-pressure is actually a Republican faction, the high-school dropout Republicans. On the other hand, when the fuller and more complex factors are used for the same analysis, as they must be in the era of divided government, three such factions surface—and they are all Democratic. The low-Protestant Democrats, the high-school dropout Democrats, and the high-school graduate Democrats, pillars of the old Democratic coalition, are now under evident (and apparently sustained) cross-pressure. Moreover, they obviously constitute a one-way directional loss to the party whenever this implicit cross-pressure can be activated.

A sense for the structure and increased strategic possibilities of the modern issue context can be additionally reinforced by rescuing the "lost" faction in our analysis, the pure partisan independents. These are the individuals who refused any party identification, even when pushed and prodded. They appeared, fleetingly, in the search for partisan attachments to policy preferences in Chapter 3. There, they proved to constitute only a small piece of the general public and to possess blandly centrist opinions. They were smaller even than some individual party factions, for example, the low-Protestant Republicans or the black Democrats. And they offered a group mean hugging the national average on the deep factors and surface dimensions (Figs. 3.1 and 3.2).

These independents were collectively too small for any internal analysis of their social composition (Chapter 4) and irrelevant to a factional analysis of the two major parties (Chapter 5). They were likewise irrelevant, by definition, to an analysis of the relationships between rank-and-file identifiers and their active fellow partisans (Chapters 6 and 7). Moreover, they produced almost no political activists of their own, at least by our available (and very modest) standards, and we know from other work that they are disproportionately unlikely even to turn out and vote.[11]

Nevertheless, the pure partisan independents are part of the audience for party political appeals, and they can vote, so that they certainly have some potential relationship to the political structure of an era of divided government. Moreover, as it develops, when this audience does respond to an issue context, their response only further reinforces the political dynamics of the modern era. For when their collective preferences are recast in the same terms as Figure 8.3, rescaling these pure partisan independents according to the mean positions of the active parties, they prove to be the archetypal population for an era of divided government (Fig. 8.4).

These partisan independents begin, by definition, with no party anchor. As a result, in the current world, liberal policy preferences ought to draw them toward the Democrats, conservative policy preferences toward the Republicans. Yet on the two great underlying factors of political opinion, these independents are actually drawn simultaneously in opposite directions (Fig. 8.4): they are clearly conservative on cultural/national issues, clearly liberal on economic/welfare concerns.

Moreover, their preferences on the surface dimensions of political opinion only embroider, while reinforcing, the basic point (Fig. 8.4.B). On the two surface dimensions most evenly balanced between the active parties, foreign relations and civil rights, the pure partisan independents sit almost exactly at the partisan midpoint (+.02 and +.01). On the two surface dimensions that most evidently benefit the Democrats, social insurance and social welfare, they are solidly liberal (+.31 on both). And on the two surface dimensions that most reliably benefit the Republicans—civil liberties and cultural values—they are, of course, solidly conservative (−.39 and −.22).

Practical Outcomes under the Modern Issue Context

There would have been no way of knowing at the time that the election of 1968 was to operationalize this new issue context and to mark the beginning of a new political era. By itself, this election could as easily have fitted into the old electoral order, as one of its intermittent Republican deviations, in what was obviously one of the worst years for the Democratic party since the coming of the New Deal. Yet Dwight Eisen-

Figure 8.4.A
Policy Preferences for the Pure Partisan Independents

The Deep Factors

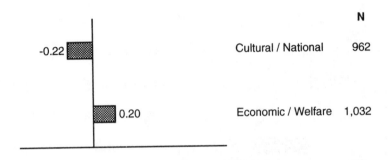

		N
-0.22	Cultural / National	962
0.20	Economic / Welfare	1,032

Figure 8.4.B
Policy Preferences for the Pure Partisan Independents

The Surface Dimensions

		N
-0.22	Cultural Values	961
0.31	Social Welfare	1,012
0.02	Foreign Relations	668
0.31	Social Insurance	1,095
0.01	Civil Rights	1,015
-0.39	Civil Liberties	1,025

hower, the last preceding beneficiary of a Republican deviation, had brought Republican congressional majorities with him. Richard Nixon did not. And twenty-five years of subsequent history, interpreted through the interaction of the two deep factors of political opinion, make it clear that this was the diagnostic point.

Thumbnail sketches of subsequent elections, once again, can elaborate the point, especially when framed by a reminder about the preferences of the rank and file *versus* the party activists in the era of divided government (Fig. 6.3, reprinted here as Fig. 8.5). Indeed, the latter is crucial to escaping an (otherwise) apparent paradox in these

Figure 8.5.A
Active Partisans and their Rank and File on the Deep Factors

Cultural/National

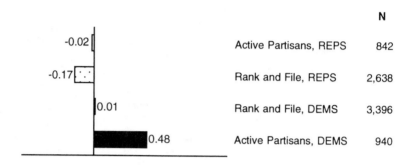

Figure 8.5.B
Active Partisans and their Rank and File on the Deep Factors

Economic/Welfare

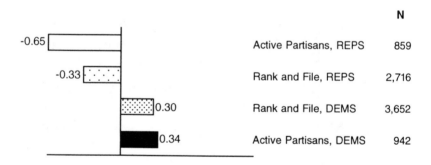

election outcomes. To wit: Public preferences on economic/welfare matters may in fact have become more conservative across the post-war years, and public preferences on cultural/national matters have almost surely become more liberal.[12] Yet economic/welfare issues continue to be a benefit for the more liberal party in the United States, the Democrats, just as cultural/national issues continue to be a major benefit to the more conservative party, the Republicans.

The interpretation which removes the paradox derives from the positional logic of the entire analysis, involving not the evolution of public preferences in their own right, but the positioning of the active parties in response. In this, the Democratic party had radically overshot the liberal drift in public preferences on cultural/national matters, making itself the distant—the deviant—party here. In turn, the active Republican party has radically overestimated the conservatizing shift on economic/welfare matters, though in truth, it may always have done so. Said differently, political strategy remains a matter of *comparative* position, having to do with a liberal or conservative posture *within the current issue context*. The active Democratic party now prefers to get this wrong on the cultural/national factor, even with the help of liberalizing trends, just as the active Republican party prefers to get it wrong on the economic/welfare factor, despite an incipient conservatizing drift.

In any case, Richard Nixon versus Hubert Humphrey, Republican versus Democrat in the presidential election of 1968, inaugurated the new era in classic fashion. In his campaign, Nixon strongly emphasized cultural/national issues. In *his* campaign, Humphrey strongly emphasized economic/welfare issues instead. It was, however, a year for cultural/national priorities if ever there was one—the war in Vietnam, urban riots, and countercultural politicking were all on the boil—and Nixon triumphed narrowly. Diagnostically, however, he gained very little at the congressional level and faced solid Democratic majorities in both houses as president.[13]

Remarkably, that situation continued after the 1972 elections. At the top of the ticket, George McGovern, the Democratic nominee, moved far to the left on cultural/national matters—farther, probably, than active party preferences—and went well left on economic/welfare issues too, to the point of promising the first governmentally guaranteed income in American history. Nixon had the superior positions on both underlying factors as a result, and his victory was overwhelming. Nevertheless, it hardly touched the (Democratic) Congress below.[14]

The election of 1976 was the stereotypical opposite, marking perhaps the only time after 1964 that the Democratic nominee seized the high ground on both underlying factors. Jimmy Carter, the Democrat, and Gerald Ford, the Republican, offered very moderate versions of orthodox party positions on economic/welfare matters, though the key point here is that they *were* the orthodox positions. Moreover, Carter managed to represent—really to incarnate—traditional values on cultural/national matters. There was little reason for the existing issue structure to produce a Republican under those conditions, and while Ford's incumbency and Carter's anonymity did narrow the margin, Carter was ultimately elected.[15]

Unified Democratic government, however, was to last for only one term, as Jimmy Carter in fact forfeited all his positional assets from the 1976 campaign. He addressed economic/welfare issues only marginally during his presidency, emphasizing little and securing less. He dissipated his apparent traditionalism on cultural/national issues, with an administration offering the general preferences of the active Democratic party. And he was saddled with the foreign-policy debacle of the Iran hostages. The campaign, even then, turned on whether Ronald Reagan, the Republican nominee, could move the perception of himself back from the active Republican position on economic/welfare matters, and back from *beyond* the active position on cultural/national affairs. In the end, he could, and he became president.[16]

The election of 1980 also marked the presidential high-water mark, to date, of Republican efforts to force cultural/national issues into congressional campaigns. Crime, foreign relations, permissiveness, and public order all became themes in a number of senatorial campaigns, and Republicans managed to capture the Senate (though not the House) in return. The experience proved heady enough and proved to be a great benefit to presidential leadership, but it was not to be long-lasting. When this same crop of senators came up for reelection in 1986, it became clear that even the partial successes of 1980 with the cultural/national factor were an aberration for Congress, so that the Senate, too, passed back into Democratic hands.

In the meantime, however, the 1984 elections had brought another classic confrontation between the two deep factors of American politics, the first pure version of that pattern since 1968. Ronald Reagan and Walter Mondale, the incumbent president and the Democratic nominee, were archetypal versions of their active parties. Mondale nevertheless communicated, in his more dramatic gestures, the orthodox Democratic position on cultural/national issues, while Reagan benefitted from a strong economic recovery which served to moderate the risks of the traditional Republican stance on economic/welfare matters. An arguably successful incumbency was added to this and brought a solid Republican victory.[17]

Before 1988, many commentators reasoned that the 1988 election would be a peculiarly "open" contest for the presidency, with no incumbent and no inescapable issue focus, and went on to conclude that it was likely to produce the first unified Democratic government since 1976. Yet Michael Dukakis, the Democratic nominee, put little emphasis on economic/welfare issues until the very end of his campaign, when polls suggested that they *were* having an effect. On the other side,

George Bush, the Republican nominee, put strong emphasis on cultural/ national issues from the start, in some of the most heavy-handed advertisements in the history of campaign television. That approach managed a double success: cultural/national issues became the theme of the contest, and the Republican candidate won. It did not, however, manage a triple success: Bush did not seriously cut Democratic margins in either house of Congress.[18]

The election of 1992 was then the stereotypical reverse. Bill Clinton, the Democratic nominee, had been emphasizing economic/welfare issues, like health insurance, since the start of his nominating campaign. George Bush, the incumbent, countered with cultural/national issues, involving foreign-policy successes and the character failings of his opponent. Yet this time, the critical influence was an environment with a protracted economic downturn at its practical and symbolic core, an environment which sapped consumer confidence disproportionately and put powerful further emphasis on economic/welfare matters. The logical outcome, in the current issue context, was a Democratic win and a period of unified Democratic government. And that was exactly what transpired.[19]

Further Implications: Alternative Future Contexts

The presidential campaigns of 1984, 1988, and 1992 are representative of the three available types of contests in the era of divided government: one where the parties square off on both deep factors, one where combat is principally on cultural/national issues, and one where political combat is principally on economic/welfare issues instead. These three elections also encompass the two associated outcomes within this context to date: split partisan control of national government, with Republicans in control of the presidency and Democrats in control of Congress, or unified Democratic control. All this follows, finally, from a very straightforward connection to the internal structure of the contemporary issue context.

That structure is clear enough in its own right, with its deep factors and surface dimensions, their partisan attachments and key group memberships, and the coordinate tensions between active partisans and their rank and file. Yet the change from one issue context to another—from the late New Deal era to the era of divided government in this case—is sufficient reminder that no structure is so coherent and lasting as to defy the simple passage of time. The surface dimensions embodying the deep factors, the social groups most proximate to preferences on them, and the way political parties aggregate these preferences, as well as the character of elite translation—all these have changed in just the postwar years. They will surely change again.

Moreover, the nature of this first change—a comparatively simple and straightforward one, we suspect—warns against trying to extrapolate too far by means of an existing structure. The two eras of the late New Deal and of divided government were not unrelated in their substantive foci, so that the character of change was relatively easy to specify. Even this was so, however, only after the fact: There was no ineluctable standard by which an analyst in the immediate postwar years *should* have conceived of the social-insurance dimension as only one of several future contenders to express the economic/welfare factor, nor of the foreign-relations dimension as only one of several subsequent possibilities to express the cultural/national factor. Much less should any such analyst have been taxed with conceiving the *specific identities* of the surface dimensions that would subsequently come to play these roles.

This does not proscribe taking the current issue context, altering its dimensional expressions, and then projecting the outcome. It merely warns against putting any great credence in the result. Moreover, this *is* a comparatively simple form of projection, arguably not the sort which will characterize a successor era. Or at least, there is no reason to assume that the current surface dimensions will even serve as expressions of the same underlying factors in a different political era. Should foreign relations, for instance, cease to focus principally on defense and come to focus on trade, it might as reasonably find expression in the economic/welfare (rather than the cultural/national) factor. Or, should social welfare change its programmatic contents in a world where international competitiveness was a more dominating concern, that dimension might change its associated social dynamics and its partisan impact, as well, again, as the dimensions with which it was most nearly aligned. And so on.[20]

Such examples underline the difficulty in projecting from a current issue context. They do not argue against the need to interpret the current context, nor to isolate its role in undergirding a current, extended political era. Nor, lastly, do such difficulties suggest that some future issue context will not offer its own distinctive embodiment of the same basic characteristics—its own deep factors and surface dimensions, its own group and party attachments, its own elite-mass relations and tensions. Indeed, the central point in focusing on "what the struggle is about" is a belief that some such structure will characterize—will organize and discipline—every political era, including our own.

APPENDIX

Texts for Survey Questions

This appendix presents the full texts of the individual opinion items used in the preceding analysis, in the order in which they appeared in Table 2.1. Most of these items offered a four-category response, with agreement or disagreement in a stronger or more moderate fashion; a few offered a three-category response, in the "more," "same," or "less" format.

1. School boards ought to have the right to fire teachers who are known homosexuals. (V40206)

2. Changing the laws to make it more difficult for a woman to get an abortion. (V20101)

3. A constitutional amendment to permit prayer in the public schools. (V20103)

4. Women should return to their traditional role in society. (V40211)

5. Proposals to limit the access that AIDS patients have to public places. (V20108)

6. The government should help more needy people even if it means going deeper into debt. (40025)

7. The government should guarantee every citizen enough to eat and a place to sleep. (V40026)

8. It is the responsibility of the government to take care of people who can't take care of themselves. (V40024)

9. Spending on government assistance for the unemployed. (V20006)

10. Our society should do what is necessary to make sure that everyone has an equal opportunity to succeed. (V40022)

11. The "Star Wars" program to develop a space-based defense against nuclear attack. (V20104)

12. The best way to ensure peace is through military strength. (V40035)

13. Cutting back federal spending for defense and miliary purposes. (V20105)

14. Which of the following increases the chances of nuclear war more—a con-

tinuation of the nuclear arms build-up here and in the Soviet Union *or* the U.S. falling behind the Soviet Union in nuclear weaponry? (V210)

15. Which is the greater risk to peace—trusting the Russians to live up to their side of an arms agreement or being too suspicious of the Russians so that we never get an arms agreement with them? (V212)

16. To reduce tensions with the Soviet Union, do you think U.S. policy is too willing to compromise, not willing enough to compromise, or about right? (V209)

17. Should the U.S. be giving assistance to the Contras, that is, the guerilla forces now opposing the Marxist government in Nicaragua? (V204)

18. Resuming the military draft. (V20111)

19. Spending on improving the nation's health care. (V20009)

20. Spending on social security. (V20003)

21. Spending on aid to farmers. (V20014)

22. Proposals to increase taxes on foreign imports to protect American jobs in certain industries. (V20110)

23. Spending on programs that assist blacks and other minorities. (V20008)

24. We should make every possible effort to improve the position of blacks and other minorities, even if it means giving them preferential treatment. (V40032)

25. We have gone too far in pushing equal rights in this country. (40023)

26. Books that contain dangerous ideas should be banned from public school libraries. (V40207)

27. Freedom of speech should not extend to groups like the Communist party or the Ku Klux Klan. (V40209)

28. The police should be allowed to search the houses of known drug dealers without a court order. (V40210)

29. The government ought to be able to censor news stories that it feels threaten national security. (V40213)

30. Mandatory drug tests for government employees. (V20106)

NOTES

Chapter 1: The Notion of an Issue Context

1. Both exemplifying that tradition and integrating much of the relevant work in its time is V. O. Key, Jr., *Public Opinion and American Democracy* (New York: Knopf, 1961). Stimulating earlier views include Walter Lippman, *Public Opinion* (New York: Macmillan, 1922), and the opening article in the first journal devoted specifically to the topic, Floyd H. Allport, "Toward a Science of Public Opinion," *Public Opinion Quarterly* 1 (Jan. 1937), 7–23. Citations to some of the (voluminous) work in the years since Key can be found in subsequent footnotes; a useful and provocative attempt to give this work itself a further structure is Paul M. Sniderman, "The New Look in Public Opinion Research," in Ada W. Finifter, ed., *Political Science: The State of the Discipline, II* (Washington, D.C.: American Political Science Association, 1993).

2. Despite the obvious risks, the current moment features a wealth of impressionistic efforts along just these lines; see Michael Barone, *Our Country: The Shaping of America from Roosevelt to Reagan* (New York: Free Press, 1990); E. J. Dionne, Jr., *Why Americans Hate Politics* (New York: Simon & Schuster, 1991); Thomas Byrne Edsall and Mary D. Edsall, *Chain Reaction: The Impact of Race, Rights, and Taxes on American Politics* (New York: Norton, 1991); Alan Ehrenhalt, *The United States of Ambition: Politicians, Power, and the Pursuit of Office* (New York: Basic Books, 1991); and Kevin Phillips, *Boiling Point: Democrats, Republicans, and the Decline of Middle-Class Prosperity* (New York: Random House, 1992).

3. Perhaps the most widely recognized embodiment of this way of thinking about politics in our time is the "realignment framework," whose landmarks include V. O. Key, Jr., "A Theory of Critical Elections," *Journal of Politics* 17 (Feb. 1955), 3–18; Walter Dean Burnham, *Critical Elections and the Mainsprings of American Politics* (New York: Norton, 1970); and James L. Sundquist, *Dynamics of the Party System: Alignment and Realignment of Political Parties in the United States* (Washington, D.C.: Brookings Institution, 1973). Yet critics who do not share the substantive conclusions of this framework normally do share this general way of thinking about issue contexts; see, for example, the essays in Richard L. McCormick, *The Party Period and Public Policy: American Politics from the Age of Jackson to the Progressive Era* (New York: Oxford, 1986), or Edward

G. Carmines and James A. Stimson, "On the Structure and Sequence of Issue Evolution," *American Political Science Review* 80 (Sept. 1986), 901–20. See also Samuel P. Huntington, *American Politics: The Promise of Disharmony* (Cambridge: Harvard UP, 1981).

4. This is a major theme in Benjamin I. Page and Robert Y. Shapiro, *The Rational Public: Fifty Years of Trends in Americans' Policy Preferences* (Chicago: U of Chicago P, 1991). It is reinforced in two otherwise quite different works: James A. Stimson, *Public Opinion in America: Moods, Cycles, and Swings* (Boulder: Westview Press, 1991), and Samuel L. Popkin, *The Reasoning Voter: Communication and Persuasion in Presidential Campaigns* (Chicago: U of Chicago P, 1991). The classic elaboration of the larger argument remains Vilfredo Pareto, *Trattato di Sociologia Generale*, 3 vols. (Florence: Barbera, 1916); an English translation is Pareto, *Compendium of General Sociology*, abr. Giulio Farina, trans. Elizabeth Abbott (Minneapolis: U of Minnesota P, 1980).

5. A powerful version of this argument, noting extended stability *and* ultimate change across the sweep of American history, is Joel H. Silbey, *The American Political Nation, 1838–1893* (Stanford: Stanford UP, 1991). Two very different works which, again, reinforce the argument from their titles onward are Eric R. A. N. Smith, *The Unchanging American Voter* (Berkeley: U of California P, 1989), and the classic, with a particularly apt subtitle, David B. Truman, *The Governmental Process: Political Interests and Public Opinion* (New York: Knopf, 1951). For even deeper roots, see Pareto, *Trattato*.

6. Useful contemporary overviews of American political opinion include Page and Shapiro, *The Rational Public*, and Stimson, *Public Opinion in America*. A powerful addition is William G. Mayer, *The Changing American Mind: How and Why American Public Opinion Changed between 1960 and 1988* (Ann Arbor: U of Michigan P, 1992). An earlier version is Lloyd A. Free and Hadley Cantril, *The Political Beliefs of Americans* (New Brunswick: Rutgers UP, 1967). These are all analyses working from the opinion data itself; the classic analyses working the other way around, from political or social structure *through* public opinion, remain Truman, *The Governmental Process*, and Key, *Public Opinion and American Democracy*. Different yet again, but powerfully suggestive, is Stanley Feldman, "Structure and Consistency in Public Opinion: The Role of Core Beliefs and Values," *American Journal of Political Science* 32 (May 1988), 416–40.

7. Possibly the classic work in the social sciences on American distinctiveness is Seymour Martin Lipset, *The First New Nation: The United States in Historical and Comparative Perspective* (New York: Basic Books, 1963). A recent return to the same issues is Byron E. Shafer, ed., *Is America Different? A New Look at American Exceptionalism* (Oxford: Oxford UP, 1991). Most students of the topic, however, would probably acknowledge the primacy of Alexis de Tocqueville, *Democracy in America*, ed. Phillips Bradley (New York: Knopf, 1945). See also Herbert McClosky and John Zaller, *The American Ethos: Public Attitudes toward Capitalism and Democracy* (Cambridge: Harvard UP, 1988).

8. The assertion that environment shapes strategy seems uncontroversial,

verging on definitional. Yet analyses of the way in which political structure shapes what candidates actually *talk about* are nevertheless in short supply. Aspects of the analytic story can be found in Marjorie Randon Hershey, *Running for Office: The Political Education of Campaigners* (Chatham: Chatham House, 1984); Byron E. Shafer, *Bifurcated Politics: Evolution and Reform in the National Party Convention* (Cambridge: Harvard UP, 1988); and Nelson W. Polsby and Aaron Wildavsky, *Presidential Elections: Contemporary Strategies of American Electoral Politics*, 8th ed. (New York: Free Press, 1991). For rich and diverse examples, see especially Richard F. Fenno, Jr., *Home Style: House Members in Their Districts* (Boston: Little, Brown, 1978).

9. The most pointed and persistent inquiries into the nature of this process have probably come through the work of William H. Riker, perhaps most diagnostically in his inquiry into what he calls "heresthetic"—the logic of political strategy and the strategic value of presentation; see especially his *Art of Political Manipulation* (New Haven: Yale UP, 1986). Practical elements (or at least analogs) of the process can be found, however, in work on "agenda-setting" and "priming," as with John W. Kingdon, *Agendas, Alternatives, and Public Policy* (Boston: Little, Brown, 1984), and Shanto Iyengar and Donald R. Kinder, *News That Matters: Television and American Opinion* (Chicago: U of Chicago P, 1987).

10. Nevertheless, some overviews with this as a partial focus can be found in Byron E. Shafer, ed., *Postwar Politics in the G-7: Orders and Eras in Comparative Perspective* (Madison: U of Wisconsin P, forthcoming [1995]).

Chapter 2: Dimensions of Political Opinion

1. William E. Leuchtenberg, *Franklin D. Roosevelt and the New Deal, 1932–1940* (New York: Harper & Row, 1963), and Arthur M. Schlesinger, Jr., *The Coming of the New Deal* (Boston: Houghton Mifflin, 1959).

2. James MacGregor Burns, *Roosevelt: The Soldier of Freedom* (New York: Harcourt Brace Jovanovich, 1970), and John Morton Blum, *V was for Victory: Politics and American Culture during World War II* (New York: Harcourt Brace Jovanovich, 1976). See also Eric F. Goldman, *The Crucial Decade: America, 1945–1955* (New York: Knopf, 1956).

3. Thomas R. Brooks, *Walls Come Tumbling Down: A History of the Civil Rights Movement, 1940–1970* (Englewood Cliffs: Prentice-Hall, 1974); Harvard Sitkoff, *The Struggle for Black Equality, 1954–1980* (New York: Hill and Wang, 1981); Juan Williams, *Eyes on the Prize: America's Civil Rights Years, 1954–1965* (New York: Viking, 1987).

4. Richard M. Scammon and Ben J. Wattenberg, *The Real Majority* (New York: Coward-McCann, 1970); Todd Gitlin, *The Sixties: Years of Hope, Days of Rage* (New York: Bantam, 1987); John Kenneth White, *The New Politics of Old Values* (Hanover, N.H.: UP of New England, 1988); James Davison Hunter, *Culture Wars: The Struggle to Define America* (New York: Basic, 1991).

5. Edward D. Berkowitz, *America's Welfare State: From Roosevelt to Reagan* (Baltimore: Johns Hopkins UP, 1991); and Theodore R. Marmor, Jerry L. Mashaw, and Philip L. Harvey, *America's Misunderstood Welfare State: Persisting Myths, Enduring Realities* (New York: Basic Books, 1990).

6. David M. O'Brien, *Storm Center: The Supreme Court in American Politics* (New York: Norton, 1986), and Richard L. Pacelle, Jr., *The Transformation of the Supreme Court's Agenda: From the New Deal to the Reagan Administration* (Boulder: Westview Press, 1991). See also Daniel Yankelovich, *New Rules: Searching for Self-Fulfillment in a World Turned Upside Down* (New York: Random House, 1981).

7. Angus Campbell, Philip E. Converse, Warren E. Miller, and Donald E. Stokes, *The American Voter* (New York: Wiley, 1960).

8. Ibid., p. 50.

9. The simplest way to track these changes is to consult the codebook, *National Election Studies: 1952–1988 Cumulative Data File* (Ann Arbor: Center for Political Studies, n.d. but released in 1990). Alternatively, Warren E. Miller and Santa A. Traugott, comps., *American National Election Studies Data Sourcebook, 1952–1986* (Cambridge: Harvard UP, 1989).

10. For attitudinal divisions, Ronald Inglehart, for example, uses the "left/right" and "materialist/postmaterialist" divisions, in Inglehart, *The Silent Revolution: Changing Values and Political Styles among Western Publics* (Princeton: Princeton UP, 1977). For societal cleavages, Seymour Martin Lipset and Stein Rokkan begin with "The Two Revolutions: The National and the Industrial," which become "territorial" and "functional" divisions in "Cleavage Structures, Party Systems, and Voter Alignments: An Introduction," from Lipset and Rokkan, eds., *Party Systems and Voter Alignments: Cross-National Perspectives* (New York: Free Press, 1967). Finally, for divisions over basic forms of social organization, Robert E. Lane may have the most precise analogy with his distinction between "consumer" (i.e., distributional) versus "producer" (experiential) values, in Lane, *The Market Experience* (Cambridge: Cambridge UP, 1991), especially chaps. 21 and 29.

11. Many of these impressions are gathered in Seymour Martin Lipset, *The First New Nation: The United States in Historical and Comparative Perspective* (New York: Basic Books, 1963). See also Louis Hartz, *The Liberal Tradition in America: An Interpretation of American Political Thought since the Revolution* (New York: Harcourt, Brace, & World, 1955).

12. It was this dimension, albeit not under this explicit heading, that received particular attention in the immediate postwar years: see David Riesman, with Nathan Glazer and Reuel Denny, *The Lonely Crowd: A Study of the Changing American Character* (New Haven: Yale UP, 1950); David M. Potter, *People of Plenty* (Chicago: U of Chicago P, 1954); and William H. Whyte, Jr., *The Organization Man* (New York: Simon & Schuster, 1956).

13. The key survey involved a telephone pilot of 508 adult Americans,

completed between January 28 and February 1, 1987. This was followed by the survey proper, involving face-to-face interviews with 4,224 adults. That personal survey took the form of a replicated probability sample down to the block level within urban areas and down to township segments within rural counterparts. It was completed between April 25 and May 10, 1987, requiring three callbacks for any initial nonrespondents, and using a modest "times-at-home" weighting procedure after the fact to contain any bias resulting from ease or difficulty of locating respondents. Further details on sampling procedure can be found in the Technical Appendix to *The People, the Press, & Politics* (Los Angeles: Times Mirror Co., Sept. 1987), esp. pp. 115–16. A revised and expanded publication growing out of this is The Gallup Organization Staff, eds., *The People, the Press, & Politics: The Times Mirror Study of the American Electorate* (Reading: Addison-Wesley, 1988).

14. Gary King, "How Not to Lie with Statistics: Avoiding Common Mistakes in Quantitative Political Science," *American Journal of Political Science* 30 (Aug. 1986), 682. For the procedure generally, see Jae-On Kim and Charles W. Mueller, *Introduction to Factor Analysis: What It Is and How To Do It* (Beverly Hills: Sage, 1978), plus Kim and Mueller, *Factor Analysis: Statistical Methods and Practical Issues* (Beverly Hills: Sage, 1978). The precise operationalization in our analysis was SPSSX. A very different approach, with many analogous concerns, is Mark A. Peffley and Jon Hurwitz, "A Hierarchical Model of Attitude Constraint," *American Journal of Political Science* 29 (Nov. 1985), 871–90.

15. In order to permit the resulting dimensions, whether or not they accorded with initial hypotheses, to have an open-ended and potentially varying relationship *to each other*—to be related or not, in the degree that public perceptions decreed—we used oblique rotation in the factor analysis itself.

In preliminary investigations, a few stray items did not load substantially on any of these dimensions, and were thus dropped from the final analysis. The one among them that probably gets most attention elsewhere, capital punishment ("A mandatory death penalty for anyone convicted of premeditated murder"), offered some mild attachment to nearly all of these dimensions, but no strong attachment to any. For a further use of this particular item, however, see William J. M. Claggett and Byron E. Shafer, "Life and Death as Public Policy: Capital Punishment and Abortion in American Political Opinion," *International Journal of Public Opinion Research* 3 (Spring 1991), 32–52.

16. This point should probably be repeated: these dimensions are being presented in terms of a small number of leading items *for purposes of naming only*. The actual tables developed from them, in Chapter 2 through the Conclusion, use scale scores adapted from the full relevant factor, thereby taking into account the potential for a given item to load differentially on several dimensions and much more accurately reflecting the underlying logic of the method—and the analysis. See esp. n. 12 to Chapter 3.

17. It is not difficult to find work after the fact that might (in principle) have foreshadowed this "surprise." Contemporary policy analyses of the cor-

nerstone of the U.S. welfare state—social security—describe a politics which bespeaks the divide between social insurance and social welfare, as with Martha Derthick, *Policymaking for Social Security* (Washington: Brookings Institution, 1979), or Derthick, *Agency under Stress: The Social Security Administration in American Government* (Washington: Brookings Institution, 1990). So does historical work about the evolution of this welfare state, when it asks why its programs did not go farther, as with many of the essays in Margaret Weir, Ann Shola Orloff, and Theda Skocpol, eds., *The Politics of Social Policy in the United States* (Princeton: Princeton UP, 1988).

18. In naming this dimension, we have obviously followed popular usage, dubbing it "civil rights" rather than "racial policy." In some abstract sense, civil rights is indeed only a subset of civil liberties, as the items in the Times Mirror survey are arguably more about racial policy than civil rights. Yet popular convention accords with the former usage (apparently shared by all of the major social groups in our sample; see Chapter 3), and in a study of political opinion—*public* political opinion—it seemed better for us to conform as well. For more on various policies themselves, see Hugh Davis Graham, *The Civil Rights Era: Origin and Development of National Policy, 1960–1972* (New York: Oxford UP, 1990).

19. Such scholarly work spans, at the very least, Samuel A. Stouffer, *Communism, Conformity, and Civil Liberties* (New York: Doubleday, 1955), through Herbert McClosky and Alida Brill, *Dimensions of Tolerance: What Americans Believe about Civil Liberties* (New York: Russell Sage, 1983). One examination of the political contours of the area is Jonathan Casper, *The Politics of Civil Liberties* (New York: Harper & Row, 1972). For one of the central specific incarnations in postwar politics, McCarthyism, see David M. Oshinsky, *A Conspiracy So Immense: The World of Joe McCarthy* (New York: Free Press, 1983), and Thomas C. Reeves, *The Life and Times of Joe McCarthy* (Melbourne: Krieger, 1982).

20. For this analysis, we inverted some of the first-order factors so that all positive scores would convey liberal preferences (and all negative scores, conservative preferences). Many contemporary analysts, with other purposes in mind, would turn at this point to a two-factor solution to avoid some of the statistical ambiguities of second-order factors. Given the approach to political opinion that guides our larger argument—individual issues, reflecting surface dimensions, reflecting deeper factors—*and* given a strong desire not to predetermine the number and/or nature of the resulting factors, we felt that a second-order factor analysis was the appropriate procedure here. On the other hand, it was also easy, after the fact, to impose a forced two-factor solution on these same data, as a kind of additional check. The result was effectively indistinguishable, yielding correlations between the two measures for the cultural/national factor of .97 and between the two measures for the economic/welfare factor of .98.

21. This is a frequent subtext in journalistic analyses which assert that a given (reliably losing) candidate failed either through nonresponse or through

"wrong" answers; see, for example, Jack W. Germond and Jules Witcover, *Whose Broad Stripes and Bright Stars? The Trivial Pursuit of the Presidency* (New York: Warner, 1989). At the opposite pole of systematic concern and intellectual rigor, a concentration on positioning and repositioning was central to the fountainhead of work on spatial modeling in politics, Anthony Downs, *An Economic Theory of Democracy* (New York: Harper & Row, 1957).

Chapter 3: Political Parties and Partisan Preferences

1. For this particular brave new world in general, see Jean H. Converse, *Survey Research in the United States: Roots and Emergence, 1890–1960* (Berkeley: U of California P, 1987), and Herbert H. Hyman, *Taking Society's Measure: A Personal History of Survey Research* (New York: Russell Sage, 1985).

2. Paul F. Lazarsfeld, Bernard Berelson, and Hazel Gaudet, *The People's Choice: How the Voter Makes Up His Mind in a Presidential Campaign* (New York: Duell, Sloan & Pearce, 1944); Bernard F. Berelson, Paul F. Lazarsfeld, and William N. McPhee, *Voting: A Study of Opinion Formation in a Presidential Campaign* (Chicago: U of Chicago P, 1954).

3. Lazarsfeld, Berelson, and Gaudet, *The People's Choice*, p. 27.

4. Berelson, Lazarsfeld, and McPhee, *Voting*, p. 73.

5. Angus Campbell, Gerald Gurin, and Warren E. Miller, *The Voter Decides* (Evanston: Row, Peterson, 1954), pp. 85–86.

6. Angus Campbell, Philip E. Converse, Warren E. Miller, and Donald E. Stokes, *The American Voter* (New York: Wiley, 1960); Angus Campbell, Philip E. Converse, Warren E. Miller, and Donald E. Stokes, *Elections and the Political Order* (New York: Wiley, 1966).

7. Angus Campbell et al., *The American Voter: An Abridgment* (New York: Wiley, 1964), p. 73.

8. Ibid., p. 273.

9. Three extremely consequential pieces of this edifice are collected as the first three substantive chapters of Campbell et al., *Elections and the Political Order:* Philip E. Converse, "The Concept of a Normal Vote"; Angus Campbell, "Surge and Decline: A Study of Electoral Change"; and Campbell, "A Classification of the Presidential Elections." See also John R. Petrocik, "An Expected Party Vote: New Data for an Old Concept," *American Journal of Political Science* 33 (Feb. 1989), 44–66.

10. Campbell, Gurin, and Miller, "The Questionnaires," in *The Voter Decides*, esp. pp. 217–18.

11. Other aspects of this distinction have been more controversial. See Bruce E. Keith, David B. Magleby, Candice J. Nelson, Elizabeth Orr, Mark C. Westlye, and Raymond E. Wolfinger, *The Myth of the Independent Voter* (Berkeley: U of California P, 1991), and its predecessor, Keith et al., "The Partisan Affinities of Independent 'Leaners,'" *British Journal of Political Science* 16 (April

1986), 155–84. They are dissenting both from the original formulation in Campbell et al., *The American Voter,* chap. 5 ff., and from subsequent interpretations, as with Norman H. Nie, Sidney Verba, and John R. Petrocik, *The Changing American Voter* (Cambridge: Harvard UP, 1976).

12. Precise derivations for these weighted scales are presented below. In constructing them, all issue items were recoded to a range of 1 to 4. (Most items began with four-category responses; the intermediate category in three-category items was assigned the value of 2.5.) The weighting itself consists of the square of the factor loading for surface dimensions and the square of the item correlation for deep factors, using the five highest loadings/correlations in each case. The full texts of these items (presented here only by their variable numbers, from Table 1.1) are offered in Appendix A. Accordingly:

Cultural values = .45 × V40206 + .41 × V40207 + .32 × V20101 + .29 × V20103 + .27 × V40211;

Social welfare = .55 × V40025 + .53 × V40026 + .50 × V40024 + .20 × V20006 + .14 × V40032;

Foreign relations = .43 × V20104 + .36 × V40035 + .32 × V20105 + .28 × V210 + .23 × V212;

Social insurance = .29 × V20009 + .28 × V20003 + .24 × V20114 + .18 × V20110 + .10 × V40022;

Civil rights = .58 × V20008 + .37 × V40032 + .27 × V40023 + .18 × V20006 + .14 × V40025;

Civil liberties = .46 × V40207 + .45 × V40209 + .38 × V40210 + .22 × V40213 + .19 × V20106;

Cultural/national = .61 × V40207 + .53 × V40206 + .38 × V20103 + .32 × V20101 + .30 × V40213;

Economic/welfare = .52 × V20008 + .49 × V 40025 + .42 × V 40026 + .36 × V 40024 + .34 × V40032.

Across the 4,820 cases for which factors scores can be obtained on the deep factors and surface dimensions, the correlations between these factor scores and their counterpart scale scores vary from .93 to .99, with a mean of .96.

13. The main risk in proceeding in this fashion involves the possibility that a greatly expanded sample would not actually put these items together in the way that the (sub)sample from the initial factor analysis did. This is the risk that not just subgroup scores but the actual factor structure might have been different had it been possible to use more respondents initially. In one check on this possibility, we took only three items for each initial (surface) dimension and factor-analyzed responses to these. This reduced the number of answers demanded, from 30 to 18; it correspondingly increased the total sample, from 4,820 to 6,997. Yet it did not change the factor structure, in its essence, at all. The eigenvalue for the sixth surface dimension, civil liberties, did skirt the conventional minimum, at .98. But its contents were identical, and if it is allowed

into the analysis, then the same six surface dimensions and the same two deep factors do appear—for a much larger sample. For an additional check on these measures, see note 17 below.

14. For scaling purposes, the two deep factors have been additionally rotated, so as to be orthogonal. Because these two factors were essentially unrelated after the original oblique rotation—scores on them correlated at .041—there is effectively no distortion in making this further adjustment, while it does make graphic displays, as in Fig. 3.3, considerably simpler.

15. Leon Epstein, *Political Parties in the American Mold* (Madison: U of Wisconsin P, 1986), and Samuel J. Eldersveld, *Political Parties in American Society* (New York: Basic Books, 1982). See also Martin J. Wattenberg, *The Decline of American Political Parties, 1952–1984* (Cambridge: Harvard UP, 1984).

16. A wide-ranging canvass of American attitudes within this orthodox theoretical categorization is Tom W. Smith, "Liberal and Conservative Trends in the United States since World War II," *Public Opinion Quarterly* 54 (Winter 1990), 479–507. A more focused application is William R. Shaffer, *Party and Ideology in the United States Congress* (Lanham, Md.: UP of America, 1980). And an emphasis on the social roots of preferences, along with a dissent from the intellectually necessary character of connections among them, is Robert E. Lane, "Patterns of Political Belief," in Jeanne N. Knutson, ed., *Handbook of Political Psychology* (San Francisco: Jossey-Bass, 1973), 83–116.

17. As an additional check on this way of proceeding, we did construct alternative weighted scales for these two deep factors. Precisely because these two factors are more comprehensive, it might be argued that they should have larger scales, encompassing more items. On the other hand, larger scales would also demand more responses, shrinking the available sample and reducing reliability. Moreover, loadings become smaller and smaller with additional items, so that such an expansion is not very likely to produce additional, different, *substantive* interpretations.

Nevertheless, we did create seven-item scales for the two deep factors, constituted as follows:

Cultural/national = .61 × V40207 + .53 × V40206 + .38 × V20103 + .32 × V20101 + .30 × V40213 + .30 × V40211 + .29 × V20106;

Economic/welfare = .52 × V20008 + .49 × V40025 + .42 × V40026 + .36 × V40024 + .34 × V40032 + .32 × V20006 + .21 × V20009.

In operation, these seven-item weighted scales actually reduced the available sample by only a little more than 300 (3%). Yet the seven-item and the five-item scales correlated at .98 and .97 for cultural/national and economic/welfare preferences, respectively; and most table entries using the two sets of scales were absolutely identical. As a result, we have retained the original five-item scales throughout.

18. James L. Sundquist, *Dynamics of the Party System: Alignment and Realignment of Political Parties in the United States* (Washington, D.C.: Brookings

Institution, 1973), chaps. 10–12; Everett C. Ladd, Jr., with Charles D. Hadley, *Transformations of the American Party System* (New York: Norton, 1975), chaps. 1–2; and Richard Jensen, "The Last Party System: Decay of Consensus, 1932–1980," chaps. 6 in Paul Kleppner et al., *The Evolution of American Electoral Systems* (Westport, Conn.: Greenwood, 1981).

19. Besides the works cited in note 3 to Chapter 2, see Stanley Feldman and John Zaller, "The Political Culture of Ambivalence: Ideological Responses to the Welfare State," *American Journal of Political Science* 36 (Feb. 1992), 268–307, and Edward G. Carmines and James A. Stimson, *Issue Evolution: Race and the Transformation of American Politics* (Princeton: Princeton UP, 1989).

20. Especially John H. Aldrich, John L. Sullivan, and Eugene Borgida, "Foreign Affairs and Issue Voting: Do Presidential Candidates Waltz before a Blind Audience?" *American Political Science Review* 83 (March 1989), 123–41. See also Jon Hurwitz and Mark Peffley, "The Means and Ends of Foreign Policy as Determinants of Presidential Support," *American Journal of Political Science* 31 (May 1987), 236–58, and a more impressionistic predecessor, Stephen Hess, "Does Foreign Policy Really Matter?" *The Wilson Quarterly* 4 (Winter 1980), 96–111.

21. Useful surveys of such views can be found in the opening sections of Epstein, *Political Parties in the American Mold*, and Eldersveld, *Political Parties in American Society*. Earlier, specific embodiments of these views, producing sharply contrasting further judgments from the same essential perceptions, are Pendleton Herring, *The Politics of Democracy: American Parties in Action* (New York: Norton, 1940), and E. E. Schattschneider, *Party Government* (New York: Holt, Rinehart and Winston, 1942).

22. This usage stems directly from V. O. Key, Jr., *Politics, Parties, and Pressure Groups*, 5th ed. (New York: Crowell, 1964), esp. pp. 163–65 but essentially throughout. For the place of the primary election in American politics, see in addition to Key's *Politics, Parties, and Pressure Groups*, his *American State Politics: An Introduction* (New York: Knopf, 1956), and Byron E. Shafer, "'Exceptionalism' in American Politics?" *PS: Political Science and Politics* 22 (Sept. 1989), 588–94.

23. Warren E. Miller and Santa A. Traugott, comps., *American National Election Studies Data Sourcebook, 1952–1986* (Cambridge: Harvard UP, 1989), p. 81.

24. A different approach, proceeding to very much the same type of conclusion, is George Rabinowitz and Stuart Elaine Macdonald, "A Directional Theory of Issue Voting," *American Political Science Review* 83 (March 1989), 93–121. See also Macdonald, Ola Listhaug, and Rabinowitz, "Issues and Party Support in Multiparty Systems," *American Political Science Review* 85 (Dec. 1991), 1107–31.

Chapter 4: Social Groups and Group Preferences

1. See esp. Henry E. Brady and Paul M. Sniderman, "Attitude Attribution: A Group Basis for Political Reasoning," *American Political Science Review* 79 (Dec. 1985), 1061–78. A further triangulation of social experience, political

opinion, and the survey process itself is sometimes noted: "For all of its techni
cal complexities, sample survey research remains an extension and elaboration
of the procedures through which ordinary people in the course of their every-
day lives acquire social knowledge. In coping with the exigencies of social life,
we are all amateur social researchers who daily survey our social terrain. Our
own well-being and the welfare of others depends on the collection, interpretation, transmission, and application of personal and social information that
enables us to live together. To acquire, construct, and employ this knowledge
we necessarily rely, as do professional survey researchers, on interviewing and
sampling." Hubert J. O'Gorman, Introduction to Herbert H. Hyman, *Taking
Society's Measure: A Personal History of Survey Research* (New York: Russell Sage,
1985), p. xvi.

2. Daniel J. Boorstin, *The Americans*, 3 vols.: *The Colonial Experience, The
National Experience*, and *The Democratic Experience* (New York: Random House,
1958–73); John Higham, *Strangers in the Land: Patterns of American Nativism,
1860–1925* (New Brunswick, N.J.: Rutgers UP, 1955); Seymour Martin Lipset,
Continental Divide: The Values and Institutions of the United States and Canada
(New York: Routledge, 1990); Richard Polenberg, *One Nation Divisible: Class,
Race, and Ethnicity in the United States* (New York: Viking, 1980); Lawrence H.
Fuchs, *The American Kaleidoscope: Race, Ethnicity, and the Civic Culture* (Hanover,
N.H.: UP of New England, 1990); Daniel J. Elazar, *The American Mosaic: The
Impact of Space, Time, and Culture on American Politics* (Boulder, Colo.: Westview
Press, 1994).

3. David A. Gerber, *The Making of an American Pluralism: Buffalo, New York,
1825–1860* (Urbana: U of Illinois P, 1989); Oscar Handlin, *The Uprooted* (Boston:
Little, Brown, 1951); Benjamin Brawley, *A Social History of the American Negro*
(New York: Collier, 1970); Stanley Lieberson, *A Piece of the Pie: Blacks and White
Immigrants since 1880* (Berkeley: U of California P, 1980); Thomas Sowell, *Ethnic
America: A History* (New York: Basic Books, 1981); Alejandro Portes and Ruben
G. Rumbaut, *Immigrant America: A Portrait* (Berkeley: U of California P, 1990).

4. Jon Butler, *Awash in a Sea of Faith: Christianizing the American People*
(Cambridge: Harvard UP, 1990); Robert Kelley, *The Cultural Pattern in American
Politics: The First Century* (Washington, D.C.: UP of America, 1979); Paul Klepp-
ner, *The Cross of Culture: A Social Analysis of Midwestern Politics, 1850–1900* (New
York: Free Press, 1970); Richard Jensen, *The Winning of the Midwest: Social and
Political Conflict, 1888–1896* (Chicago: U of Chicago P, 1971); Martin E. Marty, *A
Nation of Believers* (Chicago: U of Chicago P, 1976); Kenneth D. Wald, *Religion
and Politics in the United States*, 2nd ed. (Washington, D.C.: CQ Press, 1991).

5. Gary B. Nash, *The Urban Crucible: Social Change, Political Consciousness,
and the Origins of the American Revolution* (Cambridge: Harvard UP, 1979); Joel
H. Silbey, *The Partisan Imperative: The Dynamics of American Politics before the
Civil War* (New York: Oxford UP, 1985); Stuart M. Blumin, *The Emergence of the
Middle Class: Social Experience in America, 1760–1900* (Cambridge: Cambridge
UP, 1989); Robert H. Wiebe, *The Search for Order, 1877–1920* (New York: Hill &

Wang, 1967); Samuel P. Hays, *The Response to Industrialization, 1885–1914* (Chicago: U of Chicago P, 1957).

6. Generally, see Howard W. Odum and Harry Estell Moore, *American Regionalism: A Cultural-Historical Approach to National Integration* (New York: Henry Holt, 1938); Daniel J. Elazar, *American Federalism: A View from the States* (New York: Crowell, 1966); Richard Franklin Benzel, *Sectionalism and American Political Development: 1880–1980* (Madison: U of Wisconsin P, 1984); J. Clark Archer and Peter J. Taylor, *Section and Party: A Political Geography of American Presidential Elections from Andrew Jackson to Ronald Reagan* (New York: Research Studies, 1981). Yet for more than a hundred years, the most popular focus *within* the theme of regionalism has been the American South. See esp. W. J. Cash, *The Mind of the South* (New York: Knopf, 1941), and V. O. Key, Jr., *Southern Politics in State and Nation* (New York: Knopf, 1949).

7. Two very different types of overviews are Stanley Lieberson, *From Many Strands: Ethnic and Racial Groups in Contemporary America* (New York: Russell Sage, 1988), and Werner Sollors, *Beyond Ethnicity: Consent and Descent in American Culture* (New York: Oxford UP, 1986). More pointedly, see Richard D. Alba, *Ethnic Identity: The Transformation of White America* (New Haven: Yale UP, 1990); Guillermina Jasso and Mark R. Rosenzweig, *The New Chosen People: Immigrants in the United States* (New York: Russell Sage, 1990); Harold W. Stanley, *Voter Mobilization and the Politics of Race: The South and Universal Suffrage, 1952–1984* (New York: Praeger, 1987). See also Hugh Davis Graham, *The Civil Rights Era: Origin and Development of National Policy, 1960–1972* (New York: Oxford UP, 1990).

8. On secularization, see William S. Bainbridge, *The Future of Religion: Secularization, Revival, and Cult Formation* (Berkeley: U of California P, 1985), versus Andrew M. Greeley, *Religious Change in America* (Cambridge: Harvard UP, 1989). An extended examination of a single case is Theodore Caplow et al., *All Faithful People: Change and Continuity in Middletown's Religion* (Minneapolis: U of Minnesota P, 1983). Finally, for evangelical conservatism, Clyde Wilcox, *God's Warriors: The Christian Right in Twentieth-Century America* (Baltimore: Johns Hopkins UP, 1992), and Steve Bruce, *The Rise and Fall of the New Christian Right: Conservative Protestant Politics in America, 1978–1988* (Oxford: Oxford UP, 1988).

9. For the larger shift, Peter Blau and Otis D. Duncan, *The American Occupational Structure* (New York: Basic Books, 1967); Daniel Bell, *The Coming of Post-Industrial Society: A Venture in Social Forecasting* (New York: Basic Books, 1973); and Richard P. Coleman and Lee Rainwater, *Social Standing in America: New Dimensions of Class* (New York: Basic Books, 1978). More generally, see Richard F. Hamilton, *Class and Politics in the United States* (New York: Wiley, 1972), and Everett Carll Ladd, Jr., with Charles D. Hadley, *Transformations of the American Party System*, 2nd ed. (New York: Norton, 1978). See also Herbert H. Hyman, Charles R. Wright, and John S. Reed, *The Enduring Effects of Education* (Chicago: U of Chicago P, 1975), supplemented by Herbert S. Hyman and

Charles R. Wright, *Education's Lasting Influences on Values* (Chicago: U of Chicago P, 1979).

10. Generally, see Raymond G. Gastil, *Cultural Regions of the United States* (Seattle: Washington UP, 1975); Thad A. Brown, *Migration and Politics: The Impact of Population Mobility on American Voting Behavior* (Chapel Hill: U of North Carolina P, 1988); and William M. Lunch, *The Nationalization of American Politics* (Berkeley: U of California P, 1987). For the South specifically, see Earl Black and Merle Black, *Politics and Society in the South* (Cambridge: Harvard UP, 1987), and Alexander P. Lamis, *The Two-Party South*, 2nd expanded ed. (New York: Oxford UP, 1990).

11. The coding scheme used in the Times Mirror survey asked both "What is your religious preference?" and "Would you describe yourself as a 'born-again' or evangelical Christian?" This was not ideal for our chosen cut—we would have preferred a more specific, denominational inventory—but a blend of the two questions did allow a close approximation. In this, "non-Christians" answered "None," "Jewish," or "Other" to the first question; "Catholics" answered "Roman Catholic" or "Orthodox"; "low Protestants" answered "Protestant" to the first question and "Yes" to the second; and "High Protestants" answered "Protestant" and "No."

12. Accordingly, the Northeast encompassed Maine, New Hampshire, Vermont, Massachusetts, Rhode Island, Connecticut, New York, Pennsylvania, New Jersey, and the District of Columbia; the Midwest, Ohio, Michigan, Indiana, Illinois, Wisconsin, Minnesota, Iowa, Missouri, North Dakota, South Dakota, Nebraska, and Kansas; the South, Maryland, Delaware, Virginia, West Virginia, North Carolina, South Carolina, Georgia, Florida, Kentucky, Tennessee, Alabama, Mississippi, Arkansas, Louisiana, Oklahoma, and Texas; and the West, Montana, Idaho, Wyoming, Colorado, Utah, Nevada, New Mexico, Arizona, Washington, Oregon, California, Alaska, and Hawaii.

13. For our purposes (though not, we would emphasize, for many others), both sides of the argument over electoral nationalization can be read to support this view: that the simple concentration of other characteristics, rather than region itself, is what underpins apparent regional differences in our time. See Donald E. Stokes, "A Variance Components Model of Political Effects," in John M. Claunch, ed., *Mathematical Applications in Political Science* (Dallas: Arnold, 1965); William Claggett, William Flanigan, and Nancy Zingale, "Nationalization of the American Electorate," *American Political Science Review* 78 (March 1984), 77–91; and Laura L. Vertz, John P. Frendreis, and James L. Gibson, "Nationalization of the Electorate in the United States," *American Political Science Review* 81 (Sept. 1987), 961–66. More generally, see Lunch, *The Nationalization of American Politics;* see also Harold W. Stanley, "Southern Partisan Changes: Dealignment, Realignment, or Both?" *Journal of Politics* 50 (Feb. 1988), 64–88.

14. As ever, assuming straightforward execution, the final validation of such an approach must lie in the substantive contributions which it can offer. It

should be noted at the outset, however, that such an approach is somewhat different from isolating the *variables*—scalable social characteristics, in this case—that explain the largest amount of statistical variance. The latter is a frequent focus of related work and is often, depending on the purpose at hand, the appropriate focus. Our intention, by contrast, was to isolate opinion subgroups in American society, specific and distinctive social subcategories when judged by their composite political preferences. For a more sustained examination of the concept of "group," see David B. Truman, *The Governmental Process: Political Interests and Public Opinion* (New York: Knopf, 1951), especially chap. 2, "Groups and Society."

15. Efforts to go farther, in a variety of realms with a variety of approaches, can be found in Byron E. Shafer, ed., *Is America Different? A New Look at American Exceptionalism* (Oxford: Oxford UP, 1991). See also Nathan Glazer and Daniel P. Moynihan, *Beyond the Melting Pot: The Negroes, Puerto Ricans, Jews, Italians, and Irish of New York City* (Cambridge: MIT Press, 1963).

16. This probably reflects a sharp change from an earlier era, when regional subcultures—regionalized ways of viewing and valuing politics and public policy—were themselves substantial and distinctive. Earlier arguments about regional distinctiveness cannot be well addressed through contemporary data, however, so that the extent of the resulting change must remain unknown. Otherwise, the essence of the argument here is much akin to that of Paul Allen Beck and Paul Lopatto, "The End of Southern Distinctiveness," in Laurence W. Morehead, Tod A. Baker, and Robert P. Steed, eds., *Contemporary Southern Political Attitudes and Behavior* (New York: Praeger, 1982). An explicit dissent is John Shelton Reed, "New South or No South? Regional Culture in 2036," in Joseph S. Himes, ed., *The South Moves into Its Future: Studies in the Analysis and Prediction of Social Change* (Tuscaloosa: U of Alabama P, 1991).

17. See note 4 above.

18. The concept of "cross-pressure" is considered more critically, and used more self-consciously, at the end of Chapter 5. See also note 8 to that chapter.

Chapter 5: A Framework for Politicking

1. A different but intriguing aspect of this relationship is addressed in Arthur H. Miller and Christopher Wlezien, "The Social Group Dynamics of Partisan Evaluations," *Electoral Studies* 12 (Mar. 1993), 5–22. A more familiar aspect involves parties, groups, and the vote; see, for instance, Robert Axelrod, "Where the Vote Comes From: An Analysis of Electoral Coalitions, 1952–1968," *American Political Science Review* 66 (March 1972), 11–20; Harold W. Stanley, William T. Bianco, and Richard G. Niemi, "Partisanship and Group Support over Time: A Multivariate Analysis," *American Political Science Review* 80 (Sept. 1986), 969–76; and Robert S. Erikson, Thomas D. Lancaster, and David W. Romero, "Group Components of the Presidential Vote, 1952–1984," *Journal of Politics* 51 (May 1989), 337–46.

2. As it began for the keystone works based on public opinion surveys: for example, Angus Campbell, Philip E. Converse, Warren E. Miller, and Donald E. Stokes, "Membership in Social Groupings" and "The Role of Social Class," chaps. 11 and 12 in Campbell et al., *The American Voter* (New York: Wiley, 1960). A more contemporary overview, a generation later, is David Knoke, *Change and Continuity in American Politics: The Social Base of Political Parties* (Baltimore: Johns Hopkins UP, 1976).

3. This, too, is an established theme in writings about American political parties, as in Pendleton Herring, *The Politics of Democracy: American Parties in Action* (New York: Norton, 1940), or Austin Ranney and Willmoore Kendall, *Democracy and the American Party System* (New York: Harcourt, Brace, & World, 1956). See also Daniel J. Boorstin, *The Genius of American Politics* (Chicago: U of Chicago P, 1953).

4. The further strategic implications of this simple balance of homogeneity/heterogeneity are presumably also double-edged. On the one hand, a candidate or program capable of uniting the Democratic party presumably *is* more difficult to discover than one capable of uniting the Republicans. On the other hand, since the Democratic party remains the party of choice for the American public as a whole, Republican strategists may find that holding those members whose groups do *not* make a large contribution to their party is nevertheless more important (and more stressful). Other, highly diverse ways of thinking about this balance are gathered in Seymour Martin Lipset, ed., *Party Coalitions in the 1980s* (San Francisco: ICS, 1981). See also Andrew M. Greeley, *Building Coalitions: American Politics in the 1970s* (Chicago: U of Chicago P, 1974).

5. The small number of black Republicans in our sample (and the concomitant risk that a few more respondents would change their apparent preferences sharply) does ban them from the figures that follow. On the other hand, those Republican blacks who did surface in the Times Mirror survey provide a factional profile entirely consistent with hints implicit in the preceding analysis. First, here more than anywhere else, group membership appears to subsume all opinion differences between group partisans. Thus, for opinions on the two deep factors,

Democratic and Republican Blacks displayed the following scores:

	Cultural/ National	N	Economic/ Welfare	N
Black Democrats	−.21	913	+1.03	1,076
Black Republicans	−.35	126	+.86	136

Second, and following from this, if there were to be a substantial increase in the number and share of black Republicans, then the Republican party would not only acquire a social heterogeneity closer to that of the Democrats. It would also acquire more of the attitudinal heterogeneity on economic/welfare matters which, as we shall see, also distinguishes the Democratic from the Republican party. Or at least, existing Republican blacks are wildly liberal on these matters, in their own right but especially when compared to the entire rest of their chosen party.

6. One direct ancestor to these findings on the organizing focus of economic/ welfare versus cultural/national issues is Everett Carll Ladd, Jr., and Charles D. Hadley, *Political Parties and Political Issues: Patterns in Differentiation since the New Deal* (Beverly Hills: Sage, 1973).

7. Two alternative and highly stimulating ways to think about these same sorts of relationships are presented in John R. Petrocik, *Party Coalitions: Realignment and the Decline of the New Deal Party System* (Chicago: U of Chicago P, 1981), and Richard Rose and Ian McAllister, *The Loyalties of Voters: A Lifetime Learning Model* (London: Sage, 1990).

8. The basic concept of cross-pressure is usually attributed to Georg Simmel, *Der Konflikt der modernen Kultur* (Munich: Duncker & Humblot, 1921), available in English as Simmel, *Conflict and the Web of Group Affiliations*, trans. Kurt H. Wolff and Reinhard Bendix (New York: Free Press, 1955). The first effective empirical use of the concept is usually considered to be Paul F. Lazarsfeld, Bernard Berelson, and Hazel Gaudet, *The People's Choice: How the Voter Makes Up His Mind in a Presidential Campaign* (New York: Duell, Sloan & Pearce, 1944), esp. chap. 6, "Time of Final Decision." A lengthy modern consideration is Peter W. Sperlich, *Conflict and Harmony in Human Affairs: A Study of Cross-Pressures and Political Behavior* (Chicago: Rand-McNally, 1971).

9. For the black voting record, see the works cited in note 1, above. On the other side of the aisle, the some-college Republicans, while less stark in their preferences, could have been used to make the same point. Thus, while they are modestly liberal on cultural/national matters, at +.11, and while this does move them closer to the Democratic party on this (deep) factor, that preference (and this attraction) are dwarfed by their very conservative position on economic/ welfare concerns, at −.52—which is also, of course, far closer to Republican than to Democratic party positions overall.

10. On low Protestants in American life, see, in addition to the works cited in notes 4 and 8 to Chapter 4, George Marsden, *Fundamentalism and American Culture: The Shaping of Twentieth-Century Evangelicalism* (Oxford: Oxford UP, 1980), and James D. Hunter, *American Evangelicalism: Conservative Religion and the Quandary of Modernity* (New Brunswick: Rutgers UP, 1983).

11. One major part of this faction, Republican nonbelievers, is largely subsumed within the category of "enterprise Republicans" ("enterprisers") in the Times Mirror's own analysis of these data. See the Gallup Organization Staff, eds., *The People, the Press, and Politics: The Times Mirror Study of the American Electorate* (Reading: Addison-Wesley, 1988), pp. 13 ff. The politics of the other major part of this faction, Republican Jews, is subject to recurring debate within the American Jewish community itself. See, for example, Lucy S. Davidowicz, "Politics, the Jews, and the '84 Election," *Commentary* 79 (Feb. 1985), 25–30; Milton Himmelfarb, "American Jews: Diehard Conservatives," *Commentary*

87 (Apr. 1989), 44–49; and Jay P. Lefkowitz, "Jewish Voters and the Democrats," *Commentary* 95 (Apr. 1993), 38–41.

12. White Americans with less than a high-school education have largely disappeared as a separate focus for investigation, a fate reflecting their decline as a share of the American public. Useful information about the changing character of this declining group, however, can still be teased out of work on generational shifts in American politics more generally, esp. Paul R. Abramson, *Generational Change in American Politics* (Lexington, Mass.: D.C. Heath, 1975), and M. Kent Jennings and Richard G. Niemi, *Generations and Politics* (Princeton: Princeton UP, 1981).

13. These ambiguous "middle Americans" were restored to analytic centrality by Richard M. Scammon and Ben J. Wattenberg, who dubbed them "unyoung, unpoor, and unblack," in Scammon and Wattenberg, *The Real Majority* (New York: Coward-McCann, 1970). Their metaphorical exemplar, later sought out in real life by the news media, was "the forty-seven-year-old wife of a machinist in Dayton, Ohio" (ibid., pp. 46 ff.). Diverse further takes on the political possibilities inherent in this group include John Kenneth White, *The New Politics of Old Values* (Hanover: UP of New England, 1988); Daniel Yankelovich, *New Rules: Searching for Self-Fulfillment in a World Turned Upside Down* (New York: Random House, 1981); and Herbert J. Gans, *Middle American Individualism: Political Participation and Liberal Democracy* (New York: Oxford UP, 1988).

Chapter 6: Activists, Followers, and Political Preferences

1. A comprehensive survey and organization of related findings is Lester W. Milbrath and M. L. Goel, *Political Participation,* 2nd ed. (Chicago: Rand-McNally, 1977). A more thematic overview, for the United States, is provided by Sidney Verba and Norman H. Nie, *Participation in America: Political Democracy and Social Equality* (New York: Harper & Row, 1972). For an international overview from the elite side, see Robert D. Putnam, *The Comparative Study of Political Elites* (Englewood Cliffs, N.J.: Prentice-Hall, 1976).

2. Despite this, activists rarely achieve pride of place in studies on politics, appearing mainly in conjunction with other topics. A major exception is Warren E. Miller and M. Kent Jennings, *Parties in Transition: A Longitudinal Study of Party Elites and Party Supporters* (New York: Russell Sage, 1986). Also see the very suggestive essay by Samuel J. Eldersveld, "Party Activists: The Working Elites at the Base of the Political System," chap. 9 in Eldersveld, *Political Parties in American Society* (New York: Basic Books, 1982), and, in a somewhat different form, Alan Ware, *The Breakdown of Democratic Party Organization, 1940–1980* (Oxford: Oxford UP, 1985).

3. The landmark for "implicit representation" is surely Gabriel A. Almond and Sidney Verba, *The Civic Culture: Political Attitudes and Democracy in Five Nations* (Princeton: Princeton UP, 1963). Works on the technical end would include Larry J. Sabato, *The Rise of Political Consultants: New Ways of Winning*

Elections (New York: Basic Books, 1981); Frank I. Luntz, *Candidates, Consultants, and Campaigns: The Style and Substance of American Electioneering* (Oxford: Basil Blackwell, 1988); and Ann Beaudry and Bob Schaeffer, *Winning Local and State Elections: The Guide to Organizing Your Campaign* (New York: Free Press, 1986).

4. The fountainhead for this view is Roberto Michels, *Political Parties: A Sociological Study of the Oligarchical Tendencies of Modern Democracy*, trans. Eden Paul and Cedar Paul, introd. Seymour Martin Lipset (New York: Free Press, 1962), originally published as Michels, *Zur Soziologie des Parteiwesens in der modernen Demokratie* (Stuttgart: Alfred Kroner, 1911).

5. The great original embodiment of this view is Vilfredo Pareto, *Compendium of General Sociology*, abr. Giulio Farina, trans. Elizabeth Abbott (Minneapolis: U of Minnesota P, 1980), initially published as Pareto, *Trattato di Sociologie Generale*, 3 vols. (Florence: Barbera, 1916).

6. This perspective can be rooted, though with a bit more room for argument, in Gaetano Mosca, *The Ruling Class*, trans. Hannah D. Kahn, rev. and introd. Arthur Livingston (New York: McGraw-Hill, 1939), published originally as Mosca, *Elementi di Scienza Politica* (Turin: Bocca, 1896).

7. For example, James W. Prothro and Charles M. Grigg, "Fundamental Principles of Democracy: Bases of Agreement and Disagreement," *Journal of Politics* 22 (May 1960), 276–94, and V. O. Key, Jr., "Public Opinion and the Decay of Democracy," *Virginia Quarterly Review* 37 (Autumn 1961), 481–94. Background to these would include T. W. Adorno, Else Frenkel-Brunswick, Daniel J. Levinson, and R. Nevitt Sanford, *The Authoritarian Personality*, parts 1–2 (New York: Harper & Row, 1950), and Samuel Stouffer, *Communism, Conformity, and Civil Liberties* (New York: Doubleday, 1955).

8. The work of Herbert McClosky, extensively cited below, is perhaps most indicative of such work at the time. Successors in that tradition would certainly include Jeane J. Kirkpatrick, *The New Presidential Elite: Men and Women in National Politics* (New York: Russell Sage, 1976); Miller and Jennings, *Parties in Transition;* and even Byron E. Shafer, *Bifurcated Politics: Evolution and Reform in the National Party Convention* (Cambridge: Harvard UP, 1988), esp. pp. 100–107.

9. Herbert McClosky, Paul J. Hoffman, and Rosemary O'Hara, "Issue Conflict and Consensus among Party Leaders and Followers," *American Political Science Review* 54 (June 1960), 406–27, and Herbert McClosky, "Consensus and Ideology in American Politics," *American Political Science Review* 58 (June 1964), 361–82.

10. McClosky, "Consensus and Ideology," p. 363. Other main pieces of the same general body of work include Herbert McClosky, "Conservatism and Personality," *American Political Science Review* 52 (March 1958), 27–45, and Herbert McClosky and John Schaar, "Psychological Dimensions of Anomie," *American Sociological Review* 30 (Feb. 1965), 14–40.

11. McClosky, "Consensus and Ideology," pp. 373–74.

12. McClosky, "Issue Conflict and Consensus," pp. 425–26.

13. An early major attempt at synthesizing what we know about the varieties of political participation is Robert E. Lane, *Political Life: Why and How People Get Involved in Politics* (New York: Free Press, 1959). An early study of the variant of this activity which is most implicit (and least easily captured) is Elihu Katz and Paul F. Lazarsfeld, *Personal Influence: The Part Played by People in the Flow of Mass Communication* (New York: Free Press, 1955). What is in some sense the other end of this continuum, involving engagement with specific governmental outcomes, is Richard Rose, *Ordinary People in Public Policy: A Behavioral Analysis* (Newbury Park, Calif.: Sage, 1989).

14. This perspective can unite such otherwise diverse works from journalistic observers as David S. Broder, *Changing of the Guard: Power and Leadership in America* (New York: Simon and Schuster, 1980); Hedrick Smith, *The Power Game: How Washington Works* (New York: Random House, 1988); and Alan Ehrenhalt, *The United States of Ambition: Politicians, Power, and the Pursuit of Office* (New York: Times Books, 1991).

15. The richest exposition of this view may be Robert A. Dahl, *Who Governs? Democracy and Power in an American City* (New Haven: Yale UP, 1961); see especially the schematic rendering at p. 164. The view is further systematized in Dahl, *Modern Political Analysis* (Englewood Cliffs, N.J.: Prentice-Hall, 1963), esp. chap. 6, "Political Man." More generally, see Lester W. Milbrath, *Political Participation: How and Why Do People Get Involved in Politics?* (Chicago: Rand McNally, 1965), esp. "The General Dimension of Involvement," pp. 16–22.

16. W. Russell Neuman, *The Paradox of Mass Politics: Knowledge and Opinion in the American Electorate* (Cambridge: Harvard UP, 1986), pp. 170–71.

17. Sidney Verba and Norman H. Nie, *Participation in America: Political Democracy and Social Equality* (New York: Harper & Row, 1972), p. 80.

18. As an additional check on this procedure, beyond the substance of the items themselves, these seven items were submitted to a "principal-axis" factor analysis. A two-factor solution just barely emerged, but (a) the second factor had an initial eigenvalue of only 1.01; (b) this factor accounted for only 6.0% of variance in the rotated solution (compared with 33.3% for the first factor); and (c) the two factors were strongly correlated even then ($r = .69$). The simplicity and utility of a single dimension for participation, accordingly, does not do serious injustice to the data. Nevertheless, for an analysis employing both factors, see note 20 below.

19. See note 22 below for some additional comparisons across time and for some thoughts on the difficulties in making such comparisons with any confidence.

20. At the level which they can reach, our data in fact suggest that a single dimension of political participation does not seriously misrepresent reality. On the other hand, the factor analysis discussed in note 18 (above) did reveal a marginally two-dimensional solution, and each dimension does have a very straightforward interpretation. One attracts the three items that, on their

Specialist Elites and Their Rank and File
on the Deep Factors

A. Cultural/National

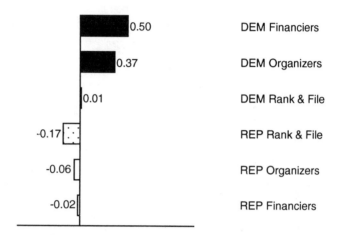

0.50	DEM Financiers
0.37	DEM Organizers
0.01	DEM Rank & File
-0.17	REP Rank & File
-0.06	REP Organizers
-0.02	REP Financiers

Specialist Elites and Their Rank and File
on the Deep Factors

B. Economic/Welfare

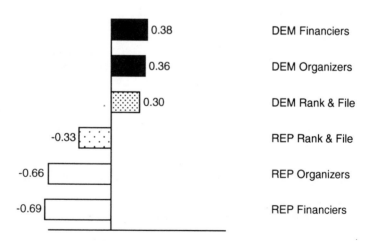

0.38	DEM Financiers
0.36	DEM Organizers
0.30	DEM Rank & File
-0.33	REP Rank & File
-0.66	REP Organizers
-0.69	REP Financiers

face, involve organizational activism; the other attracts the three involving financial activism instead. (The tax check-off item does not load strongly on either.)

Accordingly, it is possible to create two separate activism scales, for organization and for finance; to divide each into its leaders (those who engage in two or more of these activities) and its followers (those who engage in one or less); and to compare policy preferences of organizational versus financial elites, and of both groups versus the rank and file.

Certain modest but consistent distinctions between the two types of activist do surface. Thus, the financial activists are more liberal than the organizational activists on cultural/national issues in both parties, just as they are more conservative than the organizational activists in both parties on economic/welfare concerns. Yet the more consequential fact is that these differences pale into insignificance when leaders—organizational or financial—are compared to their own followers.

Indeed, from that perspective, both variants of activist look essentially like the total undifferentiated active population. Thus, Republican organizational and financial activists are still essentially clustered with the Republican as well as the Democratic rank and file on cultural/national matters, to be opposed by a cluster comprised (solely) of Democratic organizational and financial activists. Likewise, the Democratic rank and file, plus its organizational and its financial activists, are essentially clustered on economic/welfare matters, with the Republican rank and file off to their collective right, while the Republican organizational and financial activists, jointly, contribute the far right-hand end.

Again, better or more exclusive data might restore the hypothesized differences. But these data, within the limits of a national sample and with a focus on deep factors and surface dimensions, do not argue the need for a functional specialization in the analysis of our active partisans.

21. Indeed, there are some additional advantages in being able to proceed in this fashion—that is, by way of an activist population isolated through a national sample. At a minimum, this guarantees that precisely the same questions are asked of all respondents at the same point in time. Moreover, it escapes many of the peculiarities associated with the most frequent surrogate population of party activists, namely, national convention delegates, who are always selected by varying criteria and whose selection is not even reliably contingent on a continuously high level of activity.

22. The current civil liberties dimension is also the ideal opportunity to emphasize the difficulties in using contemporary measures to talk about change across the postwar years, and the need for extreme self-consciousness when doing so. On the one hand, the situation on this measure of civil liberties does parallel, strongly, the situation uncovered by McClosky in the immediate postwar years. On the other hand, this parallel is based upon a comparison to our surface dimension of civil liberties, and not to our deep factor of cultural/national values.

Indeed, careful disaggregation of the McClosky studies, by attending to individual items within them, not only emphasizes the risks in talking about "change" through dissimilar measures. It actually raises an alternative hypothesis about the issue structure of politics. To wit: Issue dimensions and alignments on them have changed remarkably little in the postwar period, but the centrality of one or another deep factor or surface dimension to practical politicking has changed substantially.

Nothing in the data—either McClosky's or ours—can comment definitively on this hypothesis. Yet there are hints. Or at least, there are individual items in the original McClosky presentation which do behave, for example, like the cultural values and social insurance dimensions of the current study. Thus, "social security benefits" and "minimum wages" feature the same liberal-to-conservative array, stretching from Democratic identifiers on the left to Republican activists on the right, as the social-insurance dimension does today.

The cultural-values dimension is more difficult to treat by analogy through the McClosky data, but "immigration to the United States," perhaps the closest single item, does feature the familiar elites-versus-masses division of this dimension. On the immigration item, Democratic elites may still be more liberal than Republican elites, yet *both* are sharply more liberal than Democratic or Republican masses, which are nearly interchangeable. See McClosky, "Issue Conflict and Consensus," esp. Table II-C, p. 413.

23. These numbers also confirm that the more active participants were those contributing most of the apparent partisan tone to cultural/national matters. Thus, these individuals show a clear partisan distinction on both deep factors, by every measure. Yet now, the other side of that coin is that less active partisans, while still showing a clear partisan connection on economic/welfare matters, no longer (in the absence of their fellow activists) show much of a (party-related) difference on cultural/national concerns.

24. The cultural/national factor also provides a precise example of the mechanics of this transformation. Thus, at Fig. 6.3 (with a midpoint of ± .00), Republican activists stood at −.02 and Democratic activists at +.48. However, the new midpoint—halfway between them—is +.23, and the two rank and files must be rescaled accordingly. The Republican rank and file, previously at −.17, is now an additional .23 *below* the new midpoint, giving it a score of −.40 (−.17 minus .23). Moreover, the Democratic rank and file, previously at +.01, is now below this new midpoint as well, giving *it* a score of −.22 (+.01 minus .23).

Chapter 7: The War inside the Parties

1. The seminal piece here is Peter B. Clark and James Q. Wilson, "Incentive Systems: A Theory of Organizations," *Administrative Science Quarterly* 6 (Sept. 1961), 219–66, elaborated and enriched in Wilson, *Political Organizations* (New York: Basic Books, 1973). See also Joseph A. Schlesinger, "On the Theory of Party Organization," *Journal of Politics* 46 (May 1984), 369–400, leading on to Schlesinger, *Political Parties and the Winning of Office* (Ann Arbor: U of Michigan P, 1991).

2. An impressionistic and a systematic look at the underlying change, respectively, are David S. Broder, *The Party's Over: The Failure of Politics in America* (New York: Harper & Row, 1971), and Jeane J. Kirkpatrick, *The New Presidential Elite: Men and Women in National Politics* (New York: Russell Sage, 1976). On the Republicans, see also Robert D. Novak, *The Agony of the GOP, 1964* (New York: Macmillan, 1965), and Nicol C. Rae, *The Decline and Fall of the Liberal Republicans: From 1952 to the Present* (New York: Oxford UP, 1989). For the Democrats, see Byron E. Shafer, *Quiet Revolution: The Struggle for the Democratic Party and the Shaping of Post-Reform Politics* (New York: Russell Sage, 1983), and Alan J. Ware, *The Breakdown of Democratic Party Organization, 1940–1980* (Oxford: Oxford UP, 1985).

3. Leon D. Epstein, *Political Parties in the American Mold* (Madison: U of Wisconsin P, 1986), pp. 5–6. An even more forceful summation comes from John H. Kessel:

> Important as these party differences are, the similarities between the parties are more consequential . . . it is clear that much more emphasis is placed on issues than on any other activity. The next most important party norms, those concerning party service and patronage, come a long way back of the issue items. As of the 1970s, most activists in electoral politics have a strong interest in the policies followed by the government once the election is over. It would be too much to say that an interest in issues draws them to political life in the first place. The activists are likely to speak of their motivations in global terms; they are attracted to politics per se. But it is also clear that an interest in issues is an important component in the attraction to politics, and in the way they participate once they become involved.
>
> Electoral activists agree with their party colleagues to a greater degree than they agree with their constituents . . . Even more important, these scores tell us we can know more about activists' attitudes by learning whether they are Republicans or Democrats than by knowing anything about attitudes in the communities from which they come. The implication is that they are not giving voice to their constituents' views. Rather, they are urging policies that their party colleagues think wise. Our electoral parties are not representative entities, but *advocacy parties.*

Kessel, *Presidential Campaign Politics: Coalition Strategies and Citizen Response* (Homewood, Ill.: Dorsey, 1980), pp. 64–66.

4. On the mechanics of this struggle, see Burdette Loomis, *The New American Politician: Ambition, Entrepreneurship, and the Changing Face of Political Life* (New York: Basic Books, 1988), and Martin P. Wattenberg, *The Rise of Candidate-Centered Politics: Presidential Elections of the 1980s* (Cambridge: Harvard UP, 1991). On the potentialities for technical substitution, see Cornelius P. Cotter, James L. Gibson, John F. Bibby, and Robert J. Huckshorn, *Party Organizations in American Politics* (New York: Praeger, 1984).

5. Because such factional over- or underrepresentation is actually correlated with policy views for the resulting factional groupings, aggregating party

factions in this way does not obscure important differences, with one partial exception. On the latter, see note 7 below.

6. The question is not an unfamiliar one in elite analysis more generally. Robert D. Putnam provides an extended framework for such an analysis in *The Comparative Study of Political Elites* (Englewood Cliffs, N.J.: Prentice-Hall, 1976), esp. chap. 5, "The Structure of Elites." For a specific application, see John L. Sullivan, Pat Walsh, Michal Shamir, David G. Barnum, and James L. Gibson, "Why Politicians Are More Tolerant: Selective Recruitment and Socialization among Political Elites in Britain, New Zealand, and the United States," *British Journal of Political Science* 23 (Jan. 1993), 51–76.

7. The Democratic party also contains the main instance where both such effects are actually being obscured—and here, reduced—by combining the overrepresented factions in a single grouping. For in fact, the some-college Democrats (the least overrepresented of the factions within this cluster) serve to moderate strongly the contribution of the other two factions, the college-graduate and non-Christian Democrats. Without their some-college brethren, these college-graduate and non-Christian Democrats would be simultaneously more overrepresented and more inclined to shift leftward at the activist level. Their combined profiles would be +1.08 for the rank and file with +1.42 for the active partisans on cultural/national issues, and +.18 for the rank and file with +.48 for the active partisans on economic/welfare concerns.

8. Analysts like Kessel would, in fact, make this a frequent and natural occurrence; see note 3 above. See also John H. Kessel, John M. Bruce, and John A. Clark, "Advocacy Politics in Presidential Parties," *American Political Science Review* 85 (Dec. 1991), 1089–1105.

9. Another way to think about the same problem uses extreme scores, in effect, as "real preferences" and moderate scores as "nonpreferences." While its genesis and rationale are clearly different, this approach would lead, we suspect, to many of the same conclusions if applied to these data. See George Rabinowitz and Stuart Elaine MacDonald, "A Directional Theory of Voting," *American Political Science Review* 83 (March 1989), 93–121. They cite, as a crucial predecessor, Donald E. Stokes, "Spatial Models of Party Competition," *American Political Science Review* 57 (June 1963), 211–26. Their own evident successor is the study by Stuart Elaine MacDonald, Olga Listhaug, and George Rabinowitz, "Issues and Party Support in Multiparty Systems," *American Political Science Review* 85 (Dec. 1991), 1107–31. Stokes's successor is Donald E. Stokes, "Valence Politics," chap. 7 in Dennis Kavanagh, ed., *Electoral Politics* (Oxford: Oxford UP, 1992).

10. Said differently, one could reasonably posit the hyperactivists as central to mounting campaigns, the partisan actives as central to determining nominations, and the total party as dominant at the general election. One could also reasonably assert that while party activists may be disproportionately influential in shaping policy options, they must still ultimately sell these policies to their nonactivist rank and file if they are to succeed. Measures built to high-

light these assertions would produce even more dramatically extended results, along the same lines as offered in the text here.

11. This picture seems fully consistent with other recent research on these issues, as with John G. Geer, "New Deal Issues and the American Electorate, 1952–1988," *Political Behavior* 14 (March 1992), 45–65.

12. Indeed, this is a central theme in the earliest summaries of relevant research, as well as in the most recent. See, for example, V. O. Key, Jr., "Public Opinion and Democratic Politics," chap. 21 in Key, *Public Opinion and American Democracy* (New York: Knopf, 1961), as well as Paul M. Sniderman, "The New Look in Public Opinion Research," chap. 9 in Ada W. Finifter, ed., *Political Science: The State of the Discipline, II* (Washington, D.C.: American Political Science Association, 1993).

13. These findings have yet a third major implication, involving the potential for addressing central strategic problems by way of deliberate structural reform. The active Republican and Democratic parties do differ explicitly in the character of their main strategic problem at the elite level. Or at least, while neither set of partisan activists would probably be willing to characterize the matter as a "problem," it is true that the main strategic "strain" for the active Republican party is its preference for economic/welfare policies well to the right of the American people, and that the counterpart strain for the active Democratic party is its preference for cultural/national policies well to the left of the same general public.

Yet the two parties also differ substantially in the roots of this problem, and thus in the possibility for addressing it through institutional tinkering— through structural reform. For the Democrats, the tendency of the active party to stand well off to the left of its rank and file on cultural/national issues does depend, in part, on simple oversampling of the more liberal rank-and-file factions at the elite level. Accordingly, institutional devices that sampled more accurately within this body could help to address a recurring structural problem. For the Republicans, on the other hand, the tendency of the active party to stand well off to the right of its rank and file on economic/welfare issues does not stem from over- and underrepresentation per se. As a result, institutional tinkering would presumably not be enough; changing elite positions in the active Republican party would necessitate actually altering activist values.

Chapter 8: An Issue Context for Contemporary Politics

1. An attempt to patch a few dramatic examples of institutional politicking into the same basic framework is included in Byron E. Shafer, "Political Orders and Political Eras," a paper presented to the conference "The Dynamics of American Politics: Approaches and Interpretations," at the Center for the Study of American Politics, University of Colorado at Boulder, February 20–22, 1992.

2. William E. Leuchtenberg, *Franklin D. Roosevelt and the New Deal, 1932–1940* (New York: Harper & Row, 1963); Arthur M. Schlesinger, Jr., *The Coming of*

the New Deal (Boston: Houghton Mifflin, 1959); James MacGregor Burns, *Roosevelt: The Soldier of Freedom* (New York: Harcourt Brace Jovanovich, 1970); John Morton Blum, *V was for Victory: Politics and American Culture during World War II* (New York: Harcourt Brace Jovanovich, 1976).

3. Eric F. Goldman, *The Crucial Decade—and After: America, 1945–1960* (New York: Vintage, 1960); Alonzo L. Hamby, *Beyond the New Deal: Harry S. Truman and American Liberalism* (New York: Columbia UP, 1973); James L. Sundquist, *Politics and Policy: The Eisenhower, Kennedy, and Johnson Years* (Washington, D.C.: Brookings Institution, 1968); John P. Diggins, *The Proud Decades: America in War and Peace, 1941–1960* (New York: Norton, 1988).

4. William G. Mayer, *The Changing American Mind: How and Why American Public Opinion Changed between 1960 and 1988* (Ann Arbor: U of Michigan P, 1992), 319–21.

5. The situation is summarized in Nelson W. Polsby and Aaron Wildavsky, "Domestic Issues, Foreign Issues," in Polsby and Wildavsky, *Presidential Elections*, 8th ed. (New York: Free Press, 1991), 232–35. Their data come most directly from "Opinion Roundup: VI. Images of the Parties," *Public Opinion* 7 (Dec./Jan. 1985), 38.

6. Irwin Ross, *The Loneliest Campaign: The Truman Victory of 1948* (New York: New American Library, 1968); Hamby, *Beyond the New Deal.*

7. Paul T. David, Malcolm Moos, and Ralph M. Goldman, *Presidential Nominating Politics in 1952,* 5 vols. (Baltimore: Johns Hopkins Press, 1954), esp. vol. 1, *The National Story;* Herbert S. Parmet, *Eisenhower and the American Crusades* (New York: Macmillan, 1972).

8. Charles A. H. Thomson and Frances M. Shattuck, *The 1956 Presidential Campaign* (Washington: Brookings, 1960); Samuel Lubell, *Revolt of the Moderates* (New York: Harper, 1956).

9. Theodore H. White, *The Making of the President, 1960* (New York: Atheneum, 1961); Paul T. David, ed., *The Presidential Election and Transition, 1960–1961* (Washington, D.C.: Brookings Institution, 1961).

10. Karl A. Lamb and Paul A. Smith, *Campaign Decision-Making: The Presidential Election of 1964* (Belmont, Calif.: Wadsworth, 1968); Milton C. Cummings, Jr., ed., *The National Election of 1964* (Washington, D.C.: Brookings Institution, 1966).

11. Key early and late texts on these pure partisan independents are Angus Campbell, Gerald Gurin, and Warren E. Miller, *The Voter Decides* (Evanston, Ill.: Row, Peterson, 1954), esp. chap. 7, "Party Identification"; Angus Campbell, Philip E. Converse, Warren E. Miller, and Donald E. Stokes, *The American Voter* (New York: Wiley, 1960), esp. chap. 5, "The Impact of Party Identification"; Norman H. Nie, Sidney Verba, and John R. Petrocik, *The Changing American Voter* (Cambridge: Harvard UP, 1976), esp. chap. 4, "The Decline of Partisanship"; and Bruce E. Keith, David R. Magleby, Candice J. Nelson, Elizabeth Orr, Mark

C. Westlye, and Raymond E. Wolfinger, *The Myth of the Independent Voter* (Berkeley: U of California P, 1991).

12. Mayer, *The Changing American Mind*, is an extremely useful overview of these trends. But see also Tom W. Smith, "General Liberalism and Social Change in Post–World War II America: A Summary of Trends," *Social Indicators Research* 10 (Jan. 1982), 1–28, and Smith, "Liberal and Conservative Trends in the United States since World War II," *Public Opinion Quarterly* 54 (Winter 1990), 479–507.

13. Theodore H. White, *The Making of the President, 1968* (New York: Atheneum, 1969); Lewis Chester, Godfrey Hodgson, and Bruce Page, *An American Melodrama: The Presidential Campaign of 1968* (New York: Viking, 1969).

14. Theodore H. White, *The Making of the President, 1972* (New York: Atheneum, 1973); A. James Reichley, *Conservatives in an Age of Change: The Nixon and Ford Administrations* (Washington, D.C.: Brookings Institution, 1981).

15. Jules Witcover, *Marathon: The Pursuit of the Presidency, 1972–1976* (New York: Viking Penguin, 1977); William Lee Miller, *Yankee from Georgia: The Emergence of Jimmy Carter* (New York: Times Books, 1978).

16. Jack W. Germond and Jules Witcover, *Blue Smoke and Mirrors: How Reagan Won and Carter Lost the Election of 1980* (New York: Viking, 1981); Austin Ranney, ed., *The American Elections of 1980* (Washington, D.C.: AEI, 1981).

17. Austin Ranney, ed., *The American Elections of 1984* (Washington, D.C.: AEI, 1985); Gerald M. Pomper, ed., *The Election of 1984: Reports and Interpretations* (Chatham, N.J.: Chatham House, 1985); William A. Henry, III, *Visions of America: How We Saw the 1984 Election* (Boston: Atlantic Monthly, 1985).

18. Gerald M. Pomper, ed., *The Election of 1988: Reports and Interpretations* (Chatham, N.J.: Chatham House, 1989); Michael Nelson, *The Elections of 1988* (Washington, D.C.: CQ Press, 1989); Jack W. Germond and Jules Witcover, *Whose Broad Stripes and Bright Stars? The Trivial Pursuit of the Presidency* (New York: Warner, 1989).

19. Gerald M. Pomper, ed., *The Election of 1992: Reports and Interpretations* (Chatham, N.J.: Chatham House, 1993); Byron E. Shafer, "The United States," chap. 1 in Shafer, ed., *Post-War Politics in the G-7* (Madison: U of Wisconsin P, forthcoming [1995]).

20. In this regard, readers of political tea leaves were powerfully intrigued by the outcome of the *congressional* elections of 1994. Because the Republicans had not managed to gain control of both houses of Congress without a presidential candidate since 1946—48 years ago—this outcome obviously raised the possibility that an entire issue context was finally changing. All it automatically represented, on the other hand, was a distinctive success at driving cultural/national concerns into and through these congressional contests, and that remains the obvious—the least demanding—interpretation. What the 1994 elections also indisputably accomplished, however, was to exaggerate the interpretive prospects from the American presidential election of *1996*.

INDEX

Library of Congress Cataloging-in-Publication Data

Shafer, Byron E.
    The two majorities : the issue context of modern American politics
/ Byron E. Shafer & William J. M. Claggett.
        p.   cm.—(Interpreting American politics)
    Includes bibliographical references and index.
    ISBN 0-8018-5018-5 (hard : acid-free paper).—ISBN 0-8018-5019-3
(pbk. : acid-free paper)
    1. Political parties—United States.   2. Political participation—United States.
3. United States—Politics and government—20th century.   I. Claggett, William J. M.
(William Jennings Mitchell)   II. Title.   III. Series.
JK2261.S43   1995
324'.0973—dc20   94-43426